D1305263

Baseball Research Journal

Volume 48, Number 2
Fall 2019

Published by the Society for American Baseball Research

BASEBALL RESEARCH JOURNAL, Volume 48, Number 2

Editor: Cecilia M. Tan
Design and Production: Lisa Hochstein
Cover Design: Lisa Hochstein
Copyediting assistance: Keith DeCandido
Proofreader: Norman L. Macht
Fact Checker: Clifford Blau

Front cover photo: Courtesy of Oakland Athletics/Michael Zagaris

Published by:
Society for American Baseball Research, Inc.
Cronkite School at ASU
555 N. Central Ave. #416
Phoenix, AZ 85004

Phone: (602) 496–1460
Web: www.sabr.org
Twitter: @sabr
Facebook: Society for American Baseball Research

Contents

Note from the Editor

A chill is in the New England air as I type this. The seasons are turning, as they always do, and I find myself looking simultaneously forward and back. In the coming year, 2020, SABR will host its 50th national convention and kick off a 50th anniversary year that we'll celebrate in myriad ways.

One will be with the publication of a SABR "greatest hits" book, *SABR 50 at 50*, by University of Nebraska Press, which compiles 50 articles spread over SABR's history. I spent some time prepping the articles for the publisher, giving myself a refresher course in SABR's own history in the process. But that's not the only reason SABR history has been on my mind.

A member wrote me last week to ask if I had a copy of a SABR publication I had never seen, *Texas is Baseball Country*. I could not locate a copy, even through Amazon or Alibris, and the main office did not have one. (If you have a copy, please let me know. In the age of the ebook I can rescue any previously "lost" book from obscurity and make it available again.) SABR's publication history is vast, and it's growing faster than ever right now.

I'm also feeling the urge to make indelible records because we lost some well-known SABR researchers in the past year. Rob Edelman, film historian and frequent BRJ contributor, passed away unexpectedly in May. Then there was Cuban baseball expert Peter Bjarkman, whom we lost this time last year. I came across his picture serendipitously: Mark Rucker's photo essay in this issue ironically entitled "Baseball Archeology" had been overlooked in the move of the SABR office from Cleveland to Phoenix, shipped to me on CD-Rom, and then unwittingly buried in my home office. I'm happy to be able to give it the light of day at last, in Peter's memory.

Another article excavated at the same time was a manual typescript from one of the longest contributing members to SABR publications, Art Ahrens. That piece on pitcher Carl Lundgren runs in this issue, but the earliest publication I could find that contained an article by Art was the second issue of the *Baseball Research Journal*, dated 1973. Also in that issue? Pete Palmer's original "On Base Average" article, a topic he revisits somewhat in this issue's "Why OPS Works."

SABR. We predict; we chronicle; we look both forward and back. I'm honored to be a part of it and I hope you are, too.

— Cecilia Tan
Publications Director

Community, Defection, and *equipo Cuba*

Baseball under Fidel Castro, 1959–93

Katie Krall

Baseball is called America's national pastime, but in Cuba baseball is a way of life. In the late 1890s during the war of independence, baseball unified the Cuban people in opposition to Spaniards, who looked down on the sport and preferred traditional European bullfighting. Sixty years later when Fidel Castro came to power, he knew that he needed to again coalesce the populace. After the 1959 revolution, Castro abolished professional baseball and created *béisbol revolucionario*. Milton Jamail writes in his book, *Full Count: Inside Cuban Baseball*, that *el comandante en jefe* thought "selling baseball players was a crude manifestation of the worst elements of capitalism, akin to slavery, and he referred to professional baseball as *la pelota esclava*."[1] Traditionally, ballplayers would travel to Havana during the offseason to play winter ball—not just major league players, but also Negro Leaguers, many of whom played in Latin America before Jackie Robinson broke the color barrier in 1947 because of the more equitable treatment they received outside of the United States. However, Castro decreed that foreign imports were no longer allowed on any of the island's diamonds.

For over four decades of this period of self-imposed isolation, the Cuban national baseball team, *equipo Cuba*, went nearly undefeated in international tournaments. Cuban baseball players competed in rickety stadiums that lacked any of the amenities associated with modern venues, but the crowds were large and loud every night. "Sports activities offered the citizen a means of individual expression, a way to compete, to achieve, and to accomplish something. In a non-capitalist, anti-individualistic society, such an opportunity was rare."[2]

Castro exploited the incredible play of *equipo Cuba* as evidence of the socialist regime's success and as a source of national pride. The creation of development academies for amateur athletes tethered baseball players to the state and made amateur baseball in Cuba a government-run operation.

Based on a cost-benefit analysis of the value of defection, I argue that strong familial and community ties prevented Cuban players from abandoning the national team after the 1959 revolution. However, after the fall of the Soviet Union in 1991 and legalization of the possession of the US dollar two years later, prominent players began defecting to the Major Leagues as those bonds started to break. A dearth of economic opportunities on the island triggered widespread player disillusionment with party ideology. Therefore, players such as Yoenis Céspedes, Aroldis Chapman, and Yasiel Puig who, had they been born decades prior, would have remained in Cuba, analyzed the incentives of defection and decided that exponentially higher salaries in MLB were worth the price of leaving the island.

My study examines the time between Castro's takeover and the legalization of the US dollar on the island in 1993. The revolution altered how players were developed and subsequently indoctrinated with the socialist creed. When René Arocha, a pitcher on *equipo Cuba*, defected in 1991, he ushered in a new era of Cuban baseball in the US, but I have found that this moment alone was not enough to encourage a widespread exodus of baseball players. Instead, it was a combination of limited economic freedoms caused by the dissolution of the Soviet Union (and their financial support to the island) that led to the proliferation of *equipo Cuba* players filling spots on Major League rosters. Defection "began happening in earnest after the collapse of the Soviet Union because the Cuban economy, which was in shambles already, took a further dip and the players saw that their future was bleak."[3]

Despite the government establishing academies for amateur volleyball, boxing, and soccer, baseball was the most popular sport on the island and deeply ingrained in the national consciousness. Castro wanted to make baseball his own in the same way he sought to reorder healthcare and education. Juan Linz explains in his book, *Totalitarian and Authoritarian Regimes*, that "the destruction, or at least decisive weakening of all the institutions, organizations, and interest groups existing before a new elite takes political power and organizes its own political structures is one of the distinguishing characteristics of totalitarian systems."[4] Castro stripped the game of its association with the

PHOTOGRAPHER: KEITH ALLISON

Aroldis Chapman is one of the highest-earning Cuban ballplayers in MLB, second only to Yoenis Céspedes.

Youngsters with potential were thus offered luxuries: better food, comfortable living quarters, modern facilities, opportunities to travel and compete, and even special bonuses such as a car or pocket money.[7]

The government had a strong influence over amateur Cuban athletes at a very impressionable age. While in the US a Little Leaguer might dream of playing shortstop for the Yankees, in Cuba there was no higher honor than being named to the national team. When players were between thirteen and sixteen, the top athletes attended Escuelas de Iniciación Deportiva (EIDE). At these sports initiation schools, students divided their day between the field and classroom. Competition was incredibly fierce at each level. "Those baseball players who show exceptional promise at the EIDEs are sent on to the Escuela Superior de Perfeccionamiento Atlético (ESPA). There is one ESPA in each of Cuba's fourteen provinces, plus one for the city of Havana."[8] Since players attend EIDEs and ESPAs in the province where they were born, strong bonds developed between a player and his community. The state made an intentional investment in its athletes both physically and ideologically with the expected dividend someday being their high level of play in international tournaments.

Wearing a jersey with "Cuba" emblazoned across your chest as a member of the national team was a tangible representation of the state, so Castro micromanaged the officials and players of *equipo Cuba*. This party oversight meant that in addition to having baseball prowess, a player had to also follow doctrine and ideology as outlined by the regime. Castro expected that anyone affiliated with *equipo Cuba* would properly represent the island—no errors were tolerated on or off the field.

Cubans had great pride and respect for their players who seemed to embody the ideals of the revolution. Player defections caused significant grief and heartbreak to fans who viewed many athletes like sons or brothers. Sigfredo Barros, a Cuban journalist, explained that "no one in the United States taught Arrojo to throw a sinker; he was taught that here in Cuba. Or the slider to Orlando, or Livan's 93-mph fastball, or to field balls like Ordóñez does. We taught them those things here."[9] The references to Rolando Arrojo, brothers Orlando and Livan Hernandez, and Rey Ordóñez, all of whom defected from Cuba in the 1990s, underscore the pain many Cubans felt when players abandoned the national team.

Baseball, and its accompanying values, proved an effective vehicle for Castro to advance the objectives of his new socialist order. "The sports hero exemplifies

United States and ushered in a new era—one completely under his control. Cuban baseball historian Roberto Gonzalez Echevarria notes that Castro took "a tremendous tradition, one that all Cubans agree is the essence of their identity, of being Cuban, and fused it with a state structure which supports the playing of the game, that creates the young ballplayers, finds them, uses them and develops them."[5]

The timeless rules of baseball were unaltered so that when *equipo Cuba* played in international competitions they would not be at a disadvantage, but Castro eliminated many of the commercial features of sports. Even in 1959, corporate sponsors had taken over most major-league ballparks with Coca-Cola signs dotting the outfield walls from New York to Los Angeles. Castro, in his crusade against all things capitalist, saw to it there were "no paid advertisements in Cuban ballparks, just political slogans."[6] Instead of team owners, the Communist Party operated all organizations and stadiums throughout the island. Baseball therefore became not only a form of recreation, but also a means through which to raise the next generation of party loyalists.

Castro implemented a system where ballplayers were developed locally, in a similar fashion to the state-sponsored sports programs of the Soviet Union. Every two to three years, depending on their abilities, young athletes were promoted to different academy levels to foster their talents. Parents were encouraged to place particularly gifted children in special sports schools for early training at the regime's expense.

the ideal disciplined worker, loyal revolutionary, and obedient soldier."[10] While there were few economic or social victories the government could cite, the Olympic gold medals in Barcelona in 1992 and Atlanta in 1996 *equipo Cuba* won seemed to vindicate the methods of the Communist Party. Castro merged sport with nationalism and ensured that the game advanced his authoritarian mission.

In a society of alleged equality, one man stood above all others. Every aspect of the Cuban regime, and baseball in particular, was meant to glorify the prowess of Fidel Castro. On the rare occasions when he spoke to American journalists, he cited multiple occasions when he was scouted as a pitcher by major league teams and even offered a contract. While most of these stories have been debunked, the narrative he constructed of himself as a legendary baseball player speaks to the importance of the game in earning the respect and devotion of Cuban citizens.

These four decades of spectacular play by *equipo Cuba* and backing by the Soviet Union resulted in a golden era for Cuban baseball. While Cuban players didn't enjoy the same material comforts as their counterparts in the United States, for some the admiration and love communities lavished on them overcame the financial gap. Carlos Rodriguez Acosta, the current Commissioner of Cuban Baseball, explained that "almost all of our athletes, not only in baseball, but in all of our sports, are all very aware of what they represent and why they're so great. They're great because they've benefited from a free education system, because sport is the right of the people, because they don't rely on sport to make a living, because health care is free and because they are given everything."[11] Rodriguez Acosta's rhetoric was a hallmark of the curriculum each player learned at all levels of the state-sponsored development academies.

Just as they were instructed in how to properly throw a curveball or steal second base, party ideology was taught to Cuban baseball players. Ronald Wintrobe explains in his essay "The Tinpot and the Totalitarian: An Economic Theory of Dictatorship" that "the Party encourages and directs loyalty by maintaining and propagandizing an exclusive ideology that promotes the Party's goals and helps establish and codify its reputation."[12] Every victory against the US was not just a win for *equipo Cuba*, but a triumph over capitalism and the Western world order. For a time, there were many Cuban athletes who believed unconditionally in Castro and the socialist state.

Omar Linares was one of those players and arguably the most talented third baseman in Cuban baseball history. He was the "poster boy for the deep-seated loyalty of the great majority of late-twentieth century Cuban diamond stars."[13] For over two decades he trumpeted the benefits of the Cuban baseball system, always remembering to pay homage to the state and development academies that taught him the game. "Linares often described his decision to remain in Cuba, making the equivalent of $20 a month plus a few perks not available to the average Cuban, as based upon the gains he and his family made through the revolution."[14]

Since Linares was frequently approached by major-league teams to play in the US and could have left the island, albeit under covert methods, on multiple occasions, Linares's cost-benefit analysis at the time favored remaining in Cuba. While the degree of his support of the system may have been amplified to serve the goals of the state, his comments to foreign journalists and *Granma*, Cuba's official government newspaper, seem to be authentic representations of his feelings. After *equipo Cuba* beat the Baltimore Orioles in 1999 in an exhibition game, Linares proclaimed, "Commander-in-chief, the mission you gave us has been completed," and he ended his battle report to the *comandante en jefe* with the words "*Socialismo o muerte!* (Socialism or death!) *Patria o muerte!* (Homeland or death!) *Venceremos!* (We will triumph!)"[15] Linares, like other amateur Cuban baseball players, received no financial incentives for winning a championship. Nevertheless, he played with a tenacity and joy that transcended economic concerns.

After the fall of the Soviet Union, however, poverty became so dire that all Cubans, athletes especially, could no longer ignore the cost of remaining in a socialist state. The *período especial* (special period), which was the excuse used for broken machinery and lack of goods and services, disproportionately impacted baseball players. While some Cubans sold cigars to tourists or took on side work to secure extra cash, members of *equipo Cuba* were closely monitored by the party and unable to engage in any illicit activities. As "Cuba's domestic GDP collapsed by an estimated 37 per cent, and 50 per cent of the economy lost purchasing power,"[16] leaving the island was less of a political stance and more of a means of survival. In addition, "the years of productivity for an athlete, for anyone who depends on his or her body or performance is limited. So, the urgency to be able to use that talent is much greater than in the case of someone who has a much more intellectual type of job. These players felt that urgency after the Cuban economy dipped, and there was a sense of despair, now communism was a religion without a Rome or a Jerusalem."[17]

Beginning in 1991, Cuban baseball players began to fully understand that other opportunities existed only ninety miles away. Once removed from the watchful eye of the party, Cuban defectors became more comfortable voicing their critiques of the government. Jorge Diaz, a defector and former member of *equipo Cuba*, explained, "in Cuba we won three straight championships. They would treat you to a beer, they'd pay for a night at the hotel with your family, but nothing more. One would ask for things that one needed and they would deceive you."[18] While national pride and love of country were ties that had kept players on the island, the tether snapped when baseball players were no longer able to scrape by on meager government handouts.

Baseball players' repudiation embarrassed the Cuban government. Castro considered members of *equipo Cuba* to be the face of the revolution. When they turned their backs on the country that raised them, it suggested to the Cuban people that the party

could be challenged. As defections have become far more common today (although the risks remain with tales of danger and bravery thoroughly outlined by the US media), the strength of the national team and its grip on amateur players has waned. Instead of staying in Cuba, top players have sought wealth and fame in Major League Baseball. (See table below.)

Inextricably linked to baseball defectors is the relationship between the United States and Cuba. "It has long been a part of American media policy to cheer on the Cuban baseball defector as a political and ideological story."[19] In this charged climate, there is more at stake than a championship or standing on the Olympic podium. Robert Huish explains in his essay, "The (Soft) Power of Sport: The Comprehensive and Contradictory Strategies of Cuba's Sport-Based Internationalism," that "Cuban sport should be understood as part of a broader development agenda, as well as an opportunity or avenue through which Cuba pursues its national interests."[20] When players leave the island,

Notable Cuban Defectors' MLB Career Earnings

Name	MLB Teams	Years in MLB	MLB Career Earnings (in US Dollars)	Accolades
Yoenis Céspedes	OAK, BOS, DET, NYM	2012–18	144,000,000	2013 Home Run Derby Winner, 2016 Silver Slugger
Aroldis Chapman	CIN, CHC, NYY	2010–19	84,810,772	6-time All-Star
Kendrys Morales	LAA, SEA, MIN, KC, TOR, OAK, NYY	2006–19	69,410,000	2015 Silver Slugger
José Abreu	CWS	2014–19	68,825,000	2014 AL Rookie of the Year
Jose Contreras	NYY, CWS, COL, PHI	2003–13	67,500,000	2006 All-Star
Rusney Castillo	BOS	2014–16	58,228,571	2018 MiLB All-Star
Yasiel Puig	LAD, CIN, CLE	2013–19	51,698,000	Finished 2nd in the 2013 NL Rookie of the Year
Alexei Ramirez	CWS, SD, TB	2008–16	41,811,666	2010, 2014 Silver Slugger
Yulieski Gurriel	HOU	2016–19	39,100,000	Finished 4th in the 2017 AL Rookie of the Year
Orlando Hernandez	NYY, CWS, ARI, NYM	1998–2007	34,525,000	Finished 4th in the 1998 AL Rookie of the Year
Lourdes Gurriel Jr.	TOR	2018–19	22,000,000	July 2018 Rookie of the Month
Adeiny Hechavarria	TOR, MIA, TB, PIT, NYY, NYM	2012–19	24,100,000	Finished 3rd in 2014 and 2015 Gold Glove voting
Jorge Soler	CHI, KC	2014–19	22,666,667	2014 and 2017 MiLB All-Star
Yuniesky Betancourt	SEA, KC, MIL	2005–13	15,755,000	Finished 3rd in 2007 and 2011 Gold Glove voting
Dayan Viciedo	CWS	2010–14	13,321,311	Finished 4th in 2012 Gold Glove voting
Jose Fernandez	MIA	2013–16	4,576,000	2013 NL Rookie of the Year
Yandy Diaz	CLE, TB	2017–19	1,093,400	2015 and 2016 MiLB All-Star

*Data through July 31, 2019. Courtesy of Baseball-Reference.com

they are fighting party ideology and therefore constitute a threat to the regime.

The Cuban state baseball apparatus is faced with the dual problem of "players with little possibility of advancement and the unwillingness to provide the necessary economic stimulus for players to remain in the country."[21] While during the Mariel exodus thousands of Cubans left the island, it was the players on *equipo Cuba* who were disproportionately ostracized. "Those who migrated from Cuba to the United States were labeled *gusanos* (worms or traitors) by the Cuban revolutionary authorities and by many compatriots who remained on the island."[22]

While great wealth and fame can await some talented baseball players who leave Cuba, it is still a harrowing journey that is difficult to execute alone. Joe Cubas has represented a number of Cuban defectors and is the mastermind behind the now famous "Joe Cubas Plan" which has become the blueprint for the entire baseball smuggling industry. After ferrying players off the island and establishing residency in a third country (thus circumventing regulations for MLB free agents and the embargo), he encourages high-priced bidding wars among the 30 major league clubs.[23]

While Cuba under Castro exhibited many of the textbook characteristics of authoritarian regimes and baseball was used by the state as a means through which to promote ideology, it is clear that defection is linked to economic considerations. After years of dynastic success on the world stage, the death blow to *equipo Cuba* was not due to a lower quality of play on the field or poor coaching but rather the political climate. The Special Period changed the variables players weighed when deciding to defect with the promise of financial security and a better quality of life trumping any debt they may have felt to their homeland.

Despite the many former *equipo Cuba* stars who now play for storied MLB franchises such as the Yankees, Red Sox, and Dodgers, the Cuban government refuses to acknowledge their achievements or forgive their transgressions. There is a fear that normalizing conversations about teams in the United States will encourage defection. Under this mentality, if the Cuban people were to know of defectors' successes, it would undermine the socialist mission. Celebrating players in MLB, a business that adheres to the rules of the free market, would be tantamount to touting the benefits of capitalism.

The reign of amateur Cuban baseball from 1959 until the early 1990s is unlikely ever to be seen again. Today, "playing conditions, fan enthusiasm, and ballplayer morale have sunk to all-time lows. The national team heroes are no longer the country's biggest news."[24] Names such as Omar Linares become the subject of debate among an older generation as the next wave of Cuban athletes set their eyes on defecting to join the major leagues. While players in Cuba's top baseball league still only earn a few hundred dollars a month, MLB stars such as Yuli Gurriel and José Abreu rake in tens of millions of dollars over their careers.[25] These major league standouts who, in a different era, under Fidel Castro, would have given anything to be a member of *equipo Cuba* now find themselves very far away from the island that first introduced them to the game. ∎

Notes

1. Milton H. Jamail, *Full Count: Inside Cuban Baseball*, Southern Illinois University Press, 2000, 29.
2. Julie Marie Bunck, "The Politics of Sports in Revolutionary Cuba," *Cuban Studies*, Vol. 20, 1990, 127.
3. "Stealing Home: The Case of Contemporary Cuban Baseball." http://www.pbs.org/stealinghome/debate/defections.html
4. Juan J. Linz, *Totalitarian and Authoritarian Regimes*, Rienner, 2009, 68.
5. "Stealing Home."
6. Jamail, 110.
7. Bunck, 120–21.
8. Jamail, 39.
9. "Stealing Home."
10. Bunck, 119.
11. "Stealing Home."
12. Ronald Wintrobe, "The Tinpot and the Totalitiarian: An Economic Theory of Dictatorship," *American Political Science Review*, 1990, 867.
13. Peter C. Bjarkman, "Omar Linares," Society for American Baseball Research, 2016. http://sabr.org/bioproj/person/ab3866fa.
14. Jamail, 32.
15. Jamail, 142.
16. Robert Huish, et al, "The (Soft) Power of Sport: The Comprehensive and Contradictory Strategies of Cuba's Sport-Based Internationalism," *International Journal of Cuban Studies*, Vol. 5 #1, 2013, 31.
17. "Stealing Home."
18. "Stealing Home."
19. Peter C. Bjarkman, *Cuba's Baseball Defectors: The Inside Story*, Rowman & Littlefield, 2017, 54.
20. Huish, et al., 27.
21. Jamail, 7.
22. "Stealing Home."
23. Bjarkman, *Cuba's Baseball Defectors*, 159.
24. Bjarkman, *Cuba's Baseball Defectors*, 199.
25. Mercer, Greg. "The Baseball Stars Who Ignore MLB to Stay Loyal to Cuba...and Canada." *The Guardian*, Guardian News and Media, 9 Aug. 2018, http://www.theguardian.com/sport/2018/aug/09/the-baseball-stars-who-ignore-mlb-to-stay-loyal-to-cuba-and-canada.

Baseball Archeology in Cuba

A Trip to Güines

Mark Rucker

Visiting Cuba is like tripping in a time machine. We're not talking about a beach vacation at Varadero, but a visitation to the living, working Cuba. A Cuba where baseball is woven into the shirts they wear, is the caffeine in their coffee, and the excitement in their voices. When you are there, you'll find the time traveler gets a different version of now and then. In Cuba there is the pre- and post-Revolutionary country, a national history more seen as a continuity today than in the recent past, but still a history divided, one capitalist and one socialist.

The passengers on this small-scale adventure include Sr. Ismael Séne, our magnificent intellectual host with his photographic memory, knowing all things baseball, old and new; the late Peter Bjarkman, the English-speaking master of Cuba's modern game; our driver; and the camera wielding author, who planned this 2007 jaunt with no guarantee of success.

The inspiration for our one-day trip was a group of photographs from the winter ball season of 1927–28. They were taken at a ballpark in Güines, a small city of now 70,000, 50 km. or so southeast of Havana. The photos—a group of sixteen 7" x 5" prints, mounted on decorative 10" x 8" boards—started turning up in the capital city a few years earlier in an astounding state of preservation, arriving in small groups, until almost the entire collection was assembled (16 of 18 are present). The sauna-like climate on the island is rampantly destructive to paper, and photos usually suffer. Though I had been doing photo research in Cuban baseball for over fifteen years at that point, no picture had ever before appeared of Estadio Tropical Cerveza (Tropical Beer Park), nor had I seen reference to it, nor had I seen any mention of the photographer, Raphael Santiago of Calle M. Gomez 120, Güines, whose name was embossed in each print.

The most exciting feature of this group of photographs was not the record of the physical features of the park, nor the parade of old automobiles entering through the decorated gateway, nor the close-up views of the well dressed fans, nor even the pre-game warm-up activity in front of the stands. Instead, it was a team shot of the Cuba Baseball Club, an integrated professional team from the top league in the country. This club, one of the most amazing to take the field in all of baseball history, was composed of big names from Cuba and an all-star contingent from the US Negro Leagues.

Managing "Cuba" was Armando Marsans, one of the first Cubans to wear a major league uniform in the twentieth century, playing eight years in the American, the National, and the Federal Leagues. Marsan's pitching staff featured Willie Foster, now of the Baseball Hall of Fame, Willie Powell, small and sturdy right-hander, along with Cuban Basilio "The Witch" Rosell. Sharing the infield and the outfield were Judy Johnson and Oscar Charleston, monster stars both in the Negro Leagues and in Cooperstown, Walter "Steel Arm" Davis, from the Chicago American Giants, Cubans Pelayo Chacón, who played in Cuba from 1908 to 1932, Cando Lopez, Francisco Correa, and José Perez. The catcher was Larry Brown, whose defensive skills and strong arm were legendary.

We were hoping we could find the site of this forgotten ballpark, as then the photos would take on more meaning, and we might even find some ghostly evidence of these long lost players. So, we headed south, past Cotorro, San Jose de las Lajas, and other suburban towns that ring the south side of Havana. Shortly after leaving the hubbub behind, we were passing horse carts on our two-lane road, along with reeking, wheezing agricultural trucks and 1930s tractors. In short order our tan colored Lada was driving along the main thoroughfare into town, where we stopped at Güines stadium, almost sparkling with its bright green grass and fresh coat of red and ochre paint. The stadium hosts a good number of games annually, involving the Havana Province's three national series teams, Industriales, Metropolitanos, and Habana during the winter season, which usually runs from November to April. There was no ball game on this day, but the guard on duty was not sure where the old field had been, so he directed us into the center of town for more information.

On we went making inquiries, and found that, indeed, there was an old ballpark outside of town, though no one seemed to know its former name. As we Headed eastward for a short while, the houses soon grew farther apart, the city street grid disappeared, and after a few twists and turns we were parking across the street from what had been Estadio Tropical Cerveza. The old entrance had been replaced by a now weather-beaten, stylized gateway, which was connected to a high cement wall painted white. That outer, higher wall joined with the outfield wall to the north, and together they encircled the entire field. "352" was painted on the outfield wall where the cement baseline intersected it, matching symmetrically the right field line. Another shorter cement wall had been constructed within and parallel to the perimeter structure, separating the field from the spectators. There were two cement above-ground dugouts. The grass was short, the pitching rubber and home plate still in place, so some kind of ball was still being played here. The baselines were composed of poured cement strips about 4 inches wide, sitting a little above ground level, no doubt a hazard for hustling runners and fielders playing close by. What we were looking at was a cement construction ballpark in total disrepair. Between the eras of the totally wood-framed Beer Park and the present day ruin, a reconstruction project had occurred, transforming the field into a 1930s–40s art deco style structure, one probably used extensively throughout the 1950s. In between the two parallel cement walls, now separated from the playing field, the crumbling cement foundations for the old grandstands were still clearly in place, forming patterns in the ground like concrete footprints.

By using the photos to match our locations on the field we were able to figure out where all the seating areas had been placed, where the cars parked, areas designated for pre-game warm-ups, and the location of the other field structures where four teams had posed. Since palm trees grow for hundreds of years, we thought we might match the trees in the photos with the trees of today, but younger palms had intervened.

We strolled about for most of an hour noting features that other photographs in the group revealed, like the location of the benches in front of the grandstands, or where the Cuba team players warming up five in a row intersected with their opponents, or the fact that the paved street we parked on did not exist in 1928, or how very large the park had been and still was. Back at the time of the photos, Tropical Cerveza could likely have held 10,000 fans. The photos from 1927 indicate that a crowd of such a large size could have witnessed the Cuba team in Güines.

We got an historical buzz, if not an ectoplasmic visitation. But as I turned my head to leave, I could have sworn that I saw from the corner of my eye long, tall Willie Foster, arms and legs in motion, throwing warm-up tosses to Larry Brown, with Oscar Charleston shouting exhortations from the beyond. ∎

On the way to Güines, heading South from Havana, we encountered the past in the form of a horse cart.

In the 1926–27 season the front gate of Estadio Cerveza Tropical was an elaborate entrance to the field, flanked by the proud owners of the facility.

The front gate of the old field at Güines in 2007, where Peter Bjarkman establishes the scale of the present day entrance.

Cars entering the complex for a game late in 1926.

(L) In front of the grandstands, a pitcher from one of the Güines teams warms up before the contest. The crowd that has packed the grandstands is ready to start.

(R) Today all that is left of the grandstands are the cement structures left in the ground. The camera is in a location which would have been behind the old stands.

The Cuba Base Ball Club warms up before a game at Güines in 1926. This remarkable team fielded stars at almost every position. (L–R) Pepín Perez, Pelayo Chacón, Walter Davis hitting fungos, and behind his bat is Oscar Charleston. The four pitchers in the distance to the right are Willie Foster, Willie Powell, Basilio "Brujo" Rosell, and an unknown southpaw.

Long gone are the cheering crowds in the bleachers, the shouts of the vendors, and the crack of the ball off the bat. Instead, we see cinder block dugouts and cement walls, in the seldom-used field on the eastern outskirts of Güines.

A gathering of rooters posed for a photograph near the grandstand at Güines without revealing their team affiliation. Not even a logo. But they do provide a before photo for the after, which was taken in the same spot in 2007.

(L) The fans in Güines came in all ages and sexes. This entertaining shot of los fanaticos, who filled the grandstand at Estadio Cerveza Tropical, shows the broad base of support the game had even in small towns in Cuba.

(R) Where the fans once jumped and shouted, only the foundations are left.

Cuba Baseball Club poses during their visit to the Estadio in Güines. This stellar crew played together for only one year, and did not win the pennant. They were: Top row (L–R) Willie Foster, Larry Brown, Cando Lopez, Armando Marsans, Oscar Charleston, Willie Powell, unknown, Cuco Correa.

Front row Pelayo Chacon, Judy Johnson, Rogelio Crespo, Basilio Rosell, Walter Davis.

Testing an RPI Ranking System for Canadian University Baseball

George S. Rigakos and Mitchell Thompson

University baseball in Canada currently lacks a true national tournament. Since 1994, Canadian university (and college) teams have competed in a limited national championship either under the umbrella of the defunct Canadian Intercollegiate Baseball Association (CIBA[1]) or from 2013 to 2019, the more recently defunct Canadian Collegiate Baseball Association (CCBA). CIBA and CCBA membership vacillated from a high of 30 teams in 2011 to about ten teams in 2019.[2] The recognition of baseball by Ontario University Athletics (OUA) and the Ontario Colleges Athletic Association (OCAA) in the last decade has helped establish baseball as a bona fide intercollegiate sport in Canada. Indeed, many current OUA member teams were part of the Ontario conference of the CIBA and participated in a national championship. But OUA and OCAA recognition has resulted in the fracturing of collegiate baseball into (1) two-year college and four-year university leagues on the one hand, and (2) recognized and non-recognized associations on the other.

Not surprisingly, geography is also an important determinant for the organization of university baseball, resulting in three regional groupings: the Canadian Collegiate Baseball Association (CCBA) operating from the Atlantic to Ottawa, the Ontario University Athletics (OUA) baseball group in Ontario, and the Canadian Colleges Baseball Conference (CCBC) in the west which lumps together colleges and universities in order to form a viable league.[3]

Finally, the monetary reality for university baseball is that while teams are often organized and compete at a varsity level, the vast majority are only partially financing "competitive clubs" because U Sports and its provincial members (e.g. the OUA) do not recognize baseball as G1 (varsity) sport.[4] In Canada, this distinction is particularly important. In the absence of either official university association recognition or NSO backing—in this case Baseball Canada, U sports, Canada's university sport governing body, will neither recognize nor organize a national championship for university baseball.[5]

THE PROBLEM

Given these geographic, financial and bureaucratic impediments, university baseball in Canada has historically been siloed into three groupings offering their own championships: the OUA's provincial championship, the CCBC's conference championship in the west, and the CCBA's "national" championship encompassing teams from Ottawa, Quebec, and the Atlantic. While the CCBA has been the closest thing to a bona fide "Canadian University World Series," it still has not been able to solve the problem of a truly national and inclusive tournament.[6]

The formation of two coach-driven conferences in the OUA (West and East) was deemed necessary for the 2019 season in order to make room for new arrivals Carleton and Ottawa. This makes it difficult for all teams to play each other the same number of times given the short 16-game Fall conference schedule. As a result, seeding for the open provincial tournament on the basis of teams' win-loss records is an inherently flawed endeavor.

Of course, in the CCBA, the Northern and Atlantic conferences never played each other in the regular season and held their own playoff eliminations to determine seeds for their joint national championship. It is unclear how this will function in the future with the departure of Carleton and Ottawa.

Between initial submission and final revision of this paper, the CCBA announced it would cease operations in July 2019. Three Quebec teams (Concordia, Montreal, and McGill) have been, at least temporarily, orphaned and unaffiliated in the 2019 season. The remaining Atlantic conference teams have formed as the new Atlantic Collegiate Baseball Association (ACBA).[7] This realignment has, for now, severed any connection between the Atlantic clubs and their former competition in central Canada.

These developments only exacerbate a longstanding problem. Even if former Atlantic Conference CCBA (now ACBA), Quebec, OUA, and CCBC university conference teams somehow found a way to work together to create a national championship of university baseball—a *unified* Canadian University World Series (CUWS)—how would eligible teams be seeded when inter-conference play is rare or absent and no agreed upon playoff format or elimination system currently exists or is ever likely to be implemented?

A POTENTIAL SOLUTION

The purpose of this article is to explore the feasibility of an RPI ranking system for Canadian university baseball.[8] In the absence of playoff eliminations, and where inter-conference play is sparse, an RPI-based ranking system has, for example, proven useful—albeit controversial—in the US college basketball context.[9]

The Rating Percentage Index (RPI) is the most commonly used method for ranking a large number of teams that play a relatively small schedule. Most famously adopted in the NCAA, RPI is used to rank teams nationally when most teams never have an opportunity to play one another. The premise of the RPI is that since most teams do not play each other, it would be unfair to rank teams based on wins and losses as in the NFL, NBA, and MLB, or based on a points system as in the NHL. Instead, RPI uses the strength of a team's schedule in order to judge the quality of their play.

RPI is a mathematical calculation of a team's strength of schedule. It is the sum of three components: Winning Percentage (WP), Opponent's Winning Percentage (OWP), and Opponent's Opponent's Winning percentage (OOWP), each of which is weighted differently. The Formula for RPI is as follows:

$$RPI = (0.25 * WP) + (0.5 * OWP) + (0.25 * OOWP)$$

A team's WP is the percentage of games that a team wins, expressed—in a form similar to batting average—as a decimal to three digits. This is calculated by dividing the total team wins by total games played. WP accounts for 25% of the RPI calculation. The following is an example of a WP calculation:

Team A: 4–0
Team B: 1–3
Team C: 1–3

Team A WP=Number of Wins/Number of Games Played=4/4=1.00
Team B WP=Number of Wins/Number of Games Played=1/4=0.25
Team C WP=Number of Wins/Number of Games Played=1/4=0.25

And so, we add 25% of each total to each team's respective RPI. That is, 0.25 for Team A and 0.0625 for Teams B and C.

A team's OWP considers the winning percentage of teams faced. The calculation is a bit longer than that of WP. It averages the winning percentages of teams faced for every game *not including* the outcomes of games including the team whose OWP is being calculated. OWP accounts for 50% of the RPI Calculation. Using the same example for the WP Calculation:

Team A: 4–0
Team B: 1–3
Team C: 1–3

Team A goes 2–0 against Team B. Team A goes 2–0 against team C. Team B goes 1–1 against Team C. To calculate Team A's OWP, we must first find the WP of teams B and C excluding games involving Team A:

Team B WP: 0.500
Team C WP: 0.500

Now we may calculate Team A's OWP:

=Team B WP (0.500) * 2 (games played between Teams A and B)
+ Team C WP (0.500) * 2 (games played between teams A and C)
/ Games Played by team A
=(1.000 + 1.000)/4
=0.500

Thus, Team A's OWP is 0.500 and 0.250 is added to their RPI. This process can be replicated to find Team B (OWP of 0.500, 0.250 added to RPI) and Team C's (OWP of 0.500, 0.250 added to RPI) OWP.

A team's OOWP considers the OWP of teams faced similar to how OWP considers the WP of teams faced. The calculation is similar in length to the OWP calculation, however, at this point in the RPI process the work has already been done and we must only average out the OWPs of the opponents. OOWP accounts for 25% of the RPI Calculation.

Expanding on the previous example in order to calculate OOWP:

Team A: 4–0
Team B: 1–3
Team C: 1–3

Team A OWP: 0.500
Team B OWP: 0.500
Team C OWP: 0.500

Team A OOWP = Team B OWP (0.500) * 2 (games played between teams A and B) + Team C OWP (0.500) * 2 (games played between teams A and C) / Games Played
= (1.000 + 1.000)/4
= 0.500

Team B OOWP = Team A OWP (0.500) * 2 (games played between teams B and A) + Team C OWP (0.500) * 2 (games played between teams B and C) / Games Played
= (1.000 + 1.000)/4
= 0.500

Team C OOWP = Team A OWP (0.500) * 2 (games played between teams C and A) + Team B OWP (0.500) * 2 (games played between teams C and B) / Games Played
= (1.000 + 1.000)/4
= 0.500

Thus, each team's OOWP is 25% of 0.500, and so 0.125 is added to their RPI.

In this example, the OWP and OOWP for each team would all have worked out to be the same. This will not be the case in every scenario, of course, but the point here is to demonstrate how to calculate these numbers. The separating factor for the teams in this particular example of RPI rankings would, of course, be their winning percentages (WP) given that all other factors were equalized. The RPI rankings for the example used would look like this:

Team A RPI = (0.25 * WP) + (0.5 * OWP) + (0.25 * OOWP)
= (0.25 * 1.0) + (0.5 * 0.5) + (0.25 * 0.5)
= 0.25 + 0.25 + 0.125
= 0.625

Team B RPI = (0.25 * WP) + (0.5 * OWP) + (0.25 * OOWP)
= (0.25 * 0.25) + (0.5 * 0.5) + (0.25 * 0.5)
= 0.0625 + 0.25 + 0.125
= 0.4375

Team C RPI = (0.25 * WP) + (0.5 * OWP) + (0.25 * OOWP)
= (0.25 * 0.25) + (0.5 * 0.5) + (0.25 * 0.5)
= 0.0625 + 0.25 + 0.125
= 0.4375

METHOD

In order for our RPI calculations to be useful we make certain assumptions. First, there must be some inter-conference competition to link teams in the standings. This is the only epistemic basis for ranking teams across Canada from 1 to 20. As a result of this presumption, CCBC teams are excluded from our analysis because while not all teams need to play one another, some teams must cross over. The CCBC, more importantly, plays in the Spring-Summer while the remainder of teams play in the Fall. This does not, however, preclude their participation in a CUWS.[10]

Second, we have used post-facto results culled from CCBA competition at national championships in 2016, 2017, and 2018. Normally, the RPI would be used to determine if teams qualified for such a tournament in the first place but, as we have noted, we needed the data for our model.

Third, regardless of overall ranking, a Canadian University World Series would likely adhere to some regional representation. Under the CCBA, seeds were awarded on the basis of finishes by Northern and Atlantic playoffs providing for an equal representation from both conferences. In U Sports competition, all national championships also proceed from regional playoff eliminations. In the following section, we follow these same assumptions for interpolating seeds for hypothetical 2016, 2017, and 2018 CUWS.

In the Tables below we rank all participating teams in the OUA and CCBA from 2016 to 2018 by season. We use all available data culled from GameChanger, Pointstreak, and OUA Presto results. We also include all available inter-conference, pre-season, and playoff scores.

RESULTS

Applying the RPI calculation to our dataset by season we arrive at the following rankings for 2016, 2017, and 2018. (See Tables 1, 2, and 3.)

The results at the top end of the spectrum are not surprising. Teams that had excellent win-loss records and success in play-offs also placed very high in the overall rankings. McGill won three CCBA championships in this period and had the best overall win-loss record. They had won 30 consecutive league games until Carleton beat them in 2018.[11] Not surprisingly, McGill ranked first in RPI in each season. The 2016 OUA champs, Western, ranked second in that year while perennially strong programs such as Laurier (2018 OUA champs) and Brock also ranked in the top five each season. Other notables include 2018 CCBA finalist New Brunswick and 2017 OUA champs University of Toronto who also finished in the top five in the years they made championship appearances.

There are some surprises from 6th to 10th however. Contrary to the common assumption that the Atlantic conference, which is made up of smaller schools, is not as strong as the Northern conference or the OUA, Atlantic teams Acadia or Saint Mary's ranked above

Table 1. 2016 Canadian University Baseball Rankings

Rank	Team	Conf.	GP	W/L	WP	OWP	OOWP	RPI
1	McGill	Northern	30	25 5	0.833	0.519	0.509	0.595
2	Western	OUA	22	18 4	0.818	0.503	0.504	0.582
3	Laurier	OUA	23	18 5	0.783	0.511	0.504	0.578
4	Brock	OUA	22	16 6	0.727	0.514	0.503	0.564
5	Saint Mary's	Atlantic	22	10 12	0.455	0.593	0.469	0.527
6	Guelph	OUA	21	12 9	0.571	0.503	0.505	0.526
7	New Brunswick	Atlantic	21	16 5	0.762	0.456	0.427	0.520
8	Waterloo	OUA	21	10 11	0.476	0.520	0.503	0.504
9	Concordia	Northern	24	13 11	0.542	0.475	0.509	0.500
10	Acadia	Atlantic	19	9 10	0.474	0.522	0.480	0.499
11	Montreal	Northern	24	9 15	0.375	0.538	0.482	0.483
12	Carleton	Northern	18	8 10	0.444	0.469	0.502	0.471
13	Toronto	OUA	20	7 12 1	0.375	0.499	0.504	0.469
14	Queen's	OUA	20	6 13 1	0.325	0.500	0.504	0.457
15	STFX	Atlantic	12	1 11	0.083	0.564	0.493	0.426
16	Ryerson	OUA	18	5 13	0.278	0.484	0.454	0.425
17	Dalhousie	Atlantic	16	7 9	0.438	0.361	0.520	0.420
18	York	OUA	18	4 14	0.222	0.497	0.453	0.417
19	McMaster	OUA	18	4 14	0.222	0.497	0.453	0.417
20	Ottawa	Northern	16	3 13	0.188	0.488	0.500	0.416
21	Crandall	Atlantic	16	2 14	0.125	0.495	0.477	0.398

Table 2. 2017 Canadian University Baseball Rankings

Rank	Team	Conf.	GP	W/L	WP	OWP	OOWP	RPI
1	McGill	Northern	32	29 2 1	0.938	0.500	0.510	0.612
2	Laurier	OUA	18	13 5	0.722	0.538	0.503	0.575
3	Brock	OUA	16	13 3	0.813	0.479	0.511	0.570
4	Toronto	OUA	20	10 9 1	0.525	0.583	0.498	0.547
5	Saint Mary's	Atlantic	12	6 6	0.500	0.547	0.497	0.523
6	Carleton	Northern	24	14 10	0.583	0.480	0.508	0.513
7	Montreal	Northern	12	7 5	0.583	0.462	0.501	0.502
8	Acadia	Atlantic	24	8 16	0.333	0.597	0.473	0.500
9	Queen's	OUA	20	8 12	0.400	0.541	0.500	0.496
10	STFX	Atlantic	9	3 6	0.333	0.571	0.507	0.496
11	Guelph	OUA	16	8 8	0.500	0.484	0.510	0.495
12	Western	OUA	16	9 7	0.563	0.446	0.515	0.493
13	New Brunswick	Atlantic	19	7 12	0.368	0.556	0.482	0.491
14	Concordia	Northern	24	11 13	0.458	0.500	0.491	0.487
15	Dalhousie	Atlantic	12	7 5	0.583	0.401	0.563	0.487
16	Ryerson	OUA	17	5 12	0.294	0.530	0.504	0.464
17	McMaster	OUA	16	5 11	0.313	0.483	0.510	0.447
18	Waterloo	OUA	16	4 12	0.250	0.481	0.511	0.431
19	Ottawa	Northern	20	0 20	0.000	0.514	0.488	0.379

Table 3. 2018 Canadian University Baseball Rankings

Rank	Team	Conf.	GP	W/L	WP	OWP	OOWP	RPI
1	McGill	Northern	36	27 7 2	0.778	0.523	0.506	0.583
2	New Brunswick	Atlantic	25	17 8	0.680	0.554	0.536	0.581
3	Brock	OUA	19	13 6	0.684	0.521	0.484	0.553
4	Laurier	OUA	25	18 7	0.720	0.500	0.488	0.552
5	Acadia	Atlantic	24	12 12	0.500	0.567	0.525	0.540
6	Carleton	Northern	28	18 10	0.643	0.490	0.518	0.535
7	Toronto	OUA	27	17 9 1	0.648	0.498	0.490	0.533
8	Guelph	OUA	22	14 8	0.636	0.467	0.491	0.515
9	Queen's	OUA	25	13 11 1	0.540	0.514	0.487	0.514
10	Concordia	Northern	27	14 13	0.519	0.515	0.506	0.514
11	Saint Mary's	Atlantic	23	8 15	0.348	0.568	0.529	0.503
12	Western	OUA	21	11 10	0.524	0.467	0.489	0.487
13	McMaster	OUA	21	10 11	0.476	0.465	0.489	0.474
14	STFX	Atlantic	21	7 14	0.333	0.496	0.548	0.468
15	Montreal	Northern	21	6 15	0.286	0.498	0.511	0.448
16	Ryerson	OUA	22	6 16	0.273	0.526	0.487	0.445
17	Dalhousie	Atlantic	16	3 13	0.188	0.505	0.537	0.444
18	Ottawa	Northern	17	3 14	0.176	0.505	0.506	0.423
19	Waterloo	OUA	18	3 15	0.167	0.469	0.488	0.398
20	Laurentian	OUA	17	1 16	0.059	0.450	0.487	0.362

CCBA Northern teams like Concordia and Carleton in RPI. This can be better understood by paying closer attention to the way RPI is calculated in our discussion on limitations. Other RPI calculations, for example, have taken into account conference strength. We do not do so in this analysis.

As the OUA did not divide its teams into Eastern and Western schedules until 2019 when Carleton and Ottawa joined the league, we use the town of Oakville, Ontario, as the geographic boundary line to divide the two regions from 2016-2018. As a result, Ontario West consists of six teams: Guelph, McMaster, Laurentian (entering in 2018), Laurier, Waterloo and Western. Ontario East is made up of five teams: Brock, Queens, Ryerson, Toronto and York. We selected the highest RPI ranked team by region. As was the practice in the CCBA, one spot is reserved for the host team. We simply reproduced those same hosts in our model. As the more isolated CCBC (West) did not play inter-conference games, included two-year colleges in its schedule, and was excluded from our calculations, we seeded the highest finishing four-year university team at the CCBC championship tournament as the western representative. Finally, as was the practice in the CCBA national championship, we made room for wild card entries. In our case, after regional seeds were determined, we took the next two highest RPI ranked teams that had not already been seeded. (See Tables 4, 5, and 6.)

Once again, given overall win-loss records, playoff success, and standings, the teams represented in these make-believe national championships of university baseball are not controversial representatives. Each of these teams had very strong records with a history of success in their respective conferences.

Table 4. Canadian University World Series 2016

Host	Montreal (11)
Atlantic	Saint Mary's (5)
Quebec	McGill (1)
Ontario West	Western (2)
Ontario East	Brock (4)
West	Thompson Rivers (NA)
WC1	Laurier (3)
WC2	Guelph (6)

Number in parentheses denotes RPI rank / Seeds based on regional representation

Table 5. Canadian University World Series 2017

Host	New Brunswick (13)
Atlantic	Saint Mary's (5)
Quebec	McGill (1)
Ontario West	Laurier (2)
Ontario East	Brock (4)
West	Thompson Rivers (NA)
WC1	Toronto (3)
WC2	Carleton (6)

Number in parentheses denotes RPI rank / Seeds based on regional representation

Table 6. Canadian University World Series 2018

Host	Carleton (6)
Atlantic	New Brunswick (2)
Quebec	McGill (1)
Ontario West	Laurier (3)
Ontario East	Brock (7)
West	Fraser Valley (NA)
WC1	Acadia (4)
WC2	Laurier (5)

Number in parentheses denotes RPI rank / Seeds based on regional representation

Despite determining seeds based on conferences/regions and including host teams, most of the teams in each of the three successive hypothetical World Series we seeded had very high RPI rankings. If we eliminate the Western seed (CCBC), for which we have no RPI score, and the host team, for which placement is automatic, of the remaining qualifying teams, 6 of 6 (or 100%) in each of 2016, 2017 and 2018 were ranked in the top eight for RPI. Thus, despite regional seeding considerations, the CUWS consisted of the top teams in the country.

Of course, these hypothetical seeds are partially a post-facto mockup. Any agreed upon process that accepted a unified Canadian University World Series would set its own parameters around qualifications, regional representations, and even the number of teams included. We have simply adopted the closest approximation of existing practices in our model. In the process, however, the RPI seems to largely confirm the strength of baseball programs across the country as demonstrated in actual playoff and championship results over the last three seasons.

LIMITATIONS

As effective and convenient as RPI is for comparing teams, it also has one foundational flaw: no ranking system can compare how two teams would stack up against one another quite like having those teams play head-to-head. There is no way to fix this. Unless, of course, the University of New Brunswick in the Atlantic flies to St. Catharines in Central Canada to play Brock in a weekend double header, or Queen's University in Eastern Ontario wants to travel to Wolfville, Nova Scotia, to play Acadia. As we mentioned, this is highly improbable as it involves significant interprovincial and trans-Canada travel. Moreover, for win-loss records to be the basis of rankings, the schedule would have to be balanced and complete so one could properly seed teams based on head-to-head competition. In the absence of such a schedule, we have the RPI.

Yet, what many analysts particularly dislike about the RPI formula is that so much weight is placed on the question: "How good are the teams you play?" There are three accompanying limitations associated with this weighting that affect the rankings we have presented in this paper: (1) conference strength, (2) the use of post-facto results, and (3) the importance given to pre-season games. We deal with each of these below.

1. Conference Strength

As mentioned, 75% of the RPI calculation has nothing to do with the team itself and everything to do with how the teams it played performed, and how the teams that those teams played performed. A key problem with the formula is that a team can be awarded more "RPI points" after losing to a great team than after defeating a bad team. This is because, as mentioned, 75% of the calculation is all about the rest of the league, and not the team in question.

From 2016 to 2018, OUA teams played CCBA Northern Conference teams 26 times in pre-season or inter-league competition. The vast majority of these games involved five-time CCBA champion McGill and, to a lesser degree, perennial runner-up Carleton—teams that posted high win percentages in league play. Not surprisingly, the CCBA Northern teams had a win percentage of .654 (16–8–2) against OUA competition over that three-year period.

Due to the limited amount of inter-conference competition, teams in the Atlantic were statistically firewalled from being beaten by their Northern conference opponents except in the CCBA national tournament. Moreover, the Atlantic conference typically had a less skewed differential in win percentage between teams resulting in higher OWP and OOWP compared to the Northern conference and OUA. Finally, Atlantic teams repeatedly benefited from taking turns losing, yes *losing*, to undefeated non-conference CCBA affiliate team Holland College that was included in results and standings but ineligible for playoff competition because of its 2-year college status. This causes significant problems for making sense of the final rankings.

For example, Saint Mary's ranked higher in RPI than every Northern conference team except McGill in 2016 and 2017. Acadia did the same in 2018. Yet from 2016 through 2018 Acadia and Saint Mary's were a combined 1–11 (.083) vs. Northern conference teams at the CCBA national championship, and were outscored 126–18.[12] Despite these asymmetrical head-to-head results, Saint Mary's (6–6) still outranked Carleton (14–10) Montreal (7–5), and Concordia (11–13) in RPI in 2017.

Conference asymmetry is a common issue faced by US ranking analysts who have built models to correct for Strength of Schedule (SOS) in RPI calculations.[13] The RPIs are calculated here without SOS correction, though there is evidence to support the need for such corrections in future ranking systems. This is especially true considering the CCBC, like the Atlantic conference, does not play any inter-conference games with other Canadian university teams and includes non-university teams in its schedule.

2. Post-facto Results

In this analysis we have used results that include CCBA nationals competition to allow for some inter-conference reliability (between Northern and Atlantic conferences of the CCBA) and to lend credibility to the notion that ranking Canadian university baseball teams from 1 to 20 is possible.

Of course, while we required these results to allow for a more robust statistical dataset, the results are based on games that should have ostensibly only taken place after RPI results were considered in deciding the teams receiving seeds to the championship. RPI scores in the future could not make use of these results except if calculations straddled two seasons as a rolling average or, more preferably, if teams intentionally played select inter-conference games as has already been happening in the OUA for 2019.

3. Pre-season Games

Inter-conference games between OUA and CCBA Northern teams have been inconsequential on standings, rank, or seeding. Unlike their relevance in US college competition, they have no bearing on how Canadian university baseball teams place, and in the absence of a unified national championship they are treated as exhibition games with little more than pride in the balance.

As a result, these games are often considered warm-ups for the season, when coaches test position players and pitchers, do not field their top lineups, and sometimes allow games to end in a tie. Given this reality, one could argue their use in our analysis is a dubious choice but, once again, without the inclusion of these results there would be no theoretical basis to rank OUA teams alongside CCBA teams.

Of course, if RPI was applied to these games and these results mattered for ranking seeds for a CUWS, this would surely change the nature of competition in these contests.

CONCLUSIONS

We have demonstrated the feasibility of using an RPI system for ranking Canadian university baseball teams across the country. No secondary ranking system can replace head-to-head play and qualifying playoffs, but in a short Fall season with limited inter-conference play the RPI could be useful for the future development of Canadian university baseball.

The RPI, as we have calculated it in this analysis, has limitations. It does not take into account conference strength, especially when inter-conference play is limited. It over-states the importance of pre-season and exhibition games and uses post-facto playoff results. All of these issues are correctable in future calculations of RPI, especially if there is a coordinated effort to make the results more reliable through planned inter-conference scheduling, as has been long-established in the NCAA.[14]

Despite its limitation, RPI is a relatively effective ranking system. While some organizations, such as NCAA basketball are using newer metrics, other programs such as state high school football associations are adopting the RPI.[15,16] Indeed, there are just as many critics of these newer metrics as the RPI.[17] Eight years ago, sabermetrics experts considered a potential ranking index (the PING) for NCAA baseball before regionals, super-regionals, and an accepted national qualification path to Omaha and the College World Series was established through head-to-head competition.[18]

Comparing a team's strength of schedule through RPI is the best available, independent method for comparing teams that cannot play one another. Future formulas could take into account conference strength and control for non-conference results. In the end, the RPI offers a tested and objective method for ranking Canadian university baseball teams toward ascertaining their qualification for a potential Canadian University World Series. ∎

Notes

1. Canadian Collegiate Baseball Association. 2019. "History." *Baseball-Reference.com* Accessed June 11, 2019. https://www.baseball-reference.com/bullpen/Canadian_Collegiate_Baseball_Association.
2. Canadian Collegiate Baseball Association. 2019. "History." Accessed July 25, 2019. http://ccba-abcc.pointstreaksites.com/view/ccba-abcc/about/history.
3. The University of Windsor, across the river from Detroit, participate in the US-based National Club Baseball Association (NCBA) but were granted entry to the OUA provincial tournament from 2017. Similarly, the University of British Columbia (UBC), based in Vancouver, also plays across the border in the National Athletic Intercollegiate Association (NAIA) and does not compete against Canadian baseball teams. As neither team plays against Canadian university opposition they are omitted from this analysis.

4. U Sports is Canada's national governing body for university sport, equivalent to the NCAA, and formerly named Canadian Intercollegiate Sport (CIS).

5. National Sport Organizations (NSOs) in Canada are legislatively recognized bodies for the management of amateur sport in the country. There are currently 58 NSOs in Canada—Baseball Canada oversees amateur baseball.

6. George Rigakos, "A beginner's guide to Canadian university baseball." Canadian Baseball Network. (December 16) Reposted. Accessed June 11, 2019. https://www.curavensbaseball.com/a-beginners-guide-to-university-baseball-in-canada/

7. The demise of the CCBA and the appearance of the ACBA were announced through social media on Facebook July 25, 2019. https://www.facebook.com/CanadianUniversityBaseball/photos/a.2070884913221857/2258906037753076/?type=3&theater and the takeover of the former CCBA account by ACBA on Instagram: https://www.instagram.com/atlanticcba.

8. "How to Calculate RPI and What it Means to Handicappers." madduxsports.com. Accessed February 3, 2019. http://www.madduxsports.com/library/cbb/how-to-calculate-rpi-and-what-it-means-to-handicappers.html.

9. Alex Kirshner, "Yes, USC should have made it to the NCAA tournament." SBNation. (March 11) Accessed July 9, 2019. https://www.sbnation.com/college-basketball/2018/3/11/17104676/usc-snub-ncaa-tournament-march-madness-2018

10. In 2018, the University of Calgary applied for membership in the CCBA and was accepted but ultimately could not participate as no other western team agreed to play them in a qualifier—a condition set out by the CCBA. The principle author of this paper is also the former President of the CCBA who received the application and membership cheque from the University of Calgary. A provisional agreement was worked out where if at least four members of the CCBC also joined the CCBA the top finisher in the preceding year would be invited to the CUWS. While these conditions were never satisfied, such staggered seedings are not alien to Canadian baseball. The same principle is applied during Baseball Canada's Sr. men's championship and in much international baseball competition. For university baseball, of course, the limitations are obvious. Depending on turn-over senior student-athletes graduate and freshmen arrive, the complexion and competitiveness of the team will also change.

11. CU Ravens Baseball. 2018. "McGill's historic winning streak snapped by Carleton at 30 games." (September 10). Reposted from CCBA. Accessed July 8, 2019. https://www.curavensbaseball.com/mcgills-historic-winning-streak-snapped-by-carleton-at-30-games.

12. Their only win came in 2016 when Saint Mary's upset McGill in round-robin play 3–2.

13. James, Crepea, "Pac-12 weighing 20 game basketball schedule, massively raising non-conference standards." Oregon Live. (May 1) Accessed July 8, 2019. https://www.oregonlive.com/collegebasketball/2019/05/pac-12-weighing-20-game-basketball-schedule-massively-raising-non-conference-standards.html.

14. Of course, it cannot go unstated that some teams will attempt to manipulate their inter-conference schedule to best boost their RPI. See: Jesse Newell, "How KU basketball won the scheduling game…again." Kansas City Star, June 29, 2018. Accessed September 12, 2019. https://www.kansascity.com/sports/college/big-12/university-of-kansas/article214096929.html.

15. Marc Tracy, "R.I.P. to the R.P.I.: Selection committee breaks out new math," The New York Times, March 15, 2019, Accessed July 8, 2019. https://www.nytimes.com/2019/03/15/sports/ncaa-bracket-selection-sunday-net-rating.html.

16. J. C. Carnahan, "Football RIP ranking system clears final hurdle for 2019." Orlando Sentinel, January 28, 2019. Accessed June 1, 2019. https://www.orlandosentinel.com/sports/highschool/os-sp-hs-fhsaa-football-0129-story.html.

17. Neil Greenberg, "The NCAA's lousy new metric is going to make March Madness even crazier," Washington Post, December 18, 2018. Accessed July 8, 2019. https://www.washingtonpost.com/sports/2018/12/18/ncaas-lousy-new-metric-is-going-make-march-madness-even-crazier/?noredirect=on&utm_term=.8a5887a2f735.

18. Philip Yates, "The PING ratings: A method for ranking NCAA baseball team," Baseball Research Journal: Fall 2011. Accessed July 9, 2019. https://sabr.org/research/ping-ratings-model-rating-ncaa-baseball-teams.

Time Between Pitches

Cause of Long Games?

David W. Smith

A major topic for MLB and the baseball press continues to be the length of the average game, which has been above three hours for several years. Many factors have been suggested to account for the longer games and I addressed several of these last year by looking at patterns over the past 110 seasons in my paper and presentation "Why Do Games Take So Long?"[1] The two strongest connections I found were increases in the number of strikeouts and in the overall number of pitches. One possibility that has received a great deal of attention is the time between pitches; in fact, MLB has considered instituting a 20-second clock with the bases empty. At the 2018 SABR convention, Eliza Richardson Malone presented the results of her study of 31 starting pitchers in 2017. Although her data set was limited, her conclusion was clear: she found very few pitch intervals exceeding 20 seconds. Therefore the proposal to force pitchers to throw within 20 seconds would not have a significant impact on game length. But could time between pitches still be a a major factor in why games are so long? With the help of Major League Baseball Advanced Media (MLBAM), I conducted the following study.

Thanks to MLBAM, I have the precise time down to the second that each pitch was thrown in every game in 2018—with the exceptions of the two games played in Puerto Rico and the three in Mexico—a total of 717,410 pitches. That works out to just under 148 pitches per team per game.

First I need to clarify exactly which pitches I studied. "Time between pitches" is the amount of time after a pitch before the next pitch is thrown. This only applies to consecutive pitches *to the same batter*. Therefore, the last pitch thrown to each batter does not apply because there is no "next pitch" to him. When these "last pitches" are excluded, the total number of relevant pitches drops to 511,728, which is still an impressive sample size. The overall average interval for all pitches across all situations in 2018 was 23.8 seconds. Of course, there are many interesting ways to subdivide this number.

In addition to the interval between pitches, I studied the time taken for the following:

- Between pitches
- Mound visits
- Between batters
- Between innings
- Substitutions
- Replay challenges
- Injuries
- Ejections

I also looked at the length of each inning since many have reported slower play in later innings.

Table 1 has the basic data for time elapsed after each different pitch result for bases empty situations and those with a runner on first alone.

Table 1.

Situation	Seconds to Next Pitch	
Pitch result	Bases Empty	Man on First
All pitches	20.3	28.4
Ball	18.7	26.0
Called strike	17.1	25.2
Swinging strike	20.2	27.5
Foul	26.3	34.1

The bases are empty for 58% of all pitches, so the first column confirms Malone's conclusion that when the ball is not hit, the proposed 20-second clock would solve a problem that doesn't actually exist. These are averages, so of course some values are less and some more, but overall the bases-empty situation provides little opportunity for a rule intervention to speed up the game; pitchers are already meeting this standard.

Table 1 also shows that the time increases after a foul ball compared to pitches when no contact is made. This is not surprising. Every foul ball results in a new ball being put in play, which takes more time than continuing to use the same ball. There is greater variation here, as well, since a ball fouled at the plate will not slow things nearly as much as a long foul into the stands.

There is a man on first alone 18% of the time and the second column presents the average intervals in this situation. All other situations combined add up to 24% of pitches. It is conventional wisdom that the game slows down when someone gets on base and these numbers certainly support that position. The average increase is 8.1 seconds across all pitch results.

PICKOFFS

We must consider another major feature of having a man on first, namely pickoff throws. I documented 11,194 throws to first in 2018, 10,755 by pitchers and 439 by catchers. The pickoffs added an average of 25 seconds to each pitch interval although there was a wide variation. When the overall average time for pickoff attempts is subtracted from the 28.4 second interval for a runner on first, then the time between pitches drops to 22.9 seconds. In other words, pickoff attempts at first account for about two thirds of the increase found with having a runner on first. To complete this thread, the other runner situations differ very little, with a combined effect of adding about 1 additional second to the time for a runner on first only.

MOUND VISITS

Mound visits were restricted in 2018 for the first time with a limit of six per game for each team. This limit has been reduced to five for 2019. I began noting mound visits in July of 2018. The average time consumed by a mound visit is 81.5 seconds, even though the rules are clear that the visit itself is limited to 30 seconds. The 81 second interval is the actual time between pitches whereas the 30 second clock starts when the manager or coach has left the dugout and does not include the return trip to the dugout, accounting for the wide difference between the rule and the reality. Player visits to the mound are also counted, but the rules do not specify how to time those. If a mound visit ends up in a pitching change, then it does not count against the limited number for the game and I did not count them in my average time.

TIME BETWEEN BATTERS

The average time between batters within an inning is 54 seconds. Again this is the time from the last pitch to the previous batter and the first pitch to the next one. I noticed interesting differences in this time for different innings as shown in Figure 1. The horizontal line is the average for all innings to allow easier comparison.

The value is low in the early innings and then it rises with a peak in the 7th to over 62 seconds, which is almost 15 seconds more than the quickest time in

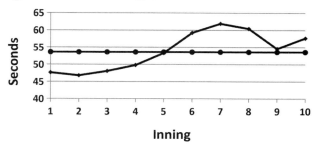

Figure 1. Time Between Batters

the second inning. The increased time in later innings makes sense as the game pressure mounts and it is reasonable for both batter and pitcher to take a little extra time to get ready. All extra innings are combined as 10. The one point that stands out is in the 9th which has a remarkable drop from the 8th and 7th innings. Two years ago in New York I showed that 47% of games had a margin of three or more runs when the 9th inning started and the team in the lead won 97% of those games. I suggest that the drop I found here reflects the reality there is less deliberate preparation by either the batter or the pitcher since so many games are clearly decided by this point. If a game goes beyond 9 innings, then it is reasonable that the time increases since the games are obviously closer.

TIME BETWEEN INNINGS

I found the average time between innings to be 2 minutes and 42 seconds. This is interesting in light of the MLB pace of play rules put into effect for 2018 which set different limits based on the nature of the television broadcast of the game, as shown in Table 2:

Table 2.

Type of Broadcast	MLB Rule	Actual
Local TV	2:05	2:41
National TV	2:25	2:55
Postseason games	2:55	Not studied

I did not look at postseason games. According to MLBAM, there were 62 games designated as national television games in 2018 as opposed to 2,368 local television games. The average time between innings for the locally televised games was 2 minutes and 41 seconds and for the nationally televised games it was 2 minutes and 55 seconds, a difference of 14 seconds. In any case, the observed times are well beyond the stated limits, especially for the locally televised games. However, we have to consider when the official clock is started at the end of each half-inning. MLB issued very precise descriptions of how the timing is to be done including different starting details when a relief pitcher is entering the game. The average time between innings also changed significantly by inning, as shown in Figure 2.

Figure 2. Time Between Innings

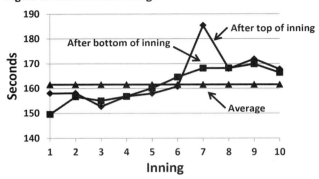

The horizontal line presents the average for all inning changes and the other two lines show the changes after the top and bottom of an inning. There are two striking features to me in this figure. First, the times get progressively longer as the game proceeds just as the breaks between batters do, and second, the break after the top of the 7th inning is much longer than all the others. In fact, it is 17 seconds longer than after the bottom of the 7th. Everyone will immediately realize this reflects the "7th inning stretch," but there is another wrinkle. You may recall that most teams now play "God Bless America" during the 7th inning stretch at Sunday games. There are three notable exceptions: the Yankees play this song in the 7th inning of every game, while the Blue Jays and A's don't play it at all. There were 391 games played on Sundays in 2018, to which I added the Yankees non-Sunday games and subtracted the Toronto and Oakland games. That gave a total of 430 games with "God Bless America" and 2,002 games without it, presumably all of which included the traditional singalong of "Take Me Out to the Ballgame" (except for the Orioles who play "Thank God I'm a Country Boy"). The breakdown for these games in shown in Table 3.

Table 3.
7th Inning Stretch times

All Games	3:06
Take Me Out to the Ballgame	2:53
God Bless America	4:04

The extra one minute and 11 seconds consumed by "God Bless America" is pretty dramatic since it is played in 17.7% of all games. Once again we need to remember that the times I found are from the last pitch

to the last batter of the inning to the first pitch of the first batter in the next inning. However, it is clear that the actual times do not correspond to the carefully prescribed timing procedures promulgated by MLB.

SUBSTITUTIONS
Substitutions are another kind of event that takes extra time, of course. The most common type is a pitcher change. Table 4 has what I considered.

Table 4. Seconds per Change

Type of Change	Start Inning	Mid-Inning
All	13	83
Pitchers	14	138
Pinch-hitters	6	14

As expected, the mid-inning substitution of a pitcher takes the greatest amount of additional time: over two minutes more than a new pitcher at the start of an inning. One of my surprising results from my previous study is that the number of mid-inning pitching changes has not changed almost at all in the last 25 years, even though the total number of relievers per game has increased steadily since 1975. This is because most pitching changes are made at the inning break rather than mid-inning.

REPLAY CHALLENGES
We now live in the age of replay challenges and they constitute another significant interruption. MLB reports the time taken for each review but by their definition the timing of the challenge starts when the umpires commit to the review. My numbers again are the actual elapsed seconds before the next batter or pitch. Once again there is a difference between challenges at the end of an inning, the end of a batter appearance or the middle of a batter appearance. These details are in Table 5.

Table 5.

Challenge Situation	Occurrences	Average Time Consumed
End of Batter	665	2:42
End of Inning	185	4:26
Mid-batter	260	3:00
Overall	1100	3:05

The "End of Batter" and "End of Inning" data have to be looked at carefully, since there is already time consumed by these events. The numbers I report in Table 5 have had these challenge times removed. The properly weighted average for these events is 3:05.

MLB reports an average of 1:28. Again, their timing starts with the request and ends with the decision from New York, but my measured average time for the interruption is more than double their reported time.

TIME TO PLAY EACH INNING

The time taken to play a given inning also changes during the course of a game, partly reflecting pitcher subs, but not entirely. Figure 3 shows the values for each inning from the first pitch of the inning to the last.

Figure 3. Time for Each Half Inning

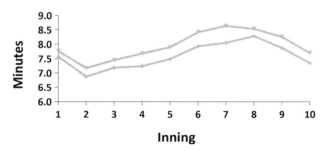

Inning

The data for the visiting team are in the bottom line and for the home team in the top line. It is interesting that the home innings take longer on average in all cases, with a difference of 12 seconds in the 1st to 35 seconds in the 7th—an average of 22 seconds. There is a drop of 36 seconds in the average from the 1st inning to the 2nd and then a fairly steady rise through the 7th. Note that this pattern mimics the differences between batters that we saw before. When these individual half-inning values are summed, we find that the average 8.5 inning game has 2 hours and 12 minutes of actual playing time and the average 9 inning game has 2 hours and 20 minutes of play.

INDIVIDUAL PITCHERS

I also looked at the time taken by individual pitchers since one would reasonably expect variation here. In order to reduce noise in the data, I only considered pitchers who threw at least 100 pitches of the "interval" type I examined here with the bases empty. There were 575 pitchers who met this criterion with the average ranging from 15.3 to 28.4 seconds between pitches.

I also looked at the ERA and WHIP (walks plus hits per inning) of these 575 pitchers to see if there were any relation between pitching success and time between pitches. There was no relation. The longest time is 8 seconds slower than overall average, which is not trivial over the course of an entire game, but it is more important to ask how often these slow times occur. Figure 4 shows a distribution that is probably

expected, with the large majority of pitchers showing little variation from the mean. In fact, the pitch intervals of 18 to 23 seconds cover 80% of all pitchers.

Figure 4. Distribution of Individual Pitchers

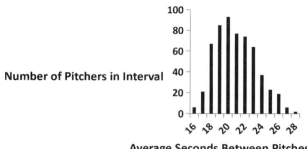

Average Seconds Between Pitches

INDIVIDUAL BATTERS

It is a logical extension to check individual batters, once again limiting the analysis to those who saw at least 100 "interval" pitches with the bases empty and excluding all pitchers. There were 513 batters in this group. Their range was 17.4 to 25.9 seconds, which is narrower than I found for pitchers. I examined batter success in terms of OPS in relation to the pitch interval and once again there was no relation.

INDIVIDUAL UMPIRES

The other party in each pitch is the plate umpire. The range here is amazingly narrow, from 19.3 to 20.5 seconds, barely a one-second difference. We can safely conclude that the identity of the umpire is of virtually no significance in the time taken between pitches

EJECTIONS

There were 87 ejection episodes in 2018 which saw the banishment of 189 players, coaches, and managers. In many cases two or more were ejected at the same time. These ejections consumed an average of one minute and 52 seconds.

INJURIES

Injuries to players and umpires were very different in their time consequences. I catalogued 528 stoppages of play for an injury to a player and these took an average of two minutes and 19 seconds. Umpire injuries are rarer—only seven in 2018. However, these took an average of nine minutes and 3 seconds. Almost all of these involved the home plate umpire hit by a foul ball, necessitating his replacement to don additional gear, which takes significant time.

SUMMARY AND HIGHLIGHTS

- Bases empty   20.3 seconds
- Man on first   28.4 seconds
- Throws to first   25 seconds

- **Mound visits**   **81 seconds**
- Between batters   54 seconds
- Between innings   162 seconds
- Seventh inning stretch   15 additional seconds
- "God Bless America"   **71 additional seconds**
- Pitcher change start inning   14 additional seconds
- Pitcher change mid-inning   **138 additional seconds**
- Challenges between plays   162 seconds
- Challenges between innings   266 seconds
- Fastest to slowest pitchers   12 seconds
- Fastest to slowest batters   7 seconds
- Injuries to players   2:19
- Injuries to umpires   9:03

CONCLUSION

As demonstrated here, there are many different factors that add to the time of games. However, the answer to the question in the title is NO, time between pitches is not the cause of long games. Time between pitches makes only a minor contribution to total time.

Table 6 breaks down the average "regulation length" game, that is, those which are either 8.5 or 9 innings.

Table 6.

	8.5 innings	9 innings
Total games	1065	1145
Average Game Time	2:56	3:05
Calculated Play	2:12	2:20
Calculated Breaks	42 min	44 min
Calculated Game Time	2:55	3:04

The "calculated" times were obtained by summing the observed average times for each half inning as well as the individual average times between innings. The nearly perfect match between the actual and calculated game times gives me great confidence that I considered the proper factors. As a final point, I looked on a per game basis at the various interruptions I identified. These are contained within the calculated play time and are listed in Table 7.

Table 7.

	Events Per Game	Total Time (minutes)
Pickoff Throws	4.6	1.9
Mound Visits	5.4	7.3
Substitutions	4.4	6.1
Challenges	0.5	1.3
Ejections	0.1	0.1
Injuries	0.2	0.5
Total	15.1	17.1

These regulation-length games average 3 hours and 1 minute, so the 17.1 minutes of interruptions comprise an average of 9.5% of the total time.

We are left with the question of where MLB could intervene to shorten games and I see no obvious target for rule changes that could mitigate this situation. There is a pending new rule requiring relievers to face a minimum of three batters instead of one, but these data suggest that will have little to no impact. It seems that the inherent structure of the game has changed to the current rate at which events flow and we should expect that to continue. ■

Note

1. David W. Smith, "Why Do Games Take So Long?" *Baseball Research Journal*, Fall 2018. See also Retrosheet: https://www.retrosheet.org/Research/SmithD/WhyDoGamesTakeSoLong.pdf.

WAA vs. WAR

Which is the Better Measure for Overall Performance in MLB, Wins Above Average or Wins Above Replacement?

Campbell Gibson, PhD

Among the many statistical analyses of baseball that have been published during the last four decades, the single most important in my opinion is *The Hidden Game of Baseball* (1984) by Peter Palmer and John Thorn. Their research, based on a large-scale regression analysis of baseball statistics, led to the development of summary measures for overall performance (including batting, base running, pitching, and fielding) standardized to account for several factors. These factors included changes over time in the average number of runs scored per game, differences in players' home parks, and the relative difficulty of a player's fielding position. This last factor reflects the fact that for two players with identical offensive performance, the one playing a more difficult position (e.g., catcher or shortstop) is more valuable than one playing a less difficult position (e.g., left field).

The beauty of Palmer's and Thorn's two primary summary measures—Total Player Rating (TPR) and Total Pitcher Index (TPI)—was that they quantified the performance of players (both pitchers and non-pitchers) in terms of wins contributed to the team relative to average performance. Thus the values of these measures could be positive, zero, or negative, and totals for teams correlated very highly with team performance. Since team performance is primarily a function of how well the team's players perform, these measures were in fact good predictors of team performance.

Eight editions of *Total Baseball* were published next, 1989 through 2004, authored by Palmer, Thorn, and others. *TB* was more comprehensive than previous baseball encyclopedias, and starting with the 4th edition was recognized as the official encyclopedia of Major League Baseball. *Total Baseball* included other measures of overall performance in addition to those developed by Palmer and Thorn. The 8th edition introduced the term Total Player Wins (TPW): "The 'MVP' of statistics, this ranks pitchers and position players by their total wins contributed in all their endeavors, revealing the most valuable performers in a given year." (Page 2,673.) TPW replaced the terms TPR and

TPI used previously. The TPW concept was continued in five editions of the *ESPN Baseball Encyclopedia* through 2008 where it was referred to as Batter-Fielder Wins (BFW).

As with many print publications, *Total Baseball* became antiquated in the wake of the Internet. Baseball-Reference.com, developed by Sean Forman, went public in 2000. The B-R.com database was developed originally using the same data underlying the issues of *Total Baseball*.[1] At B-R.com, the concept of TPR has been relabeled Wins Above Average (WAA). While there have been many refinements in computing values of WAA, the basic concept is the same: WAA quantifies the performance of players (both pitchers and non-pitchers) in terms of wins contributed to the player's team compared with average performance.[2]

SOURCES OF THE DATA

Most of the data included in this paper are from Baseball-Reference.com, and many were obtained using the Play Index on the website. The Play Index is a feature of Baseball-Reference.com that enables a researcher to develop a wide range of custom tabulations. Without the Play Index, it would not have been feasible to calculate many of the statistics presented here.

WINS ABOVE AVERAGE (WAA)

To illustrate how WAA relates values for players to team performance, we can start with the 2018 season, using an average team, the best team, and the weakest team, as defined by their won-lost records. The most average team was the Los Angeles Angels with an 80–82 record. They had a team WAA of +0.2 (essentially zero), composed of a +5.2 for the non-pitching position players and designated hitters—hereafter called "position players"—and a –5.0 for pitchers. Not surprisingly, the best player on the team was Mike Trout with a WAA of +8.1. With just an average player in place of Trout, the team would probably have won about eight fewer games, which would have produced a 72–90 record. (It should be noted that a team's WAA is not expected to predict its won-lost record exactly;

differences can occur for various reasons, for example how well or poorly a team did in one-run games.)

The best team in 2018 was the Boston Red Sox with a won-lost record of 108–54 and a team WAA of +22.3, composed of +6.2 for position players and +16.1 for pitchers. This value of WAA suggests a won-lost record of about 22 games above .500, or 103–59. While the Red Sox ranked first in the American League in runs scored with 876 and third lowest in runs allowed with 647, the values of WAA indicate that their pitchers were further above average than their position players. The explanation for this apparent inconsistency is one of the features of WAA, which incorporates Park Factor. As usual, Fenway Park in 2018 was more favorable to hitters and less favorable to pitchers than the average park. In 2018, Mookie Betts had a WAA value of +8.9, the highest in the major leagues. Without Mookie Betts and with an average player in his place, the total WAA value for position players on the Red Sox team would actually have been negative (–2.7, calculated as +6.2 – 8.9).

The weakest team in 2018 was the Baltimore Orioles at 47–115 with a team WAA of –22.9, composed of –15.6 for position players and –7.3 for pitchers. This suggests a won-lost record about 23 games below .500, or 58–104. As seems frequently to be the case with weak teams (such as teams losing more than twice as many games as they won), the Orioles' record in games decided by one run was also weak, with 12 wins and 29 losses.

One more example to show how WAA relates player value to team performance: the 1927 New York Yankees. Considered one of the best teams of all time, the 1927 Yankees included six future Hall of Famers: Babe Ruth, Lou Gehrig, Herb Pennock, Waite Hoyt, Earle Combs, and Tony Lazzeri, as well as their manager, Miller Huggins. The team had a won-lost record of 110–44 and a team WAA of +33.4, composed of +26.7 for position players and +6.7 for pitchers. In the 154-game season then in use (where a record of 77–77 was average), this suggests a won-lost record of about 110–44, which happens to agree exactly with the Yankees record that year. Their run-producing ability was led by outstanding seasons for Ruth (+9.9) and Gehrig (+9.3), with major contributions from Combs (+4.4) and Lazzeri (+3.8).

In brief, the WAA concept provides an excellent method that is intuitively appealing for quantifying the performance of players and connects player performance with team performance in a systematic way.

WINS ABOVE REPLACEMENT (WAR)

The summary definition of WAR from the Baseball-Reference website follows: "A single number that presents the number of wins the player added to the team above what a replacement player…would add." (This replacement player would come from the top minor league level.) A comprehensive history and discussion of the WAR concept is also provided on B-R.com. As noted in this discussion, "There is no one way to determine WAR. There are hundreds of steps to make this calculation, and dozens of places where reasonable people can disagree on the best way to implement a particular part of the framework…. WAR is necessarily an approximation and will never be as precise or accurate as one would like."

The discussion includes the concept of replacement players and states, "When computing the value of a major league player, average is a poor baseline for comparison. Average players are relatively rare and can be expensive to acquire…. Replacement level players, by their very definition, are players easy to obtain when a starter goes down. These are the players who receive non-roster invites at the start of the year, or the players who are 6-year minor league free agents."

While the computation of WAA and WAR are both complex and involve many steps, the computation of WAR is more subjective. The computation of WAR starts with WAA and adjusts the benchmark from the concept of an average (a straightforward statistical measure), to the concept of a replacement player. The replacement player concept is not at all straightforward, as reflected by the fact that it is calculated differently by different sources (e.g. Baseball Reference, Fangraphs). The calculation is further complicated by the fact that the best actual replacement player available to a team varies because the minor league players available vary from one team to another. An example of this is provided later.

It is clear from the definition of WAR and the discussion of the concept of replacement-level players that the primary motivation for developing WAR is not the performance level of baseball players in general, but rather the performance level as it pertains to replacing a major league player with an available minor league player.

The problem with this approach is that while the replacement-level concept may be very useful with regard to replacing a player, this does not mean that the replacement-level concept is preferable in general, or that WAR is preferable to WAA for general evaluations of player performance. In part because the WAR concept has been used widely to analyze the financial costs of replacing players and because there is an understandable focus among baseball journalists about players' salaries, team salary totals, the financial worth of free agents, etc., WAR values are cited frequently. In contrast WAA values are rarely, if ever, seen in newspapers and magazines, but appear only (or with few exceptions) in the professional literature on the analysis of baseball performance. A related difficulty is that WAR values are used in the media with no discussion of their limitations.

LIMITATIONS OF WINS ABOVE REPLACEMENT (WAR)

We can start by looking at what using the WAR concept in place of the WAA concept does to our examples relating values for players with team performance. In the case of our average team—the 2018 Los Angeles Angels and their 80-82 record—the team WAR was $+35.0$ (composed of $+26.0$ for position players and $+9.0$ for pitchers). Unlike the team WAA value of $+0.2$, the team WAR value of $+35.0$ does not convey that this was an average team. One would have to dig into the technical details of the computation of WAR to find out that the benchmark for an average team is no longer a won-lost record of 81–81 and a .500 winning percentage, but rather a won-lost record of 47–115 and a .292 winning percentage. While a lot of research has gone into determining this benchmark, it has changed over time and reflects a lot of subjective decisions, as noted in the Wins Above Replacement Explainer quoted earlier.

Does the fact that the replacement-level benchmark of a won-lost record of 47–115 is equal to the actual performance of the 2018 Baltimore Orioles mean that they could have gone out and signed a team of replacement-level players and achieved the same result? This is highly doubtful. There is a big difference between the pool of talent at the top minor league level (noted in the summary definition of WAR) and the talent actually available (the non-roster invites and 6-year minor league free agents, as noted earlier).

Historically, there are many examples of top minor league players who were not free to sign with a major league team of their choice or a team looking for a replacement player. The 1937 Newark Bears (with a .717 winning percentage) in the International League provide one notable example. This team was owned by the New York Yankees and was the top team in its minor league farm system, with several players who were good enough to have been starters on other major league teams in 1938, including batting champion Charlie Keller. He was kept at Newark for the 1938 season because the Yankees had a starting outfield of Joe DiMaggio, Tommy Heinrich, and George Selkirk.

While the fact that there are very few major league players who are not exactly "average" and that they can be expensive to acquire, as noted above, does not mean that the average major league player is not a useful benchmark—or the most useful benchmark—for general player evaluation. While it is nice to deal with distributions of values that conform to the classic bell-shaped curve (in statistical theory, a normal distribution) where the average (more technically, the *mean*), median, and mode of the distribution are identical, these distributions exist primarily in statistical theory. A simple example would be the distribution of the expected number of heads in 100 tosses of a coin.

Statistical distributions in the real world are skewed, and the mean is most likely not the most frequent value. The distribution of US households by annual income provides another example. In this case, the distribution is skewed to the right (reflecting the fact that there are cases where the value is extremely high), and thus most cases have values below the mean.

The distribution of values of WAA provides another example. The distribution is skewed to the right with most cases having values below the mean. The primary explanation is that players who are way above average (say a WAA of 5.0 +) typically will play in the large majority, if not all, of their team's games. Players who are way below average (e.g., on pace for a WAA of –5.0 or less in a season) will not get to play very long in the major leagues. In 2018, 448 position players had 100 or more plate appearances, among whom 194 had a positive WAA (+ 0.1 or higher), 11 had a WAA of 0.0, and 243 (a majority) had a negative WAA (–0.1 or lower). In contrast, the corresponding WAR values of these 448 position players were 338 positive, 9 at 0.0, and 101 negative, reflecting that the benchmark for WAR values is well below the average major league performance.

In 2018, the top 10 position players, all of whom had over 600 plate appearances, had an average WAA of 5.8. Their average WAR was 7.9, suggesting that for full-time players, the average WAR is roughly 2.0 above the average WAA for a single season.

Three major observations about the WAR concept stand out based on the preceding discussion:

1. the WAR concept was developed originally with a focus on replacing a major league player with a minor league player, not on the general evaluation of player performance;

2. the implementation of the replacement-level concept is highly subjective; and

3. the WAR concept distorts the basic statistical properties of distributions such as the average.

These three observations led me to see if anyone had researched the issues raised by these facts. I found research published in 2012 by Adam Darowski comparing WAR and WAA at HighHeatStats.com.[3] He showed that in addition to increasing the numerical value of a player's career by switching from WAA to WAR, this increase is not consistent among players and results in tremendous differences in the ranking of players by their career performance.

His primary example of a player whose career ranking benefits from using his WAR value rather than his WAA value is Pete Rose. This is because Rose had many average or below- average seasons as measured by his WAA value—especially in the latter years of his long career—that still added to his WAR value or did not reduce it significantly. Darowski asks, when considering a player for the Hall of Fame, does one ask if "he was so much better than the AAA players of his day" or if "he was so much better than everyone else?" Darowski favors the latter criterion, and given this choice, divides a player's WAR value into two categories: his WAA wins (due to being above average compared with other major league players) and his "showing-up wins" (due to being below average among major league players but better than the minor-league benchmark). There are some cases where a major league player's performance was so far below average that his WAR value was negative (e.g., Pete Rose in 1981 and 1982, at ages 41 and 42, with WAA values of –3.4 and –4.0, and WAR values of –1.1 and –2.1, respectively.)

The term "showing-up wins" may seem a bit harsh and/or cynical since most players in any given year are likely to have WAA values below average, as explained previously. This does not mean that they do not deserve to play in the major leagues. However, Darowski's term is used here because the focus is on overall performance compared to other players overall (e.g., does the player deserve to be considered for the Hall of Fame), not on who the team might replace him with if he is no longer available (e.g., injured or opts for free agency).

Table 1 is titled "WAA and WAR Comparison for the top 65 Position Players in Career WAA and in Career WAR: 1871–2018." I limited the lists to 65 players—about the number that can be included reasonably in a one-page table. The table is designed to illustrate how WAR values relate to WAA values for top players by dividing their WAR wins into WAA wins and showing-up wins, as suggested by Darowski. The

two lists include 74 players: 56 players who appear on both lists, 9 players who appear on the WAA list only, and 9 players who appear on the WAR list only.

While the lists of the top 65 position players in WAA and in WAR include many of the same players, there is a pronounced and systematic bias. In general, players with less than the average number of career plate appearances show a drop in their ranking when switching from WAA to WAR, and vice versa. Among the top 10 players in WAA, Rogers Hornsby and Ted Williams (each with fewer than 10,000 plate appearances) drop from 5 to 9 and from 6 to 11, respectively. Among players in the top 65 in career WAA and with fewer than 8,000 career plate appearances, there were the following changes (all declines) in career ranking when switching from WAA to WAR: Dan Brouthers, 28 to 39; Joe DiMaggio, 30 to 42; Mike Trout (active), 37 to 99; Arky Vaughan (40 to 54); Johnny Mize, 45 to 61; Lou Boudreau, 50 to 104; Chase Utley, 53 to 95; Joe Jackson, 56 to 110; Gary Carter, 57 to 68; Billy Hamilton, 60 to 103; and Jackie Robinson, 62 to 114.

Among players whose rank is higher using WAR instead of WAA, Pete Rose, with the all-time record of 15,890 plate appearances, stands out (40 compared with 134). Other players with differences in rank of 20 or more include: Robin Yount, 43 versus 74; Paul Molitor, 45 versus 73; Sam Crawford, 48 versus 94; Reggie Jackson, 51 versus 89; Derek Jeter, 57 versus 114; and Rafael Palmeiro, 59 versus 122. Most of these players had over 12,000 career plate appearances.

WAA and WAR player rankings from Table 1 are shown in a scatter diagram in Figure 1 (see page 34) for 74 players. These include the 56 players who are among the top 65 in both WAA and WAR, the 9 players who are among the top 65 in WAA only, and the 9 players who are among the top 65 in WAR only. The Coefficient of Rank Correlation (rho) = 0.62. As would be expected, among the 56 players on both lists, the maximum difference in rankings between WAA and WAR is relatively small; it is 17 for both Larry Walker (WAA of 39 and WAR of 56) and Brooks Robinson (WAA of 58 and WAR of 41). For the other 18 players (those who are in the top 65 on just one of the two measures, WAA or WAR, but not both), the differences in rankings are typically much larger. The largest difference in ranking is 94 for Pete Rose (WAA of 134 and WAR of 40). The largest difference in the opposite direction is 62 for Mike Trout (WAA of 37 and WAR of 99). (This difference may well decrease as Trout's career progresses.)

The systematic bias noted above can be quantified by comparing the statistical relationship between career

Table 1. WAA and WAR Comparison for Top 65 Position Players in Career WAA and in Career WAR: 1871–2018

(WAA = wins above average, WAR = wins above replacement level, and PA = plate appearances)

Top 65 in Career WAA					WAR-WAA (showing-up wins)			Top 65 in Career WAR					WAR-WAA (showing-up wins)		
WAA rank	WAR rank	Player	WAA	WAR	Number	% of WAR	PA	WAR rank	WAA rank	Player	WAR	WAA	Number	% of WAR	PA
1	2	Babe Ruth*	125.5	162.1	36.6	22.6	10623	1	2	Barry Bonds	162.8	123.9	38.9	23.9	12606
2	1	Barry Bonds	123.9	162.8	38.9	23.9	12606	2	1	Babe Ruth*	162.1	125.5	36.6	22.6	10623
3	3	Willie Mays	110.3	156.4	46.1	29.5	12496	3	3	Willie Mays	156.4	110.3	46.1	29.5	12496
4	4	Ty Cobb	102.0	151.0	49.0	32.5	13099	4	4	Ty Cobb	151.0	102.0	49.0	32.5	13099
5	9	Rogers Hornsby	97.5	127.0	29.5	23.2	9480	5	7	Hank Aaron	143.0	92.9	50.1	35.0	13941
6	11	Ted Williams	94.1	123.1	29.0	23.6	9788	6	9	Tris Speaker	134.1	88.6	45.5	33.9	12011
7	5	Hank Aaron	92.9	143.0	50.1	35.0	13941	7	8	Honus Wagner	130.9	91.8	39.1	29.9	11746
8	7	Honus Wagner	91.8	130.9	39.1	29.9	11746	8	10	Stan Musial	128.2	81.7	46.5	36.3	12718
9	6	Tris Speaker	88.6	134.1	45.5	33.9	12011	9	5	Rogers Hornsby	127.0	97.5	29.5	23.2	9480
10	8	Stan Musial	81.7	128.2	46.5	36.3	12718	10	12	Eddie Collins	124.0	78.9	45.1	36.4	12078
11	15	Mickey Mantle	79.5	110.3	30.8	27.9	9907	11	6	Ted Williams	123.1	94.1	29.0	23.6	9788
12	10	Eddie Collins	78.9	124.0	45.1	36.4	12078	12	14	Alex Rodriguez	117.8	76.1	41.7	35.4	12207
13	13	Lou Gehrig	78.5	112.4	33.9	30.2	9665	13	13	Lou Gehrig	112.4	78.5	33.9	30.2	9665
14	12	Alex Rodriguez	76.1	117.8	41.7	35.4	12207	14	17	Rickey Henderson	111.2	69.0	42.2	37.9	13346
15	19	Mike Schmidt	73.6	106.8	33.2	31.1	10062	15	11	Mickey Mantle	110.3	79.5	30.8	27.9	9907
16	16	Mel Ott	70.6	107.8	37.2	34.5	11348	16	16	Mel Ott	107.8	70.6	37.2	34.5	11348
17	14	Rickey Henderson	69.0	111.2	42.2	37.9	13346	17	18	Nap Lajoie	107.4	67.9	39.5	36.8	10460
18	17	Nap Lajoie	67.9	107.4	39.5	36.8	10460	18	19	Frank Robinson	107.3	64.8	42.5	39.6	11742
19	18	Frank Robinson	64.8	107.3	42.5	39.6	11742	19	15	Mike Schmidt	106.8	73.6	33.2	31.1	10062
20	20	Joe Morgan	63.5	100.6	37.1	36.9	11329	20	20	Joe Morgan	100.6	63.5	37.1	36.9	11329
21	21	Albert Pujols (active)	63.2	100.0	36.8	36.8	11686	21	21	Albert Pujols (active)	100.0	63.2	36.8	36.8	11686
22	24	Jimmie Foxx	62.9	96.1	33.2	34.5	9676	22	23	Eddie Mathews	96.6	58.9	37.7	39.0	10100
23	22	Eddie Mathews	58.9	96.6	37.7	39.0	10100	23	36	Carl Yastrzemski	96.4	50.1	46.3	48.0	13992
24	30	Wade Boggs	57.4	91.4	34.0	37.2	10740	24	22	Jimmie Foxx	96.1	62.9	33.2	34.5	9676
25	27	Roberto Clemente	56.9	94.5	37.6	39.8	10211	25	32	Cal Ripken, Jr.	95.9	53.5	42.4	44.2	12883
26	29	Al Kaline	55.5	92.8	37.3	40.2	11596	26	29	Adrian Beltre (active)	95.7	54.8	40.9	42.7	12130
27	28	Cap Anson	55.2	94.2	39.0	41.4	11331	27	25	Roberto Clemente	94.5	56.9	37.6	39.8	10211
28	39	Dan Brouthers	55.1	79.8	24.7	31.0	7691	28	27	Cap Anson	94.2	55.2	39.0	41.4	11331
29	26	Adrian Beltre (active)	54.8	95.7	40.9	42.7	12130	29	26	Al Kaline	92.8	55.5	37.3	40.2	11596
30	42	Joe DiMaggio	54.5	78.1	23.6	30.2	7672	30	24	Wade Boggs	91.4	57.4	34.0	37.2	10740
31	34	Roger Connor	54.2	84.3	30.1	35.7	8847	31	35	George Brett	88.7	50.6	38.1	43.0	11625
32	25	Cal Ripken, Jr.	53.5	95.9	42.4	44.2	12883	32	33	Chipper Jones	85.2	53.4	31.8	37.3	10614
33	32	Chipper Jones	53.4	85.2	31.8	37.3	10614	33	38	George Davis	84.7	48.4	36.3	42.9	10185
34	38	Jeff Bagwell	52.1	79.9	27.8	34.8	9431	34	31	Roger Connor	84.3	54.2	30.1	35.7	8847
35	31	George Brett	50.6	88.7	38.1	43.0	11625	35	41	Ken Griffey Jr.	83.8	46.8	37.0	44.2	11304
36	23	Carl Yastrzemski	50.1	96.4	46.3	48.0	13992	36	43	Rod Carew	81.3	46.2	35.1	43.2	10550
37	99	Mike Trout (active)	48.7	64.3	15.6	24.3	4673	37	44	Charlie Gehringer	80.7	45.4	35.3	43.7	10244
38	33	George Davis	48.4	84.7	36.3	42.9	10185	38	34	Jeff Bagwell	79.9	52.1	27.8	34.8	9431
39	56	Larry Walker	48.3	72.7	24.4	33.6	8030	39	28	Dan Brouthers	79.8	55.1	24.7	31.0	7691
40	54	Arky Vaughan	47.2	72.9	25.7	35.3	7722	40	134	Pete Rose	79.7	29.1	50.6	63.5	15890
41	35	Ken Griffey, Jr.	46.8	83.8	37.0	44.2	11304	41	58	Brooks Robinson	78.4	39.7	38.7	49.4	11782
42	47	Johnny Bench	46.7	75.2	28.5	37.9	8674	42	30	Joe DiMaggio	78.1	54.5	23.6	30.2	7672
43	36	Rod Carew	46.2	81.3	35.1	43.2	10550	43	74	Robin Yount	77.3	37.4	39.9	51.6	12249
44	37	Charlie Gehringer	45.4	80.7	35.3	43.7	10244	44	51	Ozzie Smith	76.9	42.0	34.9	45.4	10778
45	61	Johnny Mize	44.7	70.9	26.2	37.0	7370	45	73	Paul Molitor	75.7	37.4	38.3	50.6	12167
46	67	Scott Rolen	44.1	70.2	26.1	37.2	8518	46	59	Bill Dahlen	75.4	39.7	35.7	47.3	10411
47	60	Bobby Grich	43.6	71.1	27.5	38.7	8220	47	39	Johnny Bench	75.2	46.7	28.5	37.9	8674
48	49	Lou Whitaker	42.8	75.1	32.3	43.0	9667	48	94	Sam Crawford	75.2	34.9	40.3	53.6	10610
49	64	Barry Larkin	42.5	70.4	27.9	39.6	9057	49	48	Lou Whitaker	75.1	42.8	32.3	43.0	9967
50	104	Lou Boudreau	42.2	63.0	20.8	33.0	7025	50	54	Luke Appling	74.4	41.4	33.0	44.4	10254
51	44	Ozzie Smith	42.0	76.9	34.9	45.4	10778	51	89	Reggie Jackson	74.0	35.4	38.6	52.2	11418
52	70	Ed Delahanty	41.9	69.7	27.8	39.9	8400	52	61	Frank Thomas	73.9	39.3	34.6	46.8	10075
53	95	Chase Utley	41.7	65.4	23.7	36.2	7863	53	95	Jim Thome	72.9	37.6	35.3	48.4	10313
54	50	Luke Appling	41.4	74.4	33.0	44.4	8856	54	40	Arky Vaughan	72.9	47.2	25.7	35.3	7722
55	62	Alan Trammel	40.4	70.7	30.3	42.9	9376	55	64	Paul Waner	72.8	38.7	34.1	46.8	10766
56	110	Joe Jackson	40.3	62.2	21.9	35.2	5693	56	39	Larry Walker	72.7	48.3	24.4	33.6	8030
57	68	Gary Carter	40.1	70.1	30.0	42.8	7971	57	114	Derek Jeter	72.4	31.0	41.4	57.2	12602
58	41	Brooks Robinson	39.7	78.4	38.7	49.4	11782	58	65	Harry Heilmann	72.2	38.7	33.5	46.4	8965
59	46	Bill Dahlen	39.7	75.4	35.7	47.3	10411	59	122	Rafael Palmeiro	71.9	30.3	41.6	57.9	12046
60	103	Billy Hamilton	39.5	63.4	23.9	37.7	7608	60	47	Bobby Grich	71.1	43.6	27.5	38.7	8220
61	52	Frank Thomas	39.3	73.9	34.6	46.8	10075	61	45	Johnny Mize	70.9	44.7	26.2	37.0	7370
62	114	Jackie Robinson	39.3	61.4	22.1	36.0	5804	62	55	Alan Trammel	70.7	40.4	30.3	42.9	9376
63	65	Frankie Frisch	39.1	70.4	31.3	44.5	10099	63	81	Ron Santo	70.5	36.8	33.7	47.8	9397
64	55	Paul Waner	38.7	72.8	34.1	46.8	10766	64	49	Barry Larkin	70.4	42.5	27.9	39.6	9057
65	58	Harry Heilmann	38.7	72.2	33.5	46.4	8965	65	63	Frankie Frisch	70.4	39.1	31.3	44.5	10099

* Babe Ruth's career pitching WAA was 9.2, and his career pitching WAR was 20.5. Thus his total career values were a WAA of 134.7 and a WAR of 182.6.

Figure 1. Scatter Diagram of Ranks in Career WAA and Career WAR for 74 Position Players: 1871–2018
(Includes players in the top 65 in WAA and/or WAR. Rank correlation coefficient (rho) = 0.62)

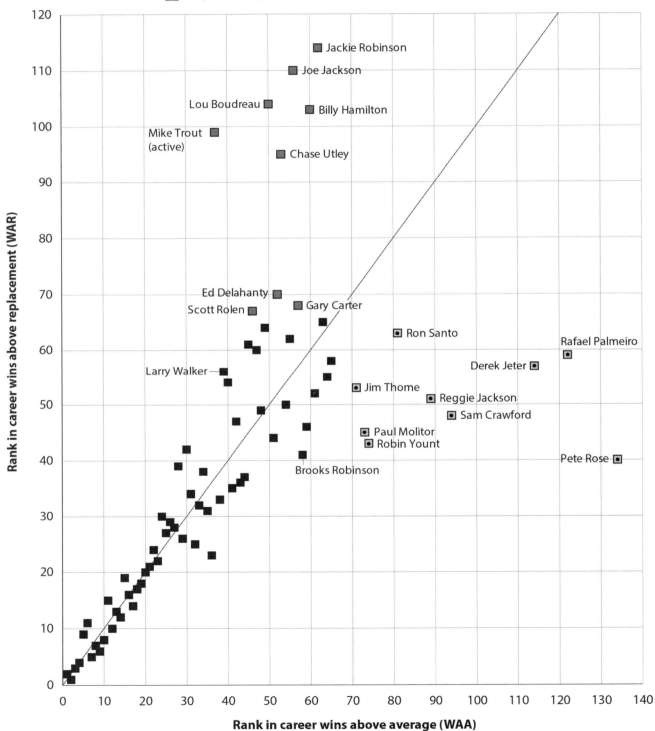

plate appearances and the change from WAA ranking to WAR ranking for the 18 players who appear on just one of the two lists. For example, Derek Jeter with 12,602 plate appearances rises 57 places (WAA rank of 114 to WAR rank of 57), and Lou Boudreau with 7,025 career plate appearances drops 54 places (WAA rank of 50 to WAR of 104). For these 18 players, the coefficient of correlation (r) between career plate appearances and change in ranking = 0.96. This means that the coefficient of determination (r squared) = 0.92. Thus 92 percent of the variation in the changes in going from WAA ranking to WAR ranking for these 18 players is due entirely to differences in their numbers of career plate appearances. This supports Darowski's conclusion as described previously. This is not to question the WAR concept for the purpose that it was developed, but to show that the WAR concept has a pronounced bias when it comes to evaluating overall career performance, including deciding which players should be considered for the Hall of Fame.

The focus in this analysis is on differences in rankings of players by WAA and WAR, as reflected in the discussion above and in Figure 1; however, it may be of interest also to summarize the statistical relationship among the values (as opposed to the rankings) of WAA and WAR. While this is not a classic case of trying to quantify the effect of an independent variable (X) on a dependent variable (Y), such as the effect of education on income), WAA is designated here as the independent variable (X), and WAR is designated as the dependent variable (Y), reflecting the fact that WAR adjusts the performance benchmark from that of an average major league player to a top minor league player. Using linear regression, the least-squares line (in the form of $Y = a + bX$) showing this relationship is WAR = 28.358 + (1.112)(WAA). Consistent with this relationship, for the 74 players, the mean value of WAA is 56.3 and the mean value of WAR is 91.0. The largest difference between a predicted value (using the least-squares line) of WAR and the actual value of WAR for any of the 74 players is for Pete Rose. Given his WAA value of 29.7, his predicted WAR value is 60.7 compared with his actual WAR value of 79.7.

Finally, it is interesting also to look at the percentage of a player's wins in his WAR value that are due to "showing up," as defined by Darowski and as discussed above. It is below 30 percent for some of the greatest players of all time: Babe Ruth (22.6 percent), Rogers Hornsby (23.2), Ted Williams (23.6), Barry Bonds (23.9), Mike Trout (24.3, active), Mickey Mantle (27.9), Willie Mays (29.5), and Honus Wagner (29.9). At the other extreme, the percentage of a player's wins as defined by his WAR value that are due to showing up, is above 50 percent for several players among the top 65 in career WAR, led by Pete Rose at 63.5 percent.

SUMMARY AND RECOMMENDATIONS

The data presented in this paper show that the Wins Above Replacement (WAR) concept seriously distorts the evaluation of player performance in Major League Baseball by systematically understating the value of players with relatively short careers and overstating the value of players with relatively long careers (as measured by plate appearances) and are consistent with the findings of Adam Darowski. It is recommended that the evaluation of player performance be shown using values based on the Wins Above Average (WAA) concept and that use of the WAR concept be restricted to its original focus on replacing a major league player with a minor league player. ∎

Acknowledgments

I appreciate the comments and suggestions of two anonymous reviewers, especially the suggestion to add a scatter diagram.

Notes

1. It should be noted that the database for Baseball-Reference.com is much larger than that original *Total Baseball* dataset, including comprehensive statistics for minor league baseball, and that the database and website are updated almost continuously. The WAR values and statistical values pulled from Baseball-Reference.com reflect what was current on February 1, 2019, and will have changed by the time of publication of this article.
2. For a detailed explanation of these measures, see *The Hidden Game of Baseball*. For a shorter explanation, see the 8th edition of *Total Baseball*, pages 976–79.
3. http://www.highheatstats.com/2012/07/wins-above-replacement-war-vs-wins-above-average-waa.

Left Out

Handedness and the Hall of Fame

Jon C. Nachtigal, PhD and John C. Barnes, PhD

Handedness historically has been of importance to how the game of baseball is played. For example, professional baseball has long alternated players at the same position of varying handedness in order to gain a competitive advantage. That advantage—the platoon effect—is in play when batters hit better when facing pitchers who throw with the opposite hand of the batter's side preference.[1] This practice dates to at least 1886 when Chicago White Stockings manager Adrian Anson used the platoon effect to maximize the effectiveness of his batters.[2]

One study found 13.5% of baseball players threw left-handed while 30.3% batted with a left-sided preference.[3] The overall percentage of left-handedness for men in the general population is just 11.6%.[4] Left-handed throwing fielders who batted with a left-sided preference were found to hit more home runs, had higher slugging percentages, but also had more strikeouts than did right-handed throwing fielders who batted with a left-sided preference.[5] The study's authors theorized that performance differences were due to hand dominance or hand specialization in the batters' swings.

In contrast, John Walsh proposed in *The Hardball Times* that performance differences in baseball based on throwing hand are largely due to positional bias.[6] Right-handed fielders dominate four positions in baseball: catcher, second base, shortstop, and third base. This positional bias exists because these positions favor a right-handed thrower. The other positions in baseball, which include first base and the outfield positions, do not favor a player by throwing hand. Therefore, according to Walsh, weak-hitting players who throw right-handed but are exceptional defenders have opportunities to play positions that weak-hitting left-handed throwers are not afforded. As a result of positional bias, the overabundance of weak-hitting right-handed throwers may skew performance data and, as a result, make it appear that left-sided batters perform better overall than right-sided batters.

We can see this positional bias demonstrated in the records of the National Baseball Hall of Fame. Only

Dan Brouthers

Lou Gehrig is the most recent of eight left-handed players in the Hall of Fame listed as playing catcher, second base, shortstop, or third base for at least one game—and he didn't actually appear in the field in the game where he was listed as shortstop.

Appearances for left-sided batters and throwers in the Hall of Fame who played Catcher/Second Base/Shortstop/Third Base[10]

Name	Bats	Throws	Years	Appearances at C/2B/SS/3B	Appearances at 1B/OF
Jake Beckley	Left	Left	1888–1907	1	2,389
Jim Bottomley	Left	Left	1922–1937	1	1,885
Dan Brouthers	Left	Left	1879–1904	2	1,671
Jesse Burkett	Left	Left	1890–1905	3	2,054
Lou Gehrig	Left	Left	1923–1939	1	2,146
Willie Keeler	Left	Left	1892–1910	65	2,039
Edd Roush	Left	Left	1913–1931	1	1,863
George Sisler	Left	Left	1915–1930	5	2,009

eight players admitted to Cooperstown threw left, batted left, and played catcher, second base, shortstop, or third base. For all eight of these players, first base or outfield were their primary positions. The most recent player in that list, Lou Gehrig, was only listed at shortstop for one game in 1934 to keep his consecutive-games-played record intact and was removed before ever taking the field.[7] Prior to Gehrig, left-hander Jim Bottomley, a career first baseman, appeared in one game at second base in 1924.[8] That appearance lasted only one inning.[9]

Examining the handedness of position players in the Hall of Fame supports Walsh's finding that positional bias, rather than intrinsic abilities associated with handedness, is largely responsible for the observed differences between right-handed and left-handed players. ∎

Notes

1. Bradbury, John Charles, and Douglas J. Drinen. "Pigou at the Plate." *Journal of Sports Economics* 9, no. 2 (September 2007): 211–24.
2. Nawrocki, Tom. "Captain Anson's Platoon." *The National Pastime*, no. 15 (1995): 34–37.
3. Grondin, Simon, Yves Guiard, Richard B. Ivry, and Stan Koren. "Manual Laterality and Hitting Performance in Major League Baseball." *Journal of Experimental Psychology: Human Perception and Performance* 25, no. 3 (1999): 747–54.
4. McManus, Chris. Right Hand, *Left Hand: The Origins of Asymmetry in Brains, Bodies, Atoms and Cultures.* London: Phoenix, 2004.
5. Grondin, et.al. "Manual Laterality."
6. Walsh, John. "The Advantage of Batting Left-Handed." The Hardball Times, November 7, 2007. https://www.fangraphs.com/tht/the-advantage-of-batting-left-handed.
7. "Biography—The Official Licensing Website of Lou Gehrig." Lou Gehrig. Accessed August 25, 2019. https://www.lougehrig.com/biography.
8. "Jim Bottomley Stats" Baseball-Reference. Accessed November 23, 2018. https://www.baseballreference.com/players/b/bottoji01.shtml.
9. The 1924 STL N Regular Season Fielding Log for Jim Bottomley. Retrosheet. Accessed September 9, 2019. https://www.retrosheet.org/boxesetc/1924/Mbottj1010031924.htm.
10. All player stats from Baseball-Reference.com.

Shifting Expectations

*An In-Depth Overview of Players' Approaches
to the Shift Based on Batted-Ball Events*

Connelly Doan, MA

One of the hottest and most polarizing topics in baseball today is the increasing implementation of the defensive shift. The idea of the shift itself is not new; teams started using the "Ted Williams Shift"—moving four infielders and two outfielders to the right side of the field—in 1946 to increase their chances of getting the great hitter out, while less dramatic shifts existed before that.[1] The strategy was used sparingly until the revolution in statistical analysis spurred a strong revival of the tactic. A glut of stats on batted-ball outcomes and defensive metrics has been coupled with data-driven processes to find efficient solutions to improving the outcomes of the games. The use of the shift has grown significantly over the past decade.[2]

Much of the focus given to the shift falls into two categories. The first is a debate between whether the shift is good or bad for baseball. Sportswriters, players, and broadcasters have voiced their displeasure over how the shift has taken away from "the way the game should be played."[3,4,5] Commissioner Rob Manfred even considered banning the shift in 2015.[6] The second category consists of various analyses, both defensively and offensively, attempting to pinpoint the effectiveness of the shift, to assess whether or not it "works" based on various statistics and metrics.[7,8]

This paper falls into the second category but will focus more on hitters' and pitchers' approaches to dealing with the shift, rather than merely the outcomes of the shift. It is easy to say that hitters could just bunt or hit to the opposite field when shifted on, but an in-depth overview of shift outcomes based on hard data would be a welcome addition to the discussion. To help fill this void, this paper will present an overview of shift batted-ball events from the beginning of the 2017 season through the first half of the 2018 season. Further, it will identify patterns in the data regarding both hitters' and pitchers' approaches to the shift. Finally, conclusions will be drawn in an attempt to explain why shift outcomes occurred as they did and to identify further topics of analysis. Understanding how players approach the shift in addition to understanding the tactic itself will offer insight into its effectiveness.

DATA OVERVIEW/METHODS

The data for this article were scraped from MLB's BaseballSavant.com using RStudio codes and packages based on Bill Petti's BaseballR.[9] Specifically, the raw data comprised complete game events from every game of the 2017 season through the first half of the 2018 season where an infield shift was on. Events are play outcomes, either batted balls, strikeouts, walks, or base-running plays such as steals.

The raw data were then loaded into Microsoft Power BI to filter the data and create interactive charts and graphs for further analysis. The data were first filtered on Baseball Savant's IF Alignment measure. This measure is broken down into three options:[10]

Standard—no shift

Shift—three infielders on one side of the
    infield ("traditional shift")

Strategic—a catch-all for plays in which
    the infield was neither standard nor
    traditionally shifted

This article uses only events featuring the traditional shift. The filtered dataset contained approximately 37,000 batted-ball events.

The data were then broken down by batter handedness as well as pitch locations of left-hand side of the plate, middle of the plate, and right-hand side of the plate. Pitch locations were labeled by aggregating Baseball Savant's Gameday zones. Various tables and graphs were then created for left-handed and right-handed batters to compare how shift performance differed in batter handedness and to compare if pitchers approached hitter handedness differently in shift situations.

RESULTS
General

Of the approximately 37,000 events in the data, 27,117 occurred against left-handed batters (referred to as lefties from here on) and 9,928 occurred against right-handed batters (referred to as righties from here on). Teams shifted about three times as often against lefties than righties. Righties hit significantly better than lefties against the shift, both in terms of batting average (.259 vs .232) and slugging average (.477 vs .429).

The differences in shift events and righties' relative success hitting against the shift compared to lefties could be explained a few ways. First, righties may just be better hitters than lefties. Second and seemingly more likely is that the physical differences in the shift benefit righties over lefties. A shift against lefties brings the shortstop closer to first base and doesn't significantly alter the second baseman's distance. A shift against righties draws both the second baseman and shortstop further away from first base, so even if a righty does put the ball in play into the shift, he has a better chance of getting a hit due to the increased difficulty of the throw to get an out.

In terms of pitch location, both lefties (.246 vs .197) and righties (.264 vs .242) had higher batting averages on pitches thrown down the middle or on the inside part of the plate compared to pitches thrown to the outside of the plate. However, pitchers pitched into the shift more often than not, regardless of batter stance (see Chart 1). Given that most of the opposite side of the infield is open when the shift is on, it may make sense intuitively for pitchers to pitch into the shift, but these data show that hitters were more successful on balls in play on middle/in pitch locations.

Approach to Hitting Against the Shift

Tables 1 and 2 show the outcomes of batted-ball events for lefties on middle/in and outside pitches, respectively. Given the imprecise reporting of batted-ball location in shifted infield positions (it is unclear where exactly the shortstop was positioned in the shift for a lefty or where the second baseman was positioned for a righty), I will only consider batted-balls to positions where the fielder's location is more clearly known. An important caveat to this is that third basemen will sometimes move into shallow right field when shifting against lefties, while the shortstop will move to the left side of the infield.[11] As noted above, a limitation of this article is the imprecise reporting of infielder positioning on batted balls. As such, I will treat the third baseman's position as "known" (where the shortstop would typically play in a non-shift situation) for lefty batted balls. Of 19,434 batted balls on middle/in pitches, lefties hit to both sides of the field fairly

Chart 1. Counts of Pitch Location by Batter Handedness

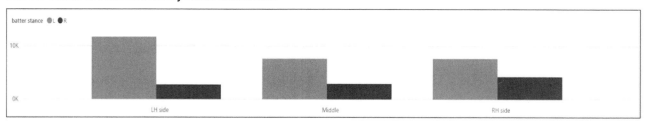

Table 1. Lefty Batted-Ball Locations on Middle/In Pitches

Events	P	C	1B	2B	3B	SS	LF	CF	RF	Total
Batted-Ball Location										
Hit Out/Error	3.25%	0.74%	8.66%	11.93%	6.59%	9.58%	11.99%	10.21%	4.80%	67.75%
Single	0.55%	0.04%	0.20%	0.54%	1.01%	0.82%	4.43%	5.35%	5.44%	18.38%
Double	-	-	0.03%	0.03%	0.01%	0.04%	2.34%	2.02%	2.53%	7.00%
Triple	-	-	-	-	-	-	0.07%	0.17%	0.18%	0.42%
Home Run	-	-	-	-	-	-	0.91%	4.29%	1.26%	6.46%
Total	3.80%	0.78%	8.89%	12.50%	7.61%	10.44%	19.74%	22.04%	14.21%	100.00%

All lefties' hit frequencies on middle/in pitches by batted-ball location. Pulled-ball locations are shaded darker.

Table 2. Lefty Batted-Ball Locations on Outside Pitches

Events	P	C	1B	2B	3B	SS	LF	CF	RF	Total
Batted-Ball Location										
Hit Out/Error	2.85%	1.72%	12.33%	12.57%	7.41%	9.29%	5.28%	9.39%	8.48%	69.32%
Single	0.40%	0.08%	0.40%	0.67%	0.99%	0.79%	3.08%	3.72%	7.25%	17.38%
Double	-	-	0.02%	0.04%	0.06%	-	0.79%	0.79%	4.76%	6.46%
Triple	0.02%	-	-	-	-	-	0.04%	0.16%	0.28%	0.50%
Home Run	-	-	-	-	-	-	0.02%	2.98%	3.34%	6.34%
Total	3.27%	1.80%	12.75%	13.28%	8.46%	10.08%	9.21%	17.04%	24.11%	100.00%

All lefties' hit frequencies on outside pitches by batted-ball location. Pulled-ball locations are shaded darker.

evenly (35.60% of balls hit to first base, second base, right field; 27.35% hit to third base, left field). On the other hand, of 7,682 batted balls on outside pitches, lefties pulled the ball much more frequently than hitting to the opposite field (50.14% of balls hit to first base, second base, right field; 17.67% hit to third base, left field). Lefties' batted balls resulted in outs or errors 67.75% of the time on middle/in pitches and 69.32% of the time on outside pitches.

Breaking down lefties' batted balls further, Table 5 shows the batted-ball locations of extra-base hits on middle/in and outside pitches. Of the 2,713 extra-base hits that occurred with the shift on for lefties, 2,056 came on middle/in pitches and 657 came on outside pitches. Of the extra-base hits on middle/in pitches, 28.65% of them were hit to right field and 23.88% to left field. Of the extra-base hits on outside pitches, 63.01% of them were hit to right field while only 6.39% were hit to left field. In sum, lefties pulled the ball significantly more often than hitting to the oppo-

site field on outside pitches and hit to both fields on middle/in pitches. Lefties hit for power by pulling the ball on outside pitches and were able to go to both fields for power on middle/in pitches.

Righties' batted-ball tendencies mirrored lefties' in many ways. Tables 3 and 4 show the outcomes of batted-ball events for righties on middle/in and outside pitches, respectively. Of 7,174 batted balls on middle/in pitches, righties pulled the ball about twice as often as going to the opposite field (41.80% of balls hit to third base, shortstop, left field; 23.40%% hit to first base, right field). Of 2,754 batted balls on outside pitches, righties pulled the ball much more frequently than hitting to the opposite field (56.31% of balls hit to third base, shortstop, left field; 16.93% hit to first base, right field). Righties' batted-balls resulted in outs or errors 66.59% of the time on middle/in pitches and 67.90% of the time on outside pitches.

Table 6 shows the batted-ball locations of extra-base hits on middle/in and outside pitches. Of the 1,084

Table 3. Righty Batted-Ball Locations on Middle/In Pitches

Events	\multicolumn{10}{c}{Batted-Ball Location}
Events	P	C	1B	2B	3B	SS	LF	CF	RF	Total
Hit Out/Error	2.60%	0.79%	4.87%	9.48%	10.66%	12.24%	4.84%	10.68%	10.43%	66.59%
Single	0.49%	0.05%	0.26%	0.70%	1.00%	0.77%	6.02%	5.00%	5.31%	19.60%
Double	-	-	0.02%	-	0.02%	0.05%	2.87%	2.22%	1.79%	6.97%
Triple	-	-	0.02%	-	0.02%	-	-	0.23%	0.23%	0.50%
Home Run	-	-	-	-	-	-	3.31%	2.55%	0.47%	6.33%
Total	3.09%	0.84%	5.17%	10.18%	11.70%	13.06%	17.04%	20.68%	18.23%	100.00%

All righties' hit frequencies on middle/in pitches by batted-ball location. Pulled-ball locations are shaded darker.

Table 4. Righty Batted-Ball Locations on Outside Pitches

Events	\multicolumn{10}{c}{Batted-Ball Location}
Events	P	C	1B	2B	3B	SS	LF	CF	RF	Total
Hit Out/Error	2.59%	1.53%	6.47%	7.10%	16.83%	12.04%	7.48%	8.20%	5.66%	67.90%
Single	0.29%	0.05%	0.38%	0.62%	1.15%	0.82%	6.43%	4.12%	3.84%	17.70%
Double	-	-	-	-	0.05%	0.10%	4.65%	1.06%	0.34%	6.20%
Triple	-	-	-	-	-	-	0.05%	0.14%	0.14%	0.33%
Home Run	-	-	-	-	-	-	6.71%	1.06%	0.10%	7.87%
Total	2.88%	1.58%	6.85%	7.72%	18.03%	12.96%	25.32%	14.58%	10.08%	100.00%

All righties' hit frequencies on outside pitches by batted-ball location. Pulled-ball locations are shaded darker.

Table 5. Lefty Batted-Ball Locations on Extra-Base Hits

\multicolumn{5}{c}{Middle/In Pitches}	\multicolumn{5}{c}{Outside Pitches}
\multicolumn{5}{c}{Batted-Ball Location}	\multicolumn{5}{c}{Batted-Ball Location}
Events	LF	CF	RF	Total	Events	LF	CF	RF	Total
Double	16.83%	14.59%	18.24%	49.66%	Double	5.94%	5.94%	35.77%	47.65%
Triple	-	1.22%	1.31%	2.53%	Triple	-	1.22%	2.13%	3.35%
Home Run	6.57%	30.89%	9.10%	46.56%	Home Run	-	22.37%	25.11%	47.48%
Total	23.40%	46.70%	28.65%	99%	Total	5.94%	29.53%	63.01%	98%

Lefties' extra-base hit frequencies on middle/in and outside pitches by batted-ball location. Data only shown where events comprised at least 1% of total data. Pulled-ball locations are shaded darker.

Table 6. Righty Batted-Ball Locations on Extra-Base Hits

\multicolumn{5}{c}{Middle/In Pitches}	\multicolumn{5}{c}{Outside Pitches}
\multicolumn{5}{c}{Batted-Ball Location}	\multicolumn{5}{c}{Batted-Ball Location}
Events	LF	CF	RF	Total	Events	LF	CF	RF	Total
Double	20.79%	16.07%	13.01%	49.87%	Double	32.33%	7.33%	2.33%	41.99%
Triple	-	1.66%	1.66%	3.32%	Triple	-	1.00%	1.00%	2.00%
Home Run	23.98%	18.49%	3.44%	45.91%	Home Run	46.67%	7.33%	-	54.00%
Total	44.77%	36.22%	18.11%	99%	Total	79.33%	15.66%	4.00%	98%

Righties' extra-base hit frequencies on middle/in and outside pitches by batted-ball location. Data only shown where events comprised at least 1% of total data. Pulled-ball locations are shaded darker.

extra-base hits that occurred with the shift on for righties, 784 came on middle/in pitches and 300 came on outside pitches. Of the extra-base hits on middle/in pitches, 44.77% of them were hit to left field while just 18.11% were hit to right field. Even more lopsided, of the extra-base hits on outside pitches, 79.33% of them were hit to left field while a mere 4% were hit to right field. Like lefties, righties hit to both fields on middle/in pitches and pulled the ball significantly more than hitting to the opposite field on outside pitches. Unlike lefties, righties hit for power mostly by pulling the ball, regardless of pitch location.

TAKEAWAYS AND EXPLANATIONS

After reviewing a season-and-a-half's worth of batted-ball shift events at a deep descriptive level, several patterns emerged. First, all hitters performed better on middle/in pitches with the shift on in terms of batting average, slugging average, and avoiding being out. More often than not, however, pitchers threw to that side of the plate. Further, hitters pulled the ball significantly more than hitting to the opposite field on outside pitches and hit to both fields somewhat evenly on middle/in pitches. Finally, lefties found success in hitting for power on outside pitches by pulling the ball and generated power to both fields on middle/in pitches. Righties, conversely, mostly generated power in the shift by pulling the ball, regardless of pitch location.

These tendencies present evidence that is counterintuitive to how one would think to approach the shift, but there may be some explanation behind how hitters and pitchers have approached it. There are several plausible explanations regarding hit location versus pitch location. First, hitters may be taking middle/in pitches to the opposite field because they are getting jammed or are slightly late on those pitches. Pitchers' average velocity has increased over the years.[12] Consequently, hitters have less time to react and are more likely to swing late. Another explanation could be that hitters are just more comfortable controlling pitches on the inner half of the plate off their bats. The data from this project indicate that all hitters had higher batting averages, greater number of extra-base hits, and a relatively equal amount of hits to both fields on middle/in pitches. Perhaps hitters can handle middle/in pitches better, and can therefore actually better strategically execute hitting the ball away from the shift on those pitches.

Two explanations arise to address batted-ball outcomes of outside pitches. First, hitters may have more trouble handling outside pitches compared to middle/in pitches; perhaps hitters are just not as successful at executing on outside pitches, especially in situations in which they are attempting to bunt for a hit.[13] What seems more likely, however, is that hitters are set on hitting over the shift to beat it. Hitters have become increasingly more strategic and calculating in terms of valuing how and where they hit the ball. The massive quantities of data that are now available have enabled coaching staffs and players to better analyze game outcomes based on attributes of their swings. A clear example of this is the prevalence of players who have increased their launch angles to hit over the shift, a phenomenon known as the Flyball Revolution.[14] A cost-benefit analysis occurs for the hitter: what is more valuable to the team, a "free" single to the opposite field or a double or home run hit into or over the shift?[15] The overwhelming number of pulled balls on outside pitches suggest that hitters may be making a conscious effort to not hit with the pitch.

Understanding pitchers' approaches to the shift is more straightforward than understanding hitters' approaches. Pitchers were pitching into the shift because it logically makes sense; if three of your infielders are gathered on one side, why not attempt to get the hitter to hit the ball to that side by pitching the ball to that side of the plate? However, based on the data presented and the above discussions on hitters' approaches to hitting against the shift, it actually seems detrimental for pitchers to pitch into the shift. Hitters perform better on middle/in pitches overall and are rarely hitting the ball to the open opposite field on outside pitches. Until hitters can make the mental or physical adjustments to make the pitcher pay for pitching to the open side of the field, pitchers should attack the outside part of the plate when the shift is on. While it may be a mental hurdle in itself for pitchers to throw to the exposed side of the field, the data show that they would be more successful doing so.

NEXT STEPS

This article provides an in-depth dive into batted-ball shift outcomes and offers insight into both hitters' and pitchers' approaches to handling the shift, but it is just the beginning in terms of understanding the shift and how players perform in it. There are several avenues of study that could follow this article.

The first could be a comparison of how hitters and pitchers perform in non-shift situations versus shift situations. While it is not necessary to identify patterns in shift situations, comparing non-shift outcomes could shed light onto how hitters and pitchers think about the shift and how they may attempt to adjust their approach (or not) to be successful. Such a comparison would also be useful at a single-player level to identify players who are relatively more successful in shift situations. This would allow for a more granular study analyzing the effectiveness of the shift.

The second could be the addition of non-batted-ball outcomes to analysis similar to that in this article. Identifying tendencies in batted-ball outcomes only provides a partial understanding of hitters' and pitchers' approaches to the shift as a whole. Russell Carleton presented analyses on shift expected outcomes at Baseball Prospectus and found that, while the shift decreased the number of singles pitchers allowed, it increased walks to a greater extent. Pitchers felt uncomfortable pitching with the shift on and, therefore, ended up pitching less effectively.[16] Analyses such as these provide key insights into players' approaches to the shift that batted-ball outcomes alone cannot. ■

Notes

1. Neil Paine, "Why Baseball Revived a 60-Year-Old Strategy Designed to Stop Ted Williams," FiveThirtyEight, October 13, 2016, https://fivethirtyeight.com/features/ahead-of-their-time-why-baseball-revived-a-60-year-old-strategy-designed-to-stop-ted-williams.

2. Travis Sawchik, "We've Reached Peak Shift," FanGraphs, November 9, 2017, https://www.fangraphs.com/blogs/weve-reached-peak-shift.

3. Matt Snyder, "MLB Shifts Are Starting to Get More and More Excessive, so Are We Headed to a Bad Place Where Positions Don't Matter?," CBS Sports, May 17, 2018, https://www.cbssports.com/mlb/news/mlb-shifts-are-starting-to-get-more-and-more-excessive-so-are-we-headed-to-a-bad-place-where-positions-dont-matter.

4. Alden Gonzalez, "How the Shift has Ruined Albert Pujols," ESPN, August 7, 2018, http://www.espn.com/mlb/story/_/id/24270231/mlb-how-shift-ruined-albert-pujols.

5. Tom Hoffarth, "Sports Media: Hall of Famer John Smoltz Not Exactly What the Viewers This Time of Year are Looking for," Los Angeles Times, October 15, 2018, https://www.latimes.com/sports/la-sp-sports-media-20181015-story.html.

6. Emma Baccellieri, "Proposing a Shift Ban is Easy, but How Would MLB Implement One?," Sports Illustrated, July 25, 2018, https://www.si.com/mlb/2018/07/25/defensive-shifts-official-baseball-rules.

7. Russell A. Carleton, "Baseball Therapy: Why the Shift Persists," Baseball Prospectus, January 3, 2018, https://www.baseballprospectus.com/news/article/36897/baseball-therapy-shift-persists.

8. Russell A. Carleton, "Baseball Therapy: The Pretty Good Case That the Shift Doesn't Work," Baseball Prospectus, May 3, 2016, https://www.baseballprospectus.com/news/article/29085/baseball-therapy-the-pretty-good-case-that-the-shift-doesnt-work.

9. "Baseballr: A Package for the R Programming Language," baseballr, last modified May 29, 2018, http://billpetti.github.io/baseballr.

10. "MLB Statcast Shifts," MLB, accessed March 3, 2019, http://m.mlb.com/glossary/statcast/shifts.

11. Ben Lindbergh, "Overthinking It: Defining Positions in the Age of the Shift," Baseball Prospectus, May 28, 2014, https://www.baseballprospectus.com/news/article/23705/overthinking-it-defining-positions-in-the-age-of-the-shift/; David Waldstein, "Who's on Third? In Baseball's Shifting Defenses, Maybe Nobody," The New York Times, May 12, 2014, https://www.nytimes.com/2014/05/13/sports/baseball/whos-on-third-in-baseballs-shifting-defenses-maybe-nobody.html.

12. Anthony Castrovince, "Speed Trap: How Velocity has Changed Baseball," MLB News, April 2, 2016, https://www.mlb.com/news/increase-in-hard-throwers-is-changing-mlb/c-170046614.

13. Jon Weisman, "Why MLB players Don't Bunt Against the Shift," Dodger Thoughts, October 9, 2018. https://www.dodgerthoughts.com/2018/10/09/why-mlb-players-dont-bunt-against-the-shift.

14. Dave Sheinin, "Why MLB Hitters Are Suddenly Obsessed With Launch Angles," Washington Post, June 1, 2017, https://www.washingtonpost.com/graphics/sports/mlb-launch-angles-story/?utm_term=.79f08e1ac9a0.

15. Jerry Crasnick, "MLB Hitters Explain Why They Can't Just Beat the Shift," ESPN, July 10, 2018, http://www.espn.com/mlb/story/_/id/24049347/mlb-hitters-explain-why-just-beat-shift.

16. Russell A. Carleton, "Baseball Therapy: How to Beat the Shift," Baseball Prospectus, May 22, 2018, https://www.baseballprospectus.com/news/article/40088/baseball-therapy-how-beat-shift.

Why OPS Works

Pete Palmer

In this paper I'll examine OPS (on-base plus slugging) and not only why I believe that the stat remains robustly in use in the twenty-first century, but how it was developed in the first place. I will recap my own early research and that of others in trying to relate batting performance to wins. Many formulas and schemes have been calculated both by me and others over the years, but the marginally more accurate methods are also more likely to be difficult to calculate or to understand, resulting in lower popularity.

I started trying to relate batting to team wins back in the Sixties. I had determined that 10 extra runs over the course of a season resulted in one more win for the team. A slightly more accurate method would be to use 10 times the square root of runs per inning by both teams—a figure usually between 9 and 11. The standard deviation of the difference between expected and actual wins from 1960 through 2018 was 4.03 for the simple method and 3.97 for the advanced one. Compare that to the "Pythagorean" method (runs squared over the sum of runs squared and runs allowed squared) where it was 4.07. This could be slightly improved to 3.99 by using 1.83 for the exponent instead of 2. Both simple and advanced methods had the same number of wins for 1016 out of 1552 teams and were off by 2 or 3 for only 47 teams. Only one team since 1971 differed by more than 2 wins: the 1996 Tigers, who allowed 1103 runs. Ten runs per win gave them 53 wins while Pythagoras had 56. They actually won 53. The runs over ten method was easier to calculate than other methods and also easier to relate individual performance to team performance.

My next step was to derive team runs from player stats. We had no play-by-play data available in those days except for World Series games as published in the annual baseball guides, so I started there. I analyzed 34 games 1956–60. I calculated the probability of scoring from each base depending on the number of outs. Later, I ran a paper-and-pencil simulation, using the various advanced data I compiled from the Series data, such as first to third on a single, first to home on a double, taking a base on an out, etc. The simulation also gave me the number of times each base-out situation occurred, so I determined how the scoring probabilities increased for each batting event. For example, a walk to lead off the inning would increase the scoring probability for that batter from .16 to .39—an increase of .23. If there was a runner on first, that runner would go from .39 to .62 for a total of .46. A single would be the same except a runner on first would go to third 45 percent of the time and the increase would be .57. I then summed up each situation weight by its frequency to get an overall value. A single came out .37 runs.

However, when I tried to project the number of team runs from its batting statistics, I did not find as close a relationship as I expected. Teams with high on base percentages would predict too low and vice-versa. I realized I was doing something wrong. A player can produce runs for his team three ways:

1. He can advance himself around the bases.

2. He can advance teammates around the bases.

3. He can cause other batters to get up by not making an out.

This third factor could never be measured by just using base advances. What I needed to calculate was the number of runs expected from each starting point through the end of the inning. These vary from year to year and league to league depending on the average batting. The expected number of runs to be scored from leadoff position is usually around .50, which is simply the league total of runs per inning. With play-by-play data for hundreds of thousands of regular season games now available through Retrosheet, we can do this easily for any season. Since I didn't have those data then, I expanded my paper-and-pencil simulation to calculate the values. Under the revised values, when a walk led off the inning, the run potential went from .48 to .82—an increase of .34.

Each positive batting event has an average increase of about .50 runs, while a negative event is around minus .25. An average player with an OBA of .333 will therefore have a net value of zero. This can be higher or lower based on the distribution of walks and hits. A portion of that comes from allowing extra batters to come up. Each batter is worth about .16 runs with none out, .12 with one out, and .08 with two outs, for an average of .12. But there is also the possibility of more than one additional batter appearing. This is a converging infinite series of $1 + 1/3 + 1/9 + 1/27$ etc…which sums to one and a half. So each time the batter gets on base, he adds 1.5 batters and when he goes out, he adds none, for an average of one half batter per appearance. Getting on base adds one batter and going out subtracts a half from the average. So of the .50 runs for a positive event, .12 is due to the extra batters and .38 is due to advances of the batters and other runners if any. That is the power of on base average (OBA).

It would still be a few more years before I would settle on the power of OPS, though. I made two mistakes in my original research. In the World Series data, there were only 5 cases of a runner on first when the batter doubled, and only one scored. So I used 20 percent for that. When more data became available, I found the real number was *40* percent, unless there were two outs when it was *60* percent. I did not consider intentional walks, since they had been first compiled in 1955. Worse, I made the bad assumption that walks occurred equally in all base-out situations. Actually walks—intentional or not—are more likely to occur in low value situations and less likely to occur in high value situations, thus the value of a walk was too high by about 10 percent. You can find a detailed study of intentional walks in the July 2017 edition of *By the Numbers*, the Statistical Analysis Committee bulletin. On average, intentional walks are worth about .15 runs.

However, you really have to look at the context of all walks, since good hitters are more apt to be walked in less favorable situations and also get more unintentional walks in intentional walk situations. Over the years the values were refined a bit, and by 1984 when John Thorn and I were writing *The Hidden Game of Baseball*, I had settled on .47 for a single, .83 for a double, 1.02 for a triple, 1.40 for a homer and .33 for a walk. The out factor was calculated to make the league total zero with pitcher batting subtracted and was usually around –.25. Thus an average player had a rating of zero. Subtracting pitcher batting puts the two leagues on an equal basis in the designated hitter era and also allows batters to be compared only with other non-pitchers for all years. Outs were defined as

at bats minus hits. I called these linear weights. Although baseball is not linear, the values remain relatively constant over the range of environments found in normal play. High scoring years would result in the positive event values slightly higher and the out value slightly more negative. You can also calculate values for various other events. Most don't have much influence on team stats. Stolen bases are more important for individuals. In the Deadball Era, everybody stole, but today they are more specialized. A few players may gain a fair number of runs from stealing. I used .22 for stolen bases and –.38 for caught stealing, although the impact on wins could be higher, since steals are more apt to occur in close games. The standard deviation in deriving team runs using the simple linear weight method is about 22 runs on the season. Adding steals and outs on base from caught stealing, double plays, and other items reduces the value to 20, which is about as low as you can get.

When correlating various measures to team runs, you can use runs per game, but a better method is to use runs *per innings batted*. Innings batted can vary based on extra innings games and games won, since a home team does not bat in the last of the ninth if ahead. In fact, you can deduce wins for the season with a standard deviation of about two if you use innings batted and innings pitched. This is half the value found by using runs scored and allowed. Wins equals games over two plus innings pitched minus innings batted.

$$W = Games/2 + IP - IB$$

It does not work for teams with an imbalance of home and away games like in the strike year of 1994, since the real difference uses home wins and road losses. Innings batted can be calculated easily if team left on base is known. LOB has been kept since 1920, although in the early years the official figures had a lot of errors. Retrosheet's box score project, headed by Tom Ruane, now has accurate LOB calculated from team data back to 1906. Innings batted is equal to plate appearances minus runs minus left on base, all divided by three.

$$IB = (PA - R - LOB)/3$$

Thus you can estimate innings batted when LOB is not available by taking innings pitched minus one half of wins minus losses. The only unknown variable is the number of outs in games won or lost in the bottom of the last inning. Innings batted per game has a standard deviation of about one percent, which would be 14 innings per year, equivalent to about 7 runs.

But getting back to OPS. Soon after SABR was founded in 1971, Dick Cramer suggested a statistical analysis committee and I became the chairman. Dick recently published his autobiography titled *When Big Data Was Small*, which covered his work in baseball and science as well as his personal life. In it he mentions a paper written by his friend Paul Bamberg in 1959 for a science project. Unfortunately, Paul was ahead of his time and did not have help from people like Bob Davids, Bill James, John Thorn, or Gary Gillette to spread the word, so his work languished in obscurity until being included in Dick's book in 2019. Others may have had the same problem of finding an outlet for their work. I was doing range factors in the 1960s and almost got an article on batting and pitching in *The Sporting News* in 1969, but they chickened out because they thought it was too complicated. George Lindsay published in *Operations Research*, but not many people noticed. Earnshaw Cook had to put out his own book and was then helped by Frank Deford, who noticed it and did a nice article in *Sports Illustrated*. Bill James also was aided when Dan Okrent did a piece there about his work.

At the time SABR's publications concentrated on historical rather than analytical work, and the Statistical Analysis Committee did not yet publish its own bulletin.[1] In 1973 Cramer contacted me about research he had done which showed that team runs were proportional to the product of on base percentage and slugging percentage. Dick created a simulation to measure this, entering individual batting data for Babe Ruth and others and calculating how many runs would score. I had reached a similar conclusion with my work with linear weights. I was looking at team runs as a function of their stats. We did a joint article in SABR's *Baseball Research Journal* in 1974, coining the term "Batter's Run Average."

On base times slugging (OxS) exaggerates the individual player's contribution when a team of nine identical players is used in the simulation. When I ran Ruth on the 1920 season, adding him to an average team added .79 runs per game while a team of nine Babes scored 14.11 runs per game—10.12 runs more than average or 1.12 runs per player per game, 44 percent higher, since he had the benefit of other Ruths on the team. Ruth's on-base was 50% higher than the league and his slugging was double. The normalized formula for OxS is OBA/lg times SLG/lg, where lg is the league average. This would mean 3 times the number of runs. For NOPS (normalized OPS) the formula is OBA/lg

plus SLG/lg minus 1, or 2.5, which is about what he had. So by 1978 I had converted to OPS, which has the advantage of being easy to calculate and relates individual performance directly to team wins.

In 1920, Ruth was 110 linear weight runs above average, but he was helped considerably by playing in the Polo Grounds. His OPS at home was an incredible 1.535. Anyone who thinks Ruth and Gehrig were helped by the short right field porch in Yankee Stadium is mistaken. Most players have an OPS at home about 5 percent better than on the road. Ruth's career figure in Yankee Stadium was only 2 percent higher, while Gehrig was actually 2 percent worse at home.

It turns out that the normalized version of OPS is directly proportional to a batter's contribution to team wins. A player with a normalized OPS of 110 percent will on average contribute 10 percent more runs than the average player. A player with an OBP and slugging each 10 percent higher than league average will have a normalized OPS that is 20 percent higher than average and will produce 20 percent more runs. Using raw OPS, 10 percent higher in each would mean the normalized version would also be 10 percent higher, which would also produce 20 percent more runs.

In OPS, a walk counts one for on-base and zero for slugging, while any hit counts one for on base and the number of bases for slugging. So counting both OBA and SLG, a single counts 2 and a homer 5. These are in about the same proportion as in linear weights. That is why OPS works almost as well.

Using an equation where OBP is multiplied by a factor (OBP times F plus SLG) gives a slightly more accurate correlation to actual team runs. However, the difference is very small. The standard deviation for the team runs projection per year for 1960–2018 is between 24.9 and 25.2 for any value of the multiplier between 1.4 and 2.4, but doing this complicates the calculation. Counting both equally is off by 26.4, only a little higher. Using OxS, you get a value of 25.4, a bit lower. If I had used 1.8 x OBP plus SLG, I don't think OPS would have caught on so well. It is possible to adjust the OBP by adding stolen bases over two minus caught stealing minus grounded into double plays. This reduces the standard deviation by about half a run.

Using the normalized method helps reduce this error, since by dividing by the league average makes 33 points of OBA equivalent to about 42 points of slugging, a factor of 1.3. OBA and slugging are highly correlated, since each is very dependent on hits over at-bats, so the multiplying factor has little effect.

Taking an average player and adding ten at-bats reduces his OPS by about 12 points. Adding 10 walks raises it by 11 points, while 10 singles adds 22 points. Doubles, triples, and homers increase the value by 40, 59, and 77 points respectively. This shows a ratio of 1–2–3–5–7, a bit higher than the 1–2–3–4–5 factors for linear weights. Thus slugging is a little heavier than it should be. Tom Tango addressed this problem in his wOBA calculation. He took the linear weight values for each event and created a pseudo OBA. The result looks very much like linear weight runs per appearance plus league average OBA. Tom also made an allowance for the fact that walks are more apt to occur in low value situations by reducing their value.

You can adjust for parks' effects for either of these. The simple way of calculating park factor (PF) is to take runs scored per game by both teams in home games compared to road games. The park adjustment factor (PA) is that ratio plus one divided by two, since half the games are played at home and the road park factor is pretty close to one. Adjusted NOPS is just NOPS/PA. But park factor itself has a rather large error due to chance. Dallas Adams had a 1983 article in the *Baseball Analyst* which showed the run distribution per game for various levels of team scoring. From that I deduced that the standard deviation of runs in a game was equal to the square root of twice the number of runs. This is very handy when figuring if a difference in runs under various conditions is significant, either in a simulation or real life. So for a particular park, if 700 runs were scored by both teams in home games, the standard deviation of the total would be around 37. But when comparing it to road games it would be higher by the square root of two, since you are comparing two samples. This comes out to be around 52. The standard deviation of the yearly park factor itself due to chance would be around 52/700, about 7 percent. The total difference in parks is only about 10 percent. So that means the real difference between parks is also 7 percent, as the total difference squared is equal to the actual difference squared plus the random difference squared. So you have to use a park factor over several years to get a better estimate of the true value. To adjust straight OPS, you divided by the square root of the park adjustment.

If you look at park factor for all decades by club since 1901, the standard deviation is 7, which means two thirds of the teams fall between 107 and 93. The random factor is reduced to about 2 by using a ten-year period.

Dick Cramer and I were far from the only ones to make attempts over the years at coming up with a formula for relating batting stats to team runs. The legendary F.C. Lane of *Baseball Magazine* had some articles in the nineteen-teens, which included run values for various events. George Lindsey did work on scoring probabilities, winning percentage, and hit values in the 1960s. Both sets of event values were very close to mine, although neither had a negative value for an out. Earnshaw Cook in the 1960s came up with a formula for what he called DX, which was number of times on base multiplied by total bases. Bill James's runs created is on-base average times slugging average times at-bats.

Branch Rickey had a famous piece in *Life* magazine in 1954 which referred to research by scientists at Princeton, although Allan Roth, longtime staff statistician for the Dodgers, told us at a SABR meeting years ago that he was actually the uncredited inventor of the formula. It was close to OPS, as it used hits plus walks plus three-quarters times extra bases over at-bats. Extra bases count one for a double, two for a triple and three for a home run, otherwise known as isolated power. I suspect he did that because he didn't want to count hits twice—however he should have. Using OBA plus three-fourths ISO gave a standard deviation of 37 runs per season, while OBA plus three-fourths SLG came out 28.

Another feature of the Rickey article was a listing of career leaders in on base average, perhaps the first time that had ever been presented. I did an article on it in the *Baseball Research Journal* in 1973 and, as a consultant to the American League, helped introduce OBA as an official statistic in 1979. The National League didn't publish it until 1984 and *The Sporting News* didn't show it in the Baseball Guide until 1987, covering 1986. I had not counted sacrifice flies as outs in the AL version, but the NL did. When it finally made the guide, the NL version was used. This had one big problem. The sacrifice fly rule was in effect from 1908 through 1930, 1939, and 1954 to date. But in the first two instances, sacrifice flies were not recorded separately from bunts. Although Retrosheet has filled in much of the older play-by-play, we can never determine the exact OBA for Babe Ruth, Ty Cobb, Lou Gehrig, or other players from that era. The only way to do it is assume no sacrifice flies. Ten sacrifice flies would reduce OBA by about five points.

Bob Creamer in *Sports Illustrated* in 1956 invented a very simple measure for players called runs produced, which was simply runs plus runs batted in minus home runs. Home runs were subtracted because that would give credit to the same run twice. However, these values turn out to be very close to the linear weight values. A walk is about .25 runs, a single .25 runs and .25 RBI, a double .4 runs and .4 RBIs, and a triple .6 run and .6 RBIs. However a homer is 1 run and 1.6 RBIs, which is 2.6, well above the linear weight value 1.4, so subtracting homers brings runs produced pretty much in line. A homer gets too much credit for RBI, since many of those runs would have scored anyway without the homer and a single too little because advancing a runner from first to second or third results in neither a run nor an RBI.

Steve Mann was one of the first analysts employed by a club—the Astros in the seventies. (Steve and I created the BACBALL program for charting batted balls and pitches which the Phillies and Braves used for a number of years in the Eighties.) He developed Run Productivity Average which was linear weights that were equal to the average number of runs and RBIs for each event. But it was fairer because it did not favor players who have more opportunities for runs or RBIs because of their team or their lineup position. However I believe it over-values home runs.

Chuck Mullen invented a system in the sixties with linear weights for each event multiplied by a clutch factor depending on the inning, score, and base-out situation. Bob Sudyk wrote a story in *The Sporting News* about it, although General Electric, who had the computer, got the credit and Chuck wasn't even mentioned. The Cardinals used it for while then, and Chuck and I revived it in the 1990s for the Astros.

And the list goes on. Barry Codell invented Base-Out Percentage in the late 1970s, basically bases over outs. Tom Boswell's Total Average came out about the same time and was similar. None of them really caught on, because I suspect people weren't ready for them. OPS combines simplicity with reasonable accuracy and I think that is why it is popular. ∎

References

Adams, Dallas (1987). The distribution of runs scored. *Baseball Analyst*, Vol. 1, Num. 1, 8–10.

Bamberg, Paul (1959). Mathematical Analysis of Batting Performance.

Codell, Barry (1979). The Base-Out Percentage. *Baseball Research Journal*, No. 8, 35–39.

Cook, Earnshaw with Wendell R. Garner (1966). *Percentage Baseball*. Cambridge, MA: MIT Press.

Cramer, Richard D. and Pete Palmer (1974). The batter's run average (BRA). *Baseball Research Journal*, No. 3, 50–57.

Cramer, Richard D. (2019). *When Big Data Was Small*, Lincoln, NE; University of Nebraska Press.

Deford, Frank (1964). Baseball is Played All Wrong, *Sports Illustrated*, Vol 20, issue 12, 14–17.

James, Bill (1978). *The 1978 Baseball Abstract*. Lawrence, KS: Bill James.

Krabbenhoft, Herm (2009). Who Invented Runs Produced? *Baseball Research Journal*, No. 38, 135–38.

Lane, F. C. (1917, January). Why the system of batting averages should be reformed. *Baseball Magazine*, 52–60.

Lane, F. C. (1917, March). The Base on Balls. *Baseball Magazine*, 93–95.

Lindsey, G. R. (1959). Statistical Data Useful for the Operation of a Baseball Team. Operations Research, Vol. 7, 197–207.

Lindsey, George R. (1963). An Investigation of Strategies in Baseball. *Operations Research*, Vol. 11, 477–501.

Mann, Steve (2005). Interview. http://hendricks-sports.com/interview2.html.

Okrent, Dan (1981). He Does It by The Numbers. *Sports Illustrated*, May 25, 1981.

Palmer, Pete (1973). On-base Average. *Baseball Research Journal*, No. 2, 87–91.

Palmer, Pete (1978). AL Home Park Effects on Performance. *Baseball Research Journal*, No. 7, 50–60.

Palmer, Pete (2009). McCracken and Wang Revisited. *By the Numbers*, Vol. 19, No. 1, 9–13.

Palmer, Pete (2017). Intentional Walks Revisited. *By the Numbers*, Vol. 27, No. 1, 16–25.

Pankin, Mark (2004). Relative value of on-base pct. and slugging avg. Presented at the annual SABR convention and available at http://www.pankin.com/baseball.htm

Pankin, Mark (2005). More on OBP vs. SLG. *By the Numbers*, Vol. 15, No. 4, 13–15.

Pankin, Mark (2006). Additional on-base worth 3x additional slugging? Presented at the 2006 SABR convention and available at the Retrosheet research page.

Rickey, Branch (1954, August 2). Goodby to some old baseball ideas. *Life*, 78–86, 89.

www.retrosheet.org, Dave Smith proprietor

Sudyk, Bob (1966, April 16). Computer Picks Top Clutch Hitters, *The Sporting News*, 13, 20.

Tango, Tom, Mitchel G. Lichtman and Andrew E. Dolphin (2006). *The Book: Playing the Percentages in Baseball*. TMA Press.

Thorn, John, and Pete Palmer (1984). *The Hidden Game of Baseball*. Garden City, NY: Doubleday.

Wang, Victor (2006). The OBP/SLG ratio: What does history say? *By the Numbers*, Vol. 16, No. 3, pages 3–4.

Wang, Victor (2007). A closer look at the OBP/SLG ratio. *By the Numbers*, Vol. 1, No. 1, pages 10–14.

Rating Baseball Agencies

Who is Delivering the Goods?

Barry Krissoff

In the summer of 2018, *Washington Post* reporter Jorge Castillo penned an article about free agent Bryce Harper's performance and his agent Scott Boras's interpretation of why Harper was experiencing a subpar year. At the time, Harper was batting a meager .215. Boras pointed out that batting average is not necessarily a good metric, and that Harper was partially a "victim of unusual circumstances," the increasingly common defensive shift, particularly against left-handed hitters. Boras focused on other positive data—Harper's impressive hard-hit and walk rates, which were at or near career bests. In the news article, the *Post* reporter refers to Scott Boras as baseball's super-agent, as have other authors.[1] Writing about eight years ago, researcher Vince Gennaro found that Boras was able to attract the top young baseball talent and was a master of marketing his players, which might be exemplified by the elucidation about Harper.[2]

For sure, Boras has been outspoken on many topics, garnering controversy on issues such as the timing and contract terms of free-agent signings, the level of team salaries in large affluent markets, the timetable of players graduating from minor to major leagues, the number of innings thrown by pitchers coming off injury, and other labor-management issues. From 2015 to 2018, the Boras Corporation has negotiated well over 200 major league baseball contracts, ranging from many one-year deals to Prince Fielder's nine-year $214 million mega-contract. The total value of all the contracts is nearly $3.5 billion. The Boras Corporation is not the only agency, though, that has substantial economic interests connected to Major League Baseball players. There are at least eight other agencies that have negotiated contracts worth over a billion dollars since 2015 and obviously have an enormous financial interest in player salaries.

The objective of this study is twofold. First, we examine the number and size of contracts that the largest baseball agencies have negotiated for their clients from the 2015 to 2018 seasons. In doing so we distinguish between single and multi-year team control and free agent agreements. The role of the agent in determining contract terms is central in the latter two cases, especially for free agents since the contract duration and salary are negotiated under open-market conditions. Second, we appraise the performance of baseball agencies. Our concentration is to gauge the extent to which player representatives have delivered value to their clients. Do some agencies have the ability to secure salary levels that exceed player performance? By the same token, do some agencies appear to sell their clients short by negotiating salary levels that end up understating their future values?

As alluded to above, batting average has limitations as indicative of a player's performance. With the aid of new technologies and advanced statistics, baseball has expanded and refined the way in which it evaluates player performance. Arguably the advanced metric that has received the most notoriety and exposure is Wins Above Replacement (WAR), which evaluates a player's overall worth by calculating the number of wins for which he is responsible compared to a replacement-level player at the same ballpark. Fangraphs, Baseball Prospectus, and Baseball-Reference.com publish WAR statistics on their websites for each major league player. Although there is not a standard WAR measure, the use of WAR has become more pervasive and it is now not unusual to see a reference to a player's WAR in a newspaper article or baseball blog. WAR has been used to estimate the future value of players and no doubt has played a role in the negotiation of player contracts.

Here, we examine players' salaries and WAR before and after signing a contract for each agency. WAR serves as a measure of on-field performance. Prior to a contract, WAR tells us about past achievements and is an indication of potential success of the player. Subsequent to the contract, WAR indicates the realization of what is accomplished. When dividing salaries by WAR, we convert a player's WAR into his monetary value.[3] Or, as Fangraphs writer Matt Swartz defines, dollars per WAR is the average cost of acquiring one win above replacement on the free-agent market.[4] A player whose WAR is 3 and receives a salary of $15 million provides a lower monetary value or higher cost to his team than a player whose WAR is 2 and receives a salary of $6 million.

We will first review the basic tenets and services provided by sports agencies. Then, we will discuss the data employed for the analysis, compare and analyze contract data and WAR levels for the clientele of a dozen of the largest baseball agencies, and review our findings and take a look at whether the conclusions found in Gennaro regarding Scott Boras as a super-agent continue to hold a decade or so later.

BRIEF BACKGROUND ON SPORTS AGENCIES

There are around 150 sports agencies representing over 2000 current and former baseball players.[5] Some of these agencies are very large and not only represent baseball players and other athletes but also artistic entertainers. A leading example is Creative Artists Agency. CAA represents well known movie and TV stars and baseball, football, basketball, hockey, soccer, golf, and tennis players. Independent Sports and Entertainment and The Wasserman Media Group are global corporate entities representing diverse sport figures including snowboarders, Olympic athletes, coaches, and managers in addition to baseball, football, and basketball players. Other agencies specialize in representing baseball players. Athletes Career Enhanced and Secured, the Boras Corporation, and Beverly Hills Sports Council represent hundreds of baseball players at the major and minor league levels in the United States, Latin America, and Asia. Other agencies represent only a few major league clients. Melvin Roman's MDR Sports Management specializes in Latin American ballplayers and represents current major leaguers Yadier Molina and Jonathan Villar. Turner Gary Sports has former major league clients Shaun Marcum, Brad Lidge, Chad Bradford and current major leaguers Lonnie Chisenhall and Shane Greene. Of course, with around 150 agencies, other examples abound.

Whether large or small, each of the agencies has specialists who focus on baseball players, usually with a background in sports, business, and/or law. The MLB Players Association (MLBPA) is the exclusive bargaining agent for players negotiating a major league contract and certifies agents. MLBPA regulates and approves General Certified Agents who can represent or advise players when negotiating a contract, Expert Agent Advisors who may assist in the negotiations, and Limited Certified Agents who can recruit and provide clients maintenance services. MLBPA explains requirements and instructions on how to apply for each type of agent.[6] Player-agent representation contracts are signed annually and there are occasional disputes about players opting for signing with new agents.[7]

Agencies offer a variety of services, usually emphasizing professionalism and individual attention in managing, marketing, and negotiating on behalf of the player. Recent innovations and guidance from MLBPA include agencies are examining players' social media posts and expunging any offensive or hurtful comments.[8] For a commission, the agency negotiates the contract, arranges for endorsement deals, and advises the player on financial planning and taxes.[9] The multisport agency, Excel Sports, for example, asserts, "From draft day, through arbitration and free agency and into retirement, we are industry leaders not only in contract negotiations, but also in meticulously building some of the most successful athlete brands in the marketplace."[10]

MLB Trade Rumors conducted player interviews prior to the 2013 season, asking what attributes players seek in choosing an agent. Not surprisingly, players indicated the importance of interpersonal relationships often developing early in their careers.[11] Players look for agents that communicate well and demonstrate an understanding of their individual and family interests and goals. Players require the agents to have the requisite legal and business expertise to represent them in negotiations with general managers and other ballclub executives. They also solicit agencies that have connections with marketing and charitable organizations to establish and enhance their "brand." Most importantly, the players seek the agencies that will be able to negotiate a contract with the largest payout.

Limited information is available on the precise figures that players compensate their agencies. The available literature suggests that agencies receive a commission of four to five percent of players' salaries.[12] This compares favorably to the National Football League and the National Basketball Association, which limit commissions to three percent of salaries. The commissions exclude fees earned from finding, negotiating, and securing endorsement contracts, where agencies typically earn 10 to 20 percent.[13]

SOURCING AND EXPLAINING THE DATA

Our main data source is Baseball Prospectus's Cots Contracts, 2015 through 2018. At the beginning of each season Cots indicates the players on every team, contract terms, and the player's agency (or agent). Contracts in effect for 2015 include single and multiyear agreements that began as early as 2008. For example, Miguel Cabrera's eight-year, $152 million contract. Multiyear contracts extend far into the future as well, such as Giancarlo Stanton's 13-year, $325 million contract from 2015 to 2027, plus an option year. Cots lists the player's agency each year and we matched those agencies with the start of each contract. For example, Elvis Andrus signed an eight-year, $120 million contract negotiated by the Boras Corporation that began in the 2015 season. In another example, early in his career, Gio Gonzalez agreed to a five-year, $42 million contract plus two years of options running from 2012 to 2016 with Athletes Career Enhanced and Secured as his agency. In 2015, Gonzalez switched agencies to the Boras Corporation. Subsequently, his 2017 and 2018 options were exercised raising the contract to seven years for $66 million. Since Athletes Career Enhanced and Secured negotiated the contract, we list them as the agency of record for the $66 million. Similarly, Creative Artists Agency represented Ryan Braun in his five-year, $105 million extension that started in 2016, although it was negotiated a few years earlier. Where data are available we attribute the player to the negotiating agency and adjust salary when options are exercised (through 2018).[14]

We source our WAR data from Fangraphs for the years 2005 through 2018. When a contract is negotiated the player, the agency, and the team base the salary and contract length on anticipated future performance. Negotiators often look at past performance to predict what might happen in the future. Rather than using a single year's WAR, an average of three years prior to the contract is used to represent a player's achievements and expected performance. For example, in a contract negotiated in 2010, we used average WAR from 2007–09.

For post contracts, we use the average WAR for up to the length of the contract. A 2015 five-year contract would be an average WAR for 2015 to 2019. However, 2019 was not available so in this case we only used four years. To the extent that a player's productivity declines in outer years of a contract, we may be overstating their productivity. Furthermore, in some instances, particularly post contract years, the number of observations are limited, and in these cases, we opt to use the one or two years of data that might be available. If no pre- or post-WAR are obtainable, then we drop this observation.

AN OVERVIEW OF AGENCY CONTRACTS

The Boras Corporation is at the head of the class for representing the most MLB players and the size of their contracts. For the 2015 season, the first year of our contract analysis, the Boras Corporation had 75 clients in which they negotiated single or multiple year major league deals starting as early as 2010. Nearly 50 additional agreements were negotiated for each of the next three years for a total of 219 contracts valued at near $3.5 billion or an average contract value of $15.9 million (Table 1). This includes multiple one year or longer contracts for the same player. Boras negotiated three contracts for Carlos Gomez: a 3-year contract in 2014 and single year contracts in 2017 and 2018. For the 2018 season, Boras had 61 MLB clients with single and multiyear contracts originating as early as 2012 (Prince Fielder) and concluding as late as 2025 (Eric Hosmer) and with a total contractual value of $2.1 billion.

Table 1. Big 12 Agencies and Their MLB Players: (Contracts Negotiated 2015–18)

Agency	Number of Contracts	Total Value*	Average Contract Value*	Average Annual Value*	Average Length	Agency Commission*
ACES	145	1501.7	10.4	3.8	1.6	60.1
BHSC	103	857.4	8.3	3.1	1.5	34.3
Boras	219	3487.0	15.9	5.0	1.7	139.5
CAA	188	2566.5	13.7	4.1	1.6	102.7
Excel	130	2016.2	15.5	4.8	1.7	80.6
ISE	204	2004.4	9.8	3.5	1.5	80.2
Jet	62	616.7	9.9	3.2	1.8	24.7
Legacy	140	1131.5	8.1	3.4	1.5	45.3
Magnus	54	251.3	4.7	2.7	1.4	10.1
Octagon	106	1148.6	10.8	3.7	1.7	45.9
Sosnick-Cobbe	62	311.1	5.0	2.0	1.4	12.4
WMG	143	1721.2	12.0	4.0	1.6	68.8

* In millions of dollars.
Average contract value = total value divided by the number of contracts
Annual average value = annual average salary
Agency commission estimated at 4 percent of the total value of contracts
Source: Data derived from Baseball Prospectus

In addition, Boras has the largest average annual value (AAV) of contracts and the largest number of contracts over $20 million per annum (Table 2). To calculate AAV we divide each player's contract value by the number of years of the contract. We then calculate an average for each agency. Boras's players have an AAV of $5 million, exceeding all the other agencies in our database. There are 34 major league players with over $20 million annual payouts, 10 of whom are Boras's clients. The list includes two players who are no longer active, Mark Teixeira (contract expired in 2016) and Fielder (contract expires in 2020), and eight current players. José Altuve, Jake Arrieta, and J.D. Martinez signed contracts in 2018. Of the 10 players, Bryce Harper was the only one in the group who was under team control. Harper had a one-year contract that expired at the end of the 2018 season. Harper's new contract with the Philadelphia Phillies that started in 2019, unsurprisingly, set a record: 13 years, $330 million, which is more than $25 million annually.

While the Boras Corporation may be the foremost agency in baseball, it is just one of four sports agencies with over $2 billion MLB player contracts in effect 2015–2018. And, at least a dozen sports agencies have had contracts over $250 million. In addition to the Boras Corporation (Boras), the agencies are: Athletes' Careers Enhanced and Secured (ACES), Beverly Hills Sports Council (BHSC), Creative Artists Agency (CAA), Excel Sports Management (Excel), Independent Sports and Entertainment (ISE), Jet Sports Management (Jet), Legacy Sports Agency (Legacy), Magnus Sports (Magnus), Octagon Baseball (Octagon), Sosnick, Cobbe, and Karon (SC), and the Wasserman Media Group (WMG). These agencies do not get as much press coverage as Boras, but along with Boras they account for approximately 40 percent of the total value of all baseball contracts. Furthermore, the dozen agencies account for nearly 75 percent of baseball contracts that exceed $20 million. Table 1 lists each of these agencies with their abbreviated names, the number, contract value, AAV, and the length of the contracts.

The next four largest agencies measured by their total value of contracts are CAA, Excel, ISE, and WSG. CAA has contracts over $2.5 billion, Excel and ISE $2 billion, and WMG $1.7 billion. AAVs are among the highest for these agencies as well, which is not surprising given that they have all but two of the remaining players under contract for our dozen agencies earning over $20 million annually. Interestingly, Zack Greinke (2013 contract) and Yoenis Cespedes (2016 contract) each earned over $20 million and had an opt out which they exercised, Greinke signing a new contract with Arizona starting in 2016 with an AAV of over $34 million and Cespedes re-signing with the New York Mets, nearly a year later than his initial contract, for an AAV of $27.5 million.

The average length of contracts is similar across all the agencies at around 1.6 years. About 20 percent of contracts are longer than one year. Boras and CAA have the most long-term contracts. They have 24 and 21 contracts four years or longer and four and three contracts eight years or longer, respectively. WMG negotiated the longest contract: Stanton for 13 years, $325 million for 2015–27, plus the option year. Jet has an average length of 1.8 years for its contracts, a little longer than the other agencies. Jet negotiated several longer-term contracts for players early in their careers: Kyle Seager's seven-year, $100 million deal and Corey Kluber's five-year, $38.5 million contract, each with option years, and both signing while they were under team control.

In the last column in Table 1 we examine the estimated commission received by each agency. Using

Table 2. Top Earners Represented by The Boras Corporation

Player	Length	Total Value*	Average Annual Value*	WAR	PostWAR
Mark Teixeira	8	180.0	22.5	4.94	2.22
Prince Fielder	9	214.0	23.8	4.46	1.50
Jacoby Ellsbury	7	153.0	21.9	4.94	1.99
Max Scherzer	7	210.0	30.0	5.24	6.31
Chris Davis	7	161.0	23.0	4.46	-0.09
Stephen Strasburg	7	175.0	25.0	3.73	3.91
J.D. Martinez	5	110.0	22.0	3.69	5.63
Jose Altuve	7	163.5	23.4	5.43	4.73
Jake Arrieta	3	75.0	25.0	4.52	1.98
Bryce Harper	1	21.6	21.6	5.74	3.38

*millions of dollars
Annual average value = annual average salary for each player
Source: Salary data from Baseball Prospectus. WAR data from Fangraphs.

the four percent estimate discussed above, Boras's commission is nearly $140 million based on the salaries of its negotiated contract players. Fielder's nine-year, $214 million 2012–20 contract generates over $8.5 million or a shade under $1 million per year. CAA's total commission is also over $100 million during this time period with the Robinson Canò 10-year, $240 million 2014–23 contract standing out with over $9.5 million commission or again a shade under $1 million per year. Isolating the 2018 season and the players' AAV of the negotiated contracts by Boras and CAA, the earned commissions are nearly $20 and $13 million, respectively.

A player's MLB status—pre-arbitration, arbitration, or free agent—significantly affects the ability to negotiate salary and the length of a contract. The AAV escalates as a player attains more experience and moves into free agency. For our sample of players for the 12 agencies, the average value for team controlled and free agent players increases from $2.5 million to $7.8 million. Clearly, players and their respective agencies have the most negotiating power in the free-agency market and this is reflected in the higher salaries and lengthier contracts. Table 3a shows that Boras has the largest number of free agent contracts (47), the highest total value ($2.2 billion), the highest AAV ($10.6 million), and the lengthiest (2.9 years) contracts.[15] Over 60 percent of the value of Boras's contracts are free agents, adding credence to the often stated comment that Boras's clients are less likely to sign a long-term contract early in their careers relative to

Scott Boras

other players. However, there are several notable exceptions mentioned below.

Team control players, who are thought to have the most upside by their teams, may coordinate with their agencies to negotiate multiyear contracts or extensions. In these cases, the role for their representatives is considerably more significant than for a one-year deal. Determining the tradeoffs between a guaranteed return of salary for a fixed number of years plus agreeing to any option years provides a player some security compared to one-year or short-term contracts and subsequently becoming a free agent. This is a paramount decision for a young aspiring player. Boras negotiated multiyear million dollar extensions for Andrus's eight-year, $120 million contract with the Texas Rangers,

Table 3a. Big 12 Agencies and Their MLB Free Agent Players: (Contracts Negotiated 2015–18)

Agency	Number of Contracts	Total Value*	Average Contract Value*	Average Annual Value*	Average Length	Agency Commission*
ACES	42	943.0	22.5	6.5	2.3	37.7
BHSC	15	396.9	26.5	7.9	2.2	15.9
Boras	47	2167.2	46.1	10.6	2.9	86.7
CAA	46	1210.8	26.3	7.0	2.3	48.4
Excel	29	897.7	31.0	8.9	2.3	35.9
ISE	41	1171.6	28.6	7.6	2.3	46.9
Jet	11	251.0	22.8	7.6	2.5	10.0
Legacy	33	691.1	20.9	7.1	2.0	27.6
Magnus	3	24.8	8.3	5.8	1.3	1.0
Octagon	29	676.0	23.3	7.4	2.2	27.0
Sosnick-Cobbe	8	102.4	12.8	4.7	1.8	4.1
WMG	39	852.7	21.9	7.5	2.0	34.1

* In millions of dollars.
Average contract value = total value divided by the number of contracts
Annual average value = annual average salary
Agency commission estimated at 4 percent of the total value of contracts
Source: Data derived from Baseball Prospectus

Stephen Strasburg's seven-year, $175 million contract with the Washington Nationals, and most recently Altuve's $163.5 million, seven-year contract with the Houston Astros. Excel negotiated multiyear million dollar extensions for Clayton Kershaw with the Los Angeles Dodgers and Homer Bailey with the Cincinnati Reds, as did CAA for Adam Jones with the Baltimore Orioles as their free agency approached. In other cases, pre-arbitration players agreed to multiyear contracts. Anthony Rendon's first contract negotiated by Boras with the Washington Nationals was for four years, plus an option year, in his first major league season. ISE negotiated a five-year contract plus an option year with the Arizona Diamondbacks for Paul Goldschmidt prior to the 2013 season, an illustration of an early major-league contract that buys out free agency years. Successful baseball stars in Japan, Korea, and Cuba have inked initial multiyear contracts without any major-league experience. Two prominent examples include Texas agreeing to terms with Japanese star Yu Darvish, represented by WMG, and Oakland coming to terms with Cuban star Yoenis Cespedes through CAA.

Boras, CAA, and Excel have the most team-controlled players with contracts of two years or longer, subsequently referred to as multiyear team control or team control 2 players (Table 3b). CAA has the highest total value ($1.1 billion) and AAV ($13.7 million) contracts, with Buster Posey's nine-year, $167 million plus option contract with the San Francisco Giants being a notable example. WMG stands out with the longest average length of contracts (7.3 years) but with only a total of eight contracts in this category. WMG clients

include New York Yankees superstar Stanton and former Japanese and Cuban players (Darvish, Kenta Maeda, Yasiel Puig, and both Yulieski and Lourdes Gurriel). The combination of free agents plus team control players accounts for approximately 85 to 90 percent of agency commissions, although only around 30 percent of the total number of contracts.

DIFFERENCES IN TALENT AND SALARIES ACROSS AGENCIES

The information examined in Tables 1, 2, and 3 demonstrates that Boras has the highest paid players on an average annual basis for all free agent players. They also tend to have lengthier contracts compared to the other large agencies. Along with Boras, CAA and Excel have the most multiyear contracts for players under team control and their AAVs for these players are among the highest. There are at least two reasons to explain the success of these agencies: they may be more adept at attracting highly-skilled players, and they may be more skillful at negotiating more lucrative contracts. To distinguish the two reasons, we must examine player achievements before inking their names on contracts.

We chose WAR to measure performance, since it is a comprehensive measure. The WAR metrics are shown in Table 4 (see following page) for free agents and team control 2 players from each of the 12 agencies. We find that Boras players earn higher WAR scores pre-contract than most other agencies for both free agents and team control 2 players, suggesting that its clients may be more talented and successful. Altuve, Harper, and Max Scherzer each have an average WAR

Table 3b. Big 12 Agencies and Their MLB Team Control Players: (Contracts 2 years or longer negotiated 2015–18)

Agency	Number of Contracts	Total Value*	Average Contract Value*	Average Annual Value*	Average Length	Agency Commission*
ACES	12	347.0	28.9	6.2	4.2	13.9
BHSC	12	347.6	29.0	6.9	3.9	13.9
Boras	16	891.0	55.7	10.6	4.6	35.6
CAA	15	1108.5	73.9	13.7	5.2	44.3
Excel	13	923.4	71.0	13.1	4.6	36.9
ISE	12	534.4	44.5	8.0	5.3	21.4
Jet	10	314.9	31.5	6.3	4.5	12.6
Legacy	11	275.4	25.0	6.3	3.9	11.0
Magnus	7	129.3	18.5	4.6	4.1	5.2
Octagon	12	372.9	31.1	6.6	4.1	14.9
Sosnick-Cobbe	6	166.0	27.7	6.8	4.5	6.6
WMG	8	663.5	82.9	9.9	7.3	26.5

* In millions of dollars.
Average contract value = total value divided by the number of contracts
Annual average value = annual average salary
Agency commission estimated at 4 percent of the total value of contracts
Source: Data derived from Baseball Prospectus

of over 5 contributing to the relatively higher average for Boras (see Table 2). The two other agencies that average over 3 WAR for team control 2 players are WMG and CAA. Notable WAR achievements elevating metrics for these two agencies are Stanton's nearly 5 WAR and Cespedes's nearly 4 WAR, respectively.

In the next two columns in Table 4 we focus on the monetary value of players. Players compensated by a higher salary per WAR prior to signing are more costly. No agency stands out, except for Jet, with most agencies having around $5 million per WAR for free agents and nearly $4 million for team control 2 players. There is some variation that can often be explained by one or two contracts per agency, where the player had limited success but still received a relatively high paying

contract. For example, Jet has represented catcher Jeff Mathis. While his most recent agreement is relatively small ($4 million for two years), his WAR averaged a meager 0.1 prior to signing. Mathis is considered to be an excellent game-caller, helpful to a pitching staff, and is considered "one of the best at something that cannot be measured but is valued."[16] In this case, WAR may not be an adequate measure of his value to a team.

In Table 5 we examine players' success after signing the contract. WAR outcomes are consistently lower than prior to the contracts. This is an expected result particularly for free agents since these players are older and their performances tend to drop off with age. Because of lower WAR, post-contract salaries per WAR

Table 4. Player Performance by Agency: Wins Above Replacement Prior to Contract

	Free Agent WAR	Team Control 2 WAR	Free Agent Salaries/WAR $ Millions	Team Control 2 Salaries/WAR $ Millions
ACES	1.28	1.62	5.04	3.85
BHSC	1.40	1.77	5.67	3.92
Boras	2.18	3.09	4.96	4.36
CAA	1.38	3.05	5.07	4.68
Excel	2.02	2.62	4.43	4.69
ISE	1.59	2.20	4.80	3.62
Jet	0.88	1.80	8.72	3.49
Legacy	1.48	2.17	4.83	2.72
Magnus	1.89	0.78	3.04	4.39
Octagon	1.83	1.86	4.08	3.69
Sosnick-Cobbe	1.02	1.66	4.62	5.02
WMG	1.45	3.28	5.18	3.93

Source: Salary data from Baseball Prospectus. WAR data from Fangraphs.

Table 5. Player Performance by Agency: Wins Above Replacement Post Contract

	Free Agent WAR	Team Control 2 WAR	Free Agent Salaries/WAR $ Millions	Team Control 2 Salaries/WAR $ Millions
ACES	0.92	1.18	7.18	5.62
BHSC	0.77	1.72	10.99	4.04
Boras	1.02	2.56	10.38	4.12
CAA	0.70	1.75	10.05	7.80
Excel	1.05	2.69	8.51	4.85
ISE	0.96	2.82	8.19	2.83
Jet	0.77	2.25	9.93	2.80
Legacy	0.58	1.79	12.40	3.53
Magnus	0.77	1.11	7.46	4.15
Octagon	0.81	2.77	9.28	2.40
Sosnick-Cobbe	0.27	1.66	19.81	4.07
WMG	0.81	2.77	9.23	3.59

Source: Salary data from Baseball Prospectus. WAR data from Fangraphs.

increase considerably for free-agent players. The average dollar cost is approximately $10 million. According to Swartz, the dollar-cost estimate of replacing a free agent is worth around $10 million over the 2015–17 period.[17] Our post-contract results are within the $10 million range for Boras and most of the other agencies. The main outlier, the nearly $20 million per WAR for Sosnick-Cobbe's free agent clients, reflects a small sample size and some players with slightly negative WARs and high salaries, most notably Jay Bruce's 2018 three-year, $39 million contract with the New York Mets combined with 2018 WAR at replacement level.

Team control 2 players exceed the achievements and are less costly than free agents; this is the case for every agency in Table 5. Coming to terms with team control 2 players for multiyear contracts relative to free agents appears to be advantageous for teams. The team owners absorb the risk of players getting injuries or subpar performances but the team control 2 clients demonstrate greater monetary value than their free agent counterparts. The team control 2 players likely receive less than free agent market rate compensation and tend to be younger.

CONCLUDING OBSERVATIONS:
GENNARO GENERALLY HAD IT CORRECT

In Gennaro's 2011 article he concludes that Boras's hype as super-agent is justified. Our analysis indicates most of the findings related to Boras's success continue to prevail. We find that Boras has the largest number of major league players under agreement, with an estimated total contract value of $3.5 billion covering contracts signed between 2015 and 2018 seasons. The firm represents clients with the highest average annual salaries and is among the agencies with the longest contracts.

Boras does appear to be a master at attracting the game's biggest stars. The company retains many of the most successful free agents. Current clients, such as Harper and Scherzer, often achieve higher WAR scores than other players. Toward the end of the 2018 season, emerging Phillies slugger Rhys Hoskins opted to hire Boras as his agent.[18] Boras's reputation as an agent who encourages his players to wait for free agency rather than sign extensions while under team control often holds. However, there are some key exceptions where Boras has negotiated extensions with players' existing teams at or near market rates. Two relatively recent examples are the seven-year extensions for Altuve and Strasburg.

In addition to Boras, we examine several other big agencies in detail. ACES, CAA, Excel, ISE, and WMG each represent major league players with well over one hundred contracts totaling at least $1.5 billion. Each has at least one star with contracts exceeding six years and $100 million. Included in this list are names like Jon Lester, Posey, Greinke, Miguel Cabrera, and Stanton.

The dozen agencies in our study appear to be competitive with each other when comparing the negotiated salaries given their clients' level of performance. Whether we are discussing free agents or multiyear contract team control players, the average annual salaries per WAR prior to signing contracts are approximately $5 and $4 million, respectively, for each of the dozen agencies. Post salaries per WAR are mostly greater than pre-salary, indicating that performance levels are often less after signing a contract. This is true for free agents in each of the dozen agencies and half of the 12 agencies of the team control 2 players.

Gennaro indicates that Boras is more successful in negotiating maximum value for his clients, achieving nearly twice their average contract values—both salaries and length of contracts—relative to performances. We find a similar result for free agents. Boras's clients have nearly 90 percent higher average contract values and 45 percent greater WAR. In contrast though, for multiyear team control players, Boras's clients attain 20 percent higher average contract values but achieve much higher WAR of 45 percent relative to other agencies. Boras may be more successful at negotiating free-agent contracts but this does not appear to be the case for multiyear team control clients.

We should add one more point: our focus has been on a metric that we can measure, namely, salary and WAR. While salaries are obviously a key component a player seeks in choosing an agency, there are likely many personal and branding factors that are important to players in enlisting agency representation. The ability of the agencies to market their players might vary and generate different streams of income. ∎

Acknowledgments

The author appreciates the careful and extensive critique and suggestions by John Wainio and two anonymous reviewers. We also benefited from correspondence with the Major League Baseball Players Association.

Notes

1. Jorge Castillo, "Scott Boras Says Shifts Are Partly Why Bryce Harper Isn't Enjoying a Typical Harper Season," *Washington Post*, July 5, 2018. https://www.washingtonpost.com/news/nationals-journal/wp/2018/07/05/scott-boras-says-shifts-are-partly-why-bryce-harper-isnt-enjoying-a-typical-harper-season/?noredirect=on.
2. Vince Gennaro, "The Scott Boras Factor: Reality or Hype?" Baseball Prospectus, April 15, 2011. https://www.baseballprospectus.com/news/article/13584/baseball-proguestus-the-scott-boras-factor-reality-or-hype.

3. Neil Paine, "Bryce Harper Should Have Made $73 Million More." FiveThirtyEight, November 9, 2015. https://fivethirtyeight.com/features/bryce-harper-nl-mvp-mlb.

4. Matt Swartz, "Foundations of the Dollars-per-WAR Evaluation Framework." Fangraphs, March 26, 2014. https://www.fangraphs.com/tht/foundations-of-the-dollars-per-war-evaluation-framework.

5. MLBTR Agency Database. Major League Baseball Trade Rumors. http://www.mlbtraderumors.com/agencydatabase.

6. See MLBPA Agent Regulations: http://mlb.mlb.com/pa/info/agent_regulations.jsp.

7. Bob Nightengale and Jorge L. Ortiz. "Scott Boras loses in grievance against Beltran," USA Today, March 26, 2014. http://www.usatoday.com/story/sports/mlb/2014/03/26/scott-boras-grievance-carlos-beltran-robinson-cano-switching-agents/6934915.

8. Jared Diamond, "Baseball Tries to Clean Up After Social-Media Fouls." Wall Street Journal, August 22, 2018, A14.

9. Wendy Thurm, "Longtime Agents Slash Fees, Try to Shake Up Industry." Fangraphs, August 26, 2014. https://www.fangraphs.com/blogs/longtime-agents-slash-fees-try-to-shake-up-industry.

10. Excel Sports Management. http://new.excelsm.com/representation-baseball.

11. See for example: B.J. Rains "Why I Chose My Agent: David Wright." Major League Baseball Trade Rumors, March 13, 2013, part of a series of interviews of players. http://www.mlbtraderumors.com/2013/03/why-i-chose-my-agency-david-wright.html.

12. See Wendy Thurm ; Marie Gentile, "The Average Sports Agent's Commission," Houston Chronicle, June 28, 2018 (updated), http://work.chron.com/average-sports-agents-commission-21083.html; and Sports Management Worldwide, "Sports Agency's Salaries," https://www.sportsmanagementworldwide.com/courses/athlete-management-sports-agent/salaries.

13. Marie Gentile.

14. If options are not exercised then the contract usually includes a relatively small payout to the player. We did not include these payouts so the value of the contracts may be slightly understated.

15. Consistent with MLB rules, the Cots database expresses MLB experience in years and days of service. A player becomes eligible for free agency if he has six years of experience at the beginning of a season. However, some players are listed between six and seven years of service who agreed to an extension before they became a free agent (see Altuve, Cots, 2018, for example). We reviewed Baseball Prospectus contract information to discern which players opted for an extension. These players are not included as free agents but are included in Table 2b.

16. R.J. Anderson, "Baseball believes in Jeff Mathis and the hidden value of game-calling by catchers." CBSsports.com, February 20, 2018. https://www.cbssports.com/mlb/news/baseball-believes-in-jeff-mathis-and-the-hidden-value-of-game-calling-by-catchers.

17. Matt Swartz, "The Recent History of Free Agency Pricing." Fangraphs, July 11, 2017. https://www.fangraphs.com/blogs/the-recent-history-of-free-agent-pricing.

18. Steve Adams, "Rhys Hoskins Hires Scott Boras." MLB Trade Rumors, Setptember 18, 2018. https://www.mlbtraderumors.com/2018/09/rhys-hoskins-hires-scott-boras.html.

Hot Streaks, Screaming Grounders, and War

Conceptual Metaphors in Baseball

Daniel Rousseau

Until my freshman year of college, the only books I'd read cover-to-cover were baseball almanacs and biographies of early and mid-twentieth century baseball players like Ed Delahanty and Satchel Paige. Throughout grade school, I spent my evenings flipping through onionskin pages full of baseball stats or studying the backs of baseball cards. An Indians fan, I would use historic home run and strikeout totals along with batting and earned run averages to construct imagined scenes from Cleveland baseball history.

In the second grade, I developed a fondness for Hall of Fame pitcher Addie Joss. He played from 1902 to 1910. His career was cut short by meningitis. There was no picture of him in my almanac, but I used his 1.89 career ERA and .968 WHIP to construct an image in my head of a sturdy and precise man—stirrups even and pressed, face placid and clean. Only a wild pitcher, I had thought, would grow an unruly beard. Indeed, if Joss were the most precise pitcher ever, he would have no facial hair. I wouldn't know for sure what his face looked like until I was in middle school when I encountered a Joss tobacco card at a collectors' convention in Chicago. In the image on the card, he was mostly as I'd imagined: straight-faced with a popped jersey collar. But I did not expect his hair parted down the middle, his bangs curled and waxed like some dorky pre-war actuary.

Each time I attend a baseball card show, I'm introduced to another of my hero's faces and can't help but imagine that player at work. In my imagined scenes, actions and dialogue are derived from a unique baseball vocabulary: bases load like guns, changeups fall off tables, and frozen ropes earn doubles. This vocabulary has influenced the way I organize and retrieve my memories. In my brain, I file cable news clips of war next to Josh Hamilton's 2008 Home Run Derby performance, tie my two weeks in the Ecuadorian jungle to Rick Ankiel's wild fastball, and place my father's death beside the 1997 World Series, which the Cleveland Indians lost. When I study baseball-related language, I am studying myself—my history, assumptions, and proximity to the world. Language and cognition are inseparable, and so our passions impact our perceptions, thought organizations, and communications.

In their book *Metaphors We Live By*, cognitive linguists George Lakoff and Mark Johnson claim that "the essence of metaphor is understanding and experiencing one kind of a thing in terms of another."[1] We cannot make sense of our complex inner and outer worlds without conceptual metaphors, through which we decipher and describe non-tactile or ambiguous concepts by comparing them to concrete objects and experiences. Metaphors are not merely "characteristic of language alone," but "pervasive in everyday life…in thought and action."[2] To strip our lives of metaphor is to live in a single dimension, to know nothing but unnamed, immediate sensations. Metaphors allow us to name and play in confounding depths—everywhere from our psyches to the cosmos—which is, I think, to be human.

Here, I'll examine orientational, ontological, and structural metaphors used to describe baseball games. As I do, I hope some of the core assumptions and perceptions that are common amongst baseball fans, and perhaps humanity as a whole, become more evident. Most importantly, I hope this basic survey will bolster my—and hopefully my readers'—ability to intentionally and effectively recognize and construct metaphors, then employ them in communication, to better describe the human experience.

I live vicariously through Dodgers pitcher Clayton Kershaw. We're about the same age, and both have four-year-old daughters. But Clayton is five inches taller than I, left-handed, and induces major-league whiffs with a swooping, 88-mph slider. At this point in my life, my fastball peaks at 73—that according to a carnival speed gun. In an alternate reality, I sometimes think, there is a tall, athletic version of myself who throws physics-bending curveballs. I watch every Kershaw start on television. He is in California while I am in Philadelphia. Our time zone difference means that I will likely stay up past midnight once every five days during the baseball season. My wife heads to bed without me on Kershaw nights.

On June 18, 2014, Clayton Kershaw no-hit the Colorado Rockies. Baseball wordsmith Vin Scully provided the color commentary. Scully began his career as a radio announcer. His descriptions of that game were so vivid that pictures weren't necessary. The baseball, according to Scully, "dips" and "drifts," gets "punched" and "speared." In the third inning, a Rockies batter hit a "soft line drive." Scully, always concerned about his words' clarity, defined his terms, "The use of the word line-drive is describing the trajectory." In the eighth inning, when it seemed the Rockies might not get a hit, the camera panned to Kershaw's wife. Scully, speaking like a proud family member, noted, "There's Ellen, applauding her hubby." In contrast to the elated Dodgers, the Rockies looked dejected. Scully used a refrain to describe struck-out Rockies: "Down he goes." "Down he goes." "Down he goes." I imagine the Colorado hitters knew their doom was inevitable, like characters in Vonnegut's *Slaughterhouse Five*: "So it goes." "So it goes." "Down he goes." Here, I am concerned about that metaphorical downward movement toward outs.

According to Lakoff and Johnson, many conceptual metaphors are the result of our spatial orientation. Indeed, they "arise from the fact that we have bodies of the sort that we have and that they function as they do in our physical world."[3] Through orientational metaphors, we "organize a whole system of concepts with respect to another." That is, we make sense of abstract ideas by way of physical perceptions, "up-down, in-out, front-back, on-off, deep-shallow, central-peripheral."[4] We often describe abstract concepts, such as emotions, as physical entities within our perceived spaces: *I am feeling down; Things are looking up; Her spirits are high.*

Based on linguist William Nagy's research (1974), Lakoff and Johnson suggest nine spatial concepts which drive orientational metaphors:

- "Happy is up; sad is down."
- "Conscious is up; unconscious is down."
- "Health and life are up; sickness and death are down."
- "Having control or force is up; being subjected to control or force is down."
- "More is up; less is down."
- "Foreseeable future events are up (and ahead)."
- "High status is up; low status is down."
- "Virtue is up; depravity is down."
- "Rational is up; emotional is down."[5]

As these orientational concepts are dependent upon subjects' immediate environments, they will not be uniform across all cultures. However, most of these concepts appear as driving forces in baseball descriptions.

In his essay collection *The Summer Game*, Roger Angell—a J.G. Taylor Spink Award winner and long-time *New Yorker* fiction editor—describes baseball in the 1960s. His book, like the sport during that decade, is dominated by images of the Yankees, Dodgers, Giants, and Cardinals—and hopeful considerations of the pitiful, fledgling Mets. Occasionally, Angell constructs essays by watching games on television, but most of the time, he writes about his first-hand experience as a fan at the ballpark.

Of a 1962 playoff game between the Giants and Dodgers, Angell writes, "One out of every three or four [Dodgers fans] carries a transistor radio in order to be told what he is seeing, and the din from these is so loud in the stands that every spectator can hear the voice of Vin Scully."[6] Like many of my own potent baseball memories, those fans' recollections—including Angell's—are forever linked to Scully's voice, his turns of phrase, his metaphors.

Using language similar to Scully's refrain from that 2014 Kershaw no-hitter—"Down he goes"—Angell describes an important moment from the '62 series: "[Maury] Wills stole second, and the Giants' catcher, in attempting to cut him down, relayed the ball to center field and to the possessor of the best arm on the club, Willie Mays, who then cut down Wills at third."[7] The speedy Maury Wills, like a tree chopped down and removed from the forest, was, when tagged out, removed from the field of play. If health and life are up and sickness and death are down, then we might conclude that the base paths on a baseball field are reserved for wellness and vitality; they are up. As such, it is common for fans, commentators, and writers to describe winning teams as *riding high* and losers as *fallen*.

Perhaps some people are attracted to baseball because it is a quick and obvious representation of their struggle to remain upright. We are all bound to the world by gravity and celebrate many human achievements which work against it: first steps and bike rides, stolen bases and home runs. Orientational metaphors, then, which are rooted in near-universal physical perceptions or at least common language related to those perceptions, are strong connecting points between the orator or writer and the audience.

In 1963, the New York Mets lost 111 games. The previous year they'd lost a historic 120. Still, Roger Angell made his way to the Polo Grounds, where he and a boisterous crowd rooted for that lovable but struggling team. Angell writes about those Mets:

Last year when the team trailed the entire league in batting…its team average was .240. So far this year, the Mets are batting .215, and a good many of the regulars display all the painful symptoms of batters in the grip of a long slump—not swinging at first pitches, taking called third strikes.[8]

Slumps, it seems, are heavy diseases which attach themselves to baseball players, then pull them downward toward outs. On the literal surface, the Mets may have looked strong and confident, but beneath a metaphorical lens, they might have appeared hunched over, straining to stand—let alone hit—in the batter's box.

Angell suggests that if the Mets' offensive woes continue, their manager "will be forced to insert any faintly warm bat into the lineup, even at the price of weakening his frail defense."[9] We understand temperature in up-down terms; it rises and falls. Cold is, perhaps, closer to rigidness or death than heat, or at least away from free movement and vitality; it is down. In baseball, the players' metaphorical temperature is equivalent to their readiness to enter the game and their likelihood to remain *upright*, which is to help their team win. Players who have consistently performed at an elite level are often described as *hot*. Struggling players are *cold*.

While hot-cold metaphors are grounded in our spatial orientations, they also draw from our direct experiences with objects: snow, campfires, coffee, etc. Lakoff and Johnson call such metaphors "ontological." Through ontological metaphors, we understand abstract concepts as concrete entities. Ontological metaphors might be richer or more specific than orientational metaphors:

One can only do so much with orientation. Our experience of physical objects and substances provides further basis for understanding…Once we can identify our experiences as entities or substances, we can refer to them, categorize them, group them, and quantify them—and, by this means, reason about them.[10]

Through ontological metaphors, we might understand a struggling baseball team as more than simply *fallen*, but rather a *defective machine*—a complex physical entity. One might describe those 1963 Mets as *rusty* or *not firing on all cylinders*. Roger Angell describes that team's manager as a novice mechanic whose "Tinkering [of the lineup] can lead to the sort of landslide that carried away the Citadel last year."[11] As machines are full of unique parts and movements, the ontological metaphors built from them—by way of direct observation or experience—might be intricate and action-packed.

If people construct ontological metaphors through specific, past physical experiences, how might they impact our physical states when called upon in the present? Do fans feel literally cold when their favorite player strikes out, stuck in a frigid slump? In a close game, do fans literally feel hotter when they see their All-Star closer warming up in the bullpen?

In their paper "Cold and Lonely: Does Social Exclusion Literally Feel Cold?" University of Toronto social psychologists Chen-Bo Zhong and Geoffrey J. Leonardelli write, "Metaphors such as *icy stare* and *cold reception* are not to be taken literally and certainly do not imply reduced temperature. Two experiments, however, revealed that social exclusion literally feels cold."[12] In one experiment, Zhong and Leonardelli asked sixty-five undergraduate students to recall "a situation in which they felt socially excluded or included."[13] Then, at the request of a supposed maintenance staff member, those students estimated the current room temperature. Consistently, students who had been asked to recall memories of social exclusion estimated lower room temperatures. For those students, social exclusion felt cold. Therefore, metaphorical concepts primed literal, physical sensations. Commenting on their experiment's results, Zhong and Leonardelli note:

[These Findings] highlight the idea that metaphors are not just linguistic elements that people use to communicate; metaphors are fundamental vessels through which people understand and experience the world around them…It is possible that people use coldness to describe social interaction patterns partly because they observe, at an abstract level, that the experience of coldness and the experience of social rejection coincide.[14]

Metaphors are bridges by which people connect abstract concepts to literal, physical perceptions. For example, uncertainty is chilling, ambitious plans are lofty, and depression is dim. In this way, abstract and concrete concepts and their connecting metaphors are tied together in our brains. When someone entertains a metaphor, they may also experience any of the abstract or concrete concepts that metaphor was initially built to bridge.

The metaphors that Vin Scully and Roger Angell use to construct images of baseball games in their listeners' or readers' minds affect their psychological, emotional, and physical states. I imagine if I were a Rockies fan watching that Kershaw no-hitter on mute, in the absence of Scully's voice, the images on the screen would frustrate me. Perhaps I'd curse at Colorado pitcher Jorge De La Rosa after he allowed five runs in the third inning. Maybe I'd pound my right fist on my knee when Rockies catcher Wilin Rosario struck out for the third time. But if I turned on the volume and let Scully tell me what I was seeing, he might lull me from mere frustration into depression. Maybe after I heard his refrain, "Down he goes," I'd hang my head, then hunch my back. Perhaps if he said that the Rockies' hitters looked "scared and lonely" at the plate, I'd also feel alone, and possibly cold. If Scully called the Rockies' offense broken, I might be moved to sadness, as I was in the third grade when my dog destroyed my Sammy Sosa rookie card, chewed beyond repair.

One of the most iconic calls of Scully's career came in Game Six of the 1986 World Series. The Red Sox led the Mets three games to two and were on the verge of their first championship since 1918. In the bottom of the 10th inning of the sixth game, with the score tied 5–5 and Mets infielder Ray Knight on third, Mookie Wilson, a speedy bean-pole-of-a-man, hit a "Little roller up along first." Before Wilson's hit, Red Sox first basemen Bill Buckner had positioned himself 20 feet from the bag. As Wilson swung, Buckner shuffled five steps to his left and crouched to receive the ball. At that time, Buckner—strong, handsome, and mustached—was one of Boston's stars. He'd won a batting title in 1980 and twice led the league in doubles. But at that point in his career, Buckner was not sure-handed and he failed to field Wilson's grounder. Vin Scully yelled, "Behind the bag! It gets through Buckner. Here comes Knight, and the Mets win it!"

In the months following his error, Buckner would receive death threats from crazed Red Sox fans who blamed him for that World Series loss. His name would become synonymous with failure. But in that moment, Scully did not say "Buckner missed it" or "Buckner made an error," but rather that the ball went "through" Buckner. Scully deemed the baseball, not a player, the main actor.

Often in baseball commentary, the ball is described as a creature. After a player swings at and misses a 95-mph fastball, an announcer might say that *the ball ate the batter up*. Or if a batter pushes a perfect bunt down the third-base line, so the ball rolls to a stop before the catcher or third baseman can field it cleanly, a writer may explain that the ball *died on the field*.

Sometimes, baseballs are described like people who *dance*, *race*, *baffle*, and *hum*. According to Lakoff and Johnson, such attributions "allow us to comprehend a wide variety of experiences with nonhuman entities in terms of human motivations, characteristics, and activities."[15] Roger Angell personifies the baseball in his description of a 1968 matchup between the Red Sox and White Sox. In the third inning, Chicago's left fielder Tommy Davis hit "a two-base screamer just inside the bag at third."[16] Maybe Davis swung so hard, made such true contact, that the baseball did not merely hiss as it usually does when rushing through wind, but yelled. Imagine standing at a street corner, an angry man shouting obscenities as he runs in your direction. Can you blame Boston's third baseman for stepping to the side of that screaming grounder, letting it pass?

Perhaps if baseballs always moved as expected, and weren't consistently fooling or injuring players, people might see them as fair and honest characters which, when batted, deserve secure *send-offs* rather than harmful *hits*. However, baseballs, so far as most baseball people know them, are crafty and unpredictable, worthy of punishment. Broadcasters happily describe batted balls as *smacked*, *crushed*, *walloped*, *destroyed*, *slapped*, *rapped*, *struck*, *banged*, *pounded*, *cracked*, *punched*, *swatted*, *belted*, and *shot*. Baseball language is often violent.

Radio commentator John Sterling creates a unique home run call for every Yankee. He often uses alliteration and rhymes. In the past, he called each Derek Jeter home run a "Jeter Jolt," and with every Chris Carter blast he exclaimed, "Carter hits it harder!" Often Sterling utilizes battle-like phrases: "Bernie goes boom!" "Kelly killed it!" "It's a nuke from Youk!" "It's an A-bomb for A-Rod!"

On March 29, 2018, when power-hitting right fielder Giancarlo Stanton hit his first home run as a Yankee, John Sterling exclaimed, "It is gone! In his first Yankee at bat! Giancarlo, non si puó stoparlo! (Giancarlo can't be stopped!) It is a Stantonian home run. A two-run blast." Many Yankees fans did not like some of the ways Sterling had described that home run. On social media, they questioned Sterling's poor Italian and dismissed his use of that added suffix in "Stanton-ian." "Ruthian" is already a common word in the Yankee vernacular, and any comparison between Stanton and Ruth might be blasphemous in the Bronx. But nobody challenged Sterling's use of the word "blast." Few people ever question his war words.

Maybe John Sterling, like many baseball fans, not only thought that Stanton's home run ball resembled a soaring weapon or that the slugger's buttoned uniform looked like battledress, but has conceptualized the entire sport as war. Maybe he's mentally organized baseball atop an existing schema of battle, and so he cannot separate the motives and strategies of literal war from his metaphorical understanding of the game. Perhaps a single structural metaphor, *baseball as war*, drives most baseball commentary.

While orientational metaphors help us to understand abstract concepts in broad physical terms, they "are not," write Lakoff and Johnson, "in themselves very rich."[17] And though we might personify inanimate objects through ontological metaphors—know ourselves and the world in more complex terms than up and down or in and out—they are limited by their necessary relationship to tangible items. We might only comprehend our inner and outer worlds as specific intangible systems through structural metaphors. Of all conceptual metaphor types,

> Structural metaphors…provide the richest source of elaboration. Structural metaphors allow us to do much more than just orient concepts, refer to them, quantify them, etc., as we do with simple orientational and ontological metaphors; they allow us, in addition, to use one highly structured and clearly delineated concept to structure another.[18]

Perhaps the most common example of a structural metaphor is *rational argument as war*. Like all animals, humans "fight to get what they want."[19] However, unlike the rest of the animal kingdom, we have instituted rational parameters around conflict and developed "sophisticated techniques for getting our way."[20] We not only participate in reckless fights but structured battles, not only physical altercations but rhetorical situations. In verbal arguments,

> Each sees himself as having something to win and something to lose, territory to establish and territory to defend. In a no-holds-barred argument, you attack, defend, counterattack, etc., using whatever verbal means you have at your disposal—intimidation, threat, invoking authority, insult, belittling, challenging authority, evading issues, bargaining, flattering, and even giving "rational reasons."[21]

We spend much of our social lives in arguments, many of them subtle and nuanced. Our default rhetorical moves in those arguments are often combat-like, designed to maneuver metaphorical battle flags toward us. As protective animals in a society often framed by war, we might perceive any two-sided contest as a battle, and so, as with rational argument, we may conceptualize and describe baseball as war.

In 1951, New York Giants utility player Bobby Thomson hit a walk-off home run to win the National League pennant, sending his team to the World Series. The following day, the *New York Daily News* dubbed Thomson's home run "The Shot Heard 'Round the Baseball World," a play on Ralph Waldo Emerson's 1837 "Concord Hymn," written to commemorate the beginning of the Revolutionary War. In that poem, Emerson writes, "Here once the embattled farmers stood/And fired the shot heard round the world."[22]

In the prologue to his novel *Underworld*, Don DeLillo imagines J. Edgar Hoover at the Polo Grounds the day Bobby Thomson hit that famed "shot." In DeLillo's fictionalized account, just before the Thomson blast, Hoover learns of a secret Russian atomic test, the deployment of an enemy "instrument of conflict…a red bomb that spouts a great white cloud like some thunder god of ancient Eurasia."[23] Hoover is not concerned with the outcome of the baseball game, but "the way our allies one by one will receive the news of the Soviet Bomb."[24] After Thomson's hit soars into the stands beyond Dodgers left fielder Andy Pafko, the Giants fans and players erupt into victorious mayhem. People toss thousands of newspaper clippings, receipts, and ripped magazine pages into the air. Paper rains over J. Edgar Hoover like confetti. Here, he stands at the intersection of the literal and metaphorical, between the tangible by-products of victory—streamers and joyous chants—and the complex intangibles which often drive war strategy and baseball language: morality, justice, purpose.

Fans who conceptualize baseball as war, their team's seasons as moral and just conquests, might employ battle terms in discussions about gameplay: *Koufax has coerced ten players to swing at his curveball; The manager should have deployed his closer earlier; Henderson evaded the tag at third; The Cubs pitching staff lacks firepower; Hershiser looks tired but will not surrender; That Cabrera double might spark a breakthrough; Griffey is patrolling center field; Acuña was plunked, but took the high ground and did not rush the mound.*

The *baseball as war* metaphor is compelling, but we might not only know the game that way. The sport is many things to many people. To some, baseball is a meticulous, practiced craft performed through improvisation, and so it is jazz. To others, baseball is athletic leaps performed by sculpted men in matching costumes, a ballet. Still, others may know the game as a matrix where player actions resemble numbers which collide and change and reveal or echo mathematical truths. Perhaps the depth and breadth of our passions apart from baseball are among the few limits on our metaphorical conceptions of it.

In her essay "I Remember, I Remember," poet and essayist Mary Ruefle writes about making a metaphor:

> I remember—I must have been eight or nine—wandering out to the ungrassed backyard of our newly constructed suburban house and seeing that the earth was dry and cracked in irregular squares and other shapes, and I felt I was looking at a map and I was completely overcome by this description, my first experience of making a metaphor, and I felt weird and shaky and went inside and wrote it down: the cracked earth is a map.[25]

Humans are miraculous metaphor-making machines. Our brains are full of beautiful, complex connections between formless mysteries and tactile or structured elements. We construct most metaphors unconsciously. But some people, like Ruefle, can make rich metaphors actively. Active metaphor construction is a practiced craft, honed through repeated and deep deliberations of undefined concepts, and perhaps bolstered by a basic understanding of how humans conceptualize their worlds: orientationally, ontologically, structurally.

When we invent metaphors, we satisfy a primal human urge to decipher and organize thought and experience. Mary Ruefle explains how she felt after constructing that first metaphor: "It was an enormous ever-expanding room of a moment, a chunk of time that has expanded ever since and that my whole life keeps fitting into." I imagine, with each new metaphor I construct, fractal-like synapse paths grow in my brain, connecting emotions, senses, and objects in new, unique ways.

Recently, my mother retired and moved in with my family. She brought boxes full of my childhood things with her: baseball cards, model cars, and wide-ruled notebooks. I did not read or write many stories as a child. My early notebooks mostly contain black and white drawings. On the first page of my fifth-grade notebook, I drew Bob Feller mid-pitch, his left toe pointed high in the air. On the second page, I drew a cartoon of Mark McGwire flexing, the word *slugger* printed across his chest. On the fourth page, I drew a hodge-podge of baseball players, only identifiable by the last names scrawled above their heads: Thomas, Vizquel, Griffey, Belle, Justice, Maddux, Bonds. Below that player lineup, I identified an important metaphor that many of my experiences keep "fitting into": baseball is my life. ■

Bibliography

Angell, Roger. *The Summer Game.* Lincoln: University of Nebraska Press, 2004.

Delillo, Don. *Underworld.* New York: Scribner, 1997.

Emerson, Ralph Waldo. "Concord Hymn by Ralph Waldo Emerson." Poetry Foundation. https://www.poetryfoundation.org/poems/45870/concord-hymn.

Lakoff, George, and Mark Johnson. *Metaphors We Live By.* Chicago: University of Chicago Press, 2017.

Ruefle, Mary. "I Remember, I Remember." Poetry Foundation, July 2, 2012. https://www.poetryfoundation.org/poetrymagazine/articles/69829/i-remember-i-remember.

Zhong, Chen-Bo, and Geoffrey J. Leonardelli. "Cold and Lonely: Does Social Exclusion Literally Feel Cold?" *Psychological Science* 19, no. 9 (2009): 838–42.

Notes

1. George Lakoff and Mark Johnson, *Metaphors We Live By* (Chicago: University of Chicago Press, 2003), 5.
2. Lakoff and Johnson, *Metaphors We Live By*, 3.
3. Lakoff and Johnson, *Metaphors We Live By*, 14.
4. Lakoff and Johnson, *Metaphors We Live By.*
5. Lakoff and Johnson, *Metaphors We Live By*, 15–17.
6. Roger Angell, *The Summer Game* (Lincoln: University of Nebraska Press, 2004), 72.
7. Angell, *The Summer Game.*
8. Angell, *The Summer Game.*
9. Angell, *The Summer Game.*
10. Lakoff and Johnson, *Metaphors We Live By*, 25.
11. Angell, *The Summer Game*, 50.
12. Chen-Bo Zhong and Geoffry J. Leonardelli, "Cold and Lonely: Does Social Exclusion Literally Feel Cold?" *Psychological Science* 19, no.9 (2008): 838.
13. Zhong and Leonardelli, 839.
14. Zhong and Leonardelli, 840.
15. Lakoff and Johnson, *Metaphors We Live By*, 33.
16. Angell, *The Summer Game*, 21.
17. Lakoff and Johnson, *Metaphors We Live By*, 61.
18. Lakoff and Johnson, *Metaphors We Live By*, 61.
19. Lakoff and Johnson, *Metaphors We Live By*, 62.
20. Lakoff and Johnson, *Metaphors We Live By*, 62.
21. Lakoff and Johnson, *Metaphors We Live By*, 62.
22. Ralph Waldo Emerson, "Concord Hymn by Ralph Waldo Emerson," Poetry Foundation, https://www.poetryfoundation.org/poems/45870/concord-hymn.
23. Don DeLillo, *Underworld* (New York: Scribner, 1997), 23.
24. DeLillo, *Underworld*, 30.
25. Mary Ruefle, "I Remember, I Remember," Poetry Foundation, July 2, 2012, https://www.poetryfoundation.org/poetrymagazine/articles/69829/i-remember-iremember.
26. Ruefle.

Did MLB Exist Before the Year 2000?

Bill Nowlin

Writers often refer to "MLB" as though it were something that has existed as long as there has been major league baseball. It has not. I decided to ask the question: Did MLB exist before 2000? Or maybe late 1999?

Some background on why I decided to delve into this question. Several odd words or constructions recur in submissions to the books I've edited for SABR over the past several years. One is the mysterious "homerun." Where did the idea that home run is a single, compound word come from? Apparently there is a "post-apocalyptic role-playing" computer game named *Fallout 4*, which users began to play on Xbox or PlayStation at the end of 2015. *Fallout 4* contains an "achievement/trophy" called a "homerun." It was indeed around that time (2015) that I noticed "homerun" cropping up in player biographies and game accounts sent in for SABR books. But were that many SABR members embracing computer gaming as well as baseball? Had they somehow forgotten the venerable history of the home run in baseball? It's almost like the misspelling was contagious. Once rare, now maybe 5% of the articles I see have this "homerun" in it.

"MLB" crops up even more often than "homerun" in articles submitted for editing. It's not uncommon to receive a manuscript with a sentence such as "In 1942, Ted Williams led MLB with 36 homers, 137 RBIs, a .356 batting average, and won the first of his two Triple Crowns."

Obviously, using "MLB" in that context is a shorthand way of referring to "major league baseball." Using the capital letters makes it appear that there was an entity known as Major League Baseball in 1942, and that "MLB" was just an abbreviated way of referring to it. As far as I've been able to determine, there was no such thing as Major League Baseball in 1942.

What was there? There were really three entities: Prior to the year 2000, American League teams were members of an unincorporated association officially called The American League of Professional Baseball Clubs, and the National League teams were members of an unincorporated association called The National League of Professional Baseball Clubs. The third entity was the Office of the Commissioner of Baseball.

Prior to 1984, the two leagues even operated out of different buildings before they were brought into the same building by Commissioner Peter Ueberroth. Each league hired its own umpires, and of course operated under different rules once the American League introduced the designated hitter. Regular in-season play did not take place between teams from separate leagues—only spring training, exhibition games, and the World Series.

Official in-season interleague play began in 1997. In September 1999 the announcement came that as of 2000 the two leagues would be consolidated into a single entity under the office of the commissioner. This is why, for instance, an umpire such as Joe West is listed on Retrosheet as a National League umpire from his debut in 1976 through the 1999 season, but beginning in 2002 he has been a "Major League" umpire.[1]

On September 10, 1999, National League president Leonard Coleman resigned, as he was seeing the consolidation of the leagues proceed under Commissioner Bud Selig. The first three functions Selig began to combine after the 1999 season were the creating of schedules, oversight of on-field discipline, and unifying the umpiring staff.

On September 15, a unanimous vote of club owners at Cooperstown's Otesaga Hotel centralized and united the two leagues into one entity.[2] They consented to re-draft the Major League Agreement.

A November 11, 1999, article in the *Los Angeles Sentinel* referred to Major League Baseball as MLB and the Major League Baseball Players Association as MLBPA. In December, the Associated Press story announcing the settlement of a lawsuit between ESPN and major league baseball did not capitalize the words "major league baseball."[3] A review of reporter Richard Sandomir's coverage of the business of baseball for the *New York Times* shows him consistently capitalizing the National Football League and the National Hockey League but only occasionally capitalizing Major League Baseball, until the middle 1990s.[4] From January 2000 forward, however, he commonly began to refer to the organization as Major League Baseball.

Does this mean MLB was only born in 1999/2000? It's more complicated than that.

EARLIER HISTORY

This isn't the place to go into the entire history of the transformation of baseball from an amateur sport to a professional, organized business, but most students of baseball history know that when the American League breached the National Agreement before the 1901 season, there was resistance from the already-established National League. There were plenty of other leagues around the country, as well, representing various levels of talent.

John Thorn reminds me of the "peace agreement in 1903 that stopped the AL from poaching NL player contracts and behaving disagreeably otherwise. This followed upon the 1902 National Agreement governing the minor league clubs, thus forming Organized Baseball. The National Commission, a three-man body that was de facto controlled by the American League (because of Garry Herrmann's friendship with Ban Johnson) was somewhat ineffective and gave way to the Commissioner system."[5]

Though there was some degree of cooperation, such as agreeing (beginning in 1905 on a regular, annual basis) to have the top team from each league play each other in a World Series, it was not until 20 years after the American League became a major league that a true compromise was reached between the leagues and on January 12, 1921, "the position of Baseball Commissioner was created with the ratification of the new Major League Agreement."[6]

Judge Kenesaw Mountain Landis was the first Commissioner. He insisted on a wide array of powers, but after his death some of those powers were diluted. There was a period of some 40 years or so during which under one Commissioner or the next, the degree of powers of the office waxed and waned. When it came to 1984, however, there was a mutual desire among the club owners of both leagues—impressed as they were with his leadership of the 1984 Summer Olympic Games—to hire Peter Ueberroth. "To entice Ueberroth, the clubs again expanded the Commissioner's powers by amending the Major League Agreement so that the two league presidents were required to answer to the Commissioner with respect to administrative matters."[7] Before this time, each league had been fairly free to go its own way. That's one of the reasons we have a designated hitter in the AL but for the past 46 years not in the NL. In 1984, there

was truly no such thing as a unified Major League Baseball.

This is not to say, however, that all administrative functions were left only to the separate leagues; the individual clubs had mutually ceded certain powers—notably through the "best interests of baseball" clause—to the Office of the Commissioner. That Office had already overseen agreements regarding network broadcasting, marketing, intellectual property, and other administrative areas.

As Commissioner Kuhn was succeeded by Commissioner Ueberroth, the Major League Agreement was amended to give the incoming Commissioner more centralized power, to become the "chief executive officer" of Major League Baseball.

CHANGE CAME SLOWLY TO THE NOMINALLY UNITED LEAGUES

In the years that followed 1984, there continued to be a number of changes to the game—exemplified, for instance, by the uneven pace of expansion—which show a lack of true centralized authority. In that very year, for instance, the National League had 12 teams and the American League had 14. It wasn't until 1993 that the NL expanded to have the same number of teams—14.

Starting in 1994, both leagues changed from two divisions to three. But in 1998, the National League added two more teams and so had 16 to the AL's 14. This sort of thing just wouldn't happen if there was one unitary body governing the two separate leagues.

Major-league ballclubs became worth hundreds of millions of dollars each. Owners understandably don't like changes that might undercut the value of their assets. Even once the two leagues were consolidated in the year 2000, it took more than a dozen years to finally—in 2013—come to an agreement where both leagues were composed of 15 teams and each division had the same number of teams in it.

USES OF THE NAME "MAJOR LEAGUE BASEBALL"

A former attorney who worked in the Office of the Commissioner wrote me, "Although it was often called 'Major League Baseball,' you are right that that was not the Commissioner's Office's official name." He added, "However, the Commissioner's Office's switchboard operator began answering the phone 'Major League Baseball' (a change from 'Baseball Commissioner's Office') early in Peter Ueberroth's term and at his instruction in order to increase the use and augment the marketing of that name."

Even though there was no legal entity by that name, there were bank accounts established, payroll taxes were filed, and there were legal proceedings of one sort or another. The name used for these was the Office of the Commissioner of Baseball, and not Major League Baseball.[8]

Legally, "Major League Baseball" is known as an unincorporated association, with each of its clubs as members. Various courts have recognized this over the years, most notably the Southern District of Ohio in the 1989 *Rose v. Giamatti* decision.[9]

As for the media, for most of the twentieth century, though writers and others often referred to "major league baseball," it was generally a descriptive term (distinguishing it from minor league baseball), rather than to identify a specific organization.

OTHER ENTITIES USING "MAJOR LEAGUE BASEBALL" AS PART OF THEIR NAMES

Were there times that "Major League Baseball" was used as more or less something of a d/b/a (doing business as)? The most definitive response would need to come from the main office in New York, but they presumably have more important things to do than answer pesky questions about legal minutiae. There are, however, several noteworthy entities which have used those three words as part of their names since 1966.

That year the Major League Baseball Players Association was founded and, with the leadership of Marvin Miller, grew to become one of the most powerful unions in the United States. Miller served as the

MLBPA's executive director 1966–83. In 1967, the 30 clubs created a Major League Baseball Player Relations Committee to negotiate with Miller and the MLBPA. Of course, the MLBPA was the name adopted by the union, not by an entity known as Major League Baseball. The Player Relations Committee was the name given to a committee; such naming was adjectival and did not necessarily reflect the existence of Major League Baseball as an actual entity.

But also in 1966, the "Major League Baseball Promotion Corporation" was incorporated. The outside attorney who incorporated it was Bowie Kuhn, later himself Commissioner of Baseball (1969–84). In March 1989 its name was changed to "Major League Baseball Properties, Inc."[10] This body handled certain licensing functions, among other things, and is a wholly-owned subsidiary of Major League Baseball Enterprises, Inc. Eleven separate entities have filed for incorporation in New York State using names that begin with "Major League Baseball." The aforementioned MLBPA, Major League Baseball Properties Inc., and Major League Baseball Enterprises, Inc. are among them. Table 1 lists all eleven and their dates of filing and whether the name/entity is still active.[11] Six of them pre-date the 1999/2000 unification.[12]

TRADEMARK FILINGS

Major League Baseball's logo has been used for some years as a long-time trademark (in particular, a "service

Name	Date of Incorporation	Active	Notes
MAJOR LEAGUE BASEBALL ACES, LLC	October 9, 2018	Yes	Jurisdiction: Delaware
MAJOR LEAGUE BASEBALL BLUE, INC.	December 20, 2007	Yes	Jurisdiction: Delaware
MAJOR LEAGUE BASEBALL CHARITIES, INC.	March 17, 2008	Yes	Domestic Not-for-profit corporation
MAJOR LEAGUE BASEBALL CHARITY, INC.	April 11, 1986	Yes	Now called MAJOR LEAGUE BASEBALL CHARITIES, INC.
MAJOR LEAGUE BASEBALL ENTERPRISES, INC.	September 23, 1996	No	Merged Out (Oct 31, 2015)
MAJOR LEAGUE BASEBALL PLAYER RELATIONS COMMITTEE, INC.	April 13, 1978	No	Dissolution (Mar 10, 1999)
MAJOR LEAGUE BASEBALL PLAYERS ALUMNI ASSOCIATION	October 4, 1994	Yes	Foreign Not-for-profit corporation
MAJOR LEAGUE BASEBALL PROMOTION CORPORATION	December 2, 1966	Yes	Now called MAJOR LEAGUE BASEBALL PROPERTIES, INC.
MAJOR LEAGUE BASEBALL PROPERTIES, INC.	December 27, 1987	Yes	Renaming
MAJOR LEAGUE BASEBALL URBAN YOUTH FOUNDATION	April 13, 2017	Yes	Now called MAJOR LEAGUE BASEBALL YOUTH FOUNDATION
MAJOR LEAGUE BASEBALL YOUTH FOUNDATION	January 22, 2018	Yes	Jurisdiction: California

Peter Ueberroth

mark"). Application #0955967 was filed on December 3, 1968, by Major League Baseball Promotion Corporation. The service mark showed the batter silhouette logo with the words MAJOR LEAGUE BASEBALL spelled out underneath it, all in capital letters.[13]

The registration was accompanied by this disclaimer:

THE TERM "MAJOR LEAGUE BASEBALL" IS DIS-CLAIMED APART FROM THE MARK AS SHOWN AND BY SUCH DISCLAIMER THE APPLICANT DOES NOT WAIVE ANY COMMON-LAW OR OTHER RIGHTS WHICH IT MAY HAVE IN THE DISCLAIMED PORTION OF THE MARK.

It appears, then, that the logo is a registered service mark, but that the registration only attempted to register the logo and not the name. That does not mean, however, that they were waiving any interest they legitimately had (and have) in the name.

On its MLB.com website, Major League Baseball also posts legal notices asserting ownership of a number of trademarks or service marks including the three words "Major League Baseball," the three letters in combination ("MLB"), and even just the two words "Major League."[14] In articles on MLB.com, MLB staff writers even use the capital letters when they refer to Major League players. Here at SABR, though, we will continue to use lower-case when referring to major league players and the major leagues, except when we're specifically talking about the post-1999 entity known as Major League Baseball, a.k.a. MLB.[15] ∎

Acknowledgements

Thanks to both Mike McCullough and John Thorn for multiple readings of this article, and suggestions for improvement.

Notes

1. Following a mass resignation as a form of protest which backfired on them, 22 umpires lost their jobs on September 1, 1999. See for instance, Murray Chass, "Umpires Accept Deal but Resignations Stand," *The New York Times*, September 2, 1999: D1. The article itself referred to Major League Baseball as though it was an entity. Though also using the words "Major League Baseball" at one point in the article, the next day's *Times* referred correctly to the actual entity in discussing another legal action, a lawsuit *ESPN v. Office of the Commissioner of Baseball*. See Richard Sandomir, "ESPN Expects to Win Baseball Suit," *The New York Times*, September 3, 1999: D3.

2. Murray Chass, "Leagues President Out As Baseball Centralizes," *The New York Times*, September 16, 1999: D3.

3. See, for instance, "Baseball has new contract with ESPN," *Chicago Daily Herald*, December 7, 1999: 7.

4. See, for instance, his mention of "major league baseball" in "Networks Back Out of TV Deal with Baseball," *The New York Times*, December 7, 1999: 7.

5. Email from John Thorn on January 25, 2019.

6. "The Commissioner: A Historical Perspective," MLB.com, accessed September 8, 2019. http://mlb.mlb.com/mlb/history/mlb_history_people.jsp?story=com.

7. "The Commissioner: A Historical Perspective."

8. Though correspondence from earlier Commissioners such as Eckert and Kuhn contained simple letterheads designating they are from the "Office of the Commissioner," Ueberroth's also added "Major League Baseball" underneath. In a March 31, 1989 letter to Jim Murray of the *Los Angeles Times*, Ueberroth also observed: "I consider myself fortunate to have been associated with two of sports' finest institutions—Major League Baseball and the Olympic Games—and hope it is the view of most that I have served those institutions well." For a copy of this letter, see www.cooperstownexpert.com/player/peter-ueberroth.

9. 721 F. Supp. 906, 917-20 (S.D. Ohio 1989). In that case, the court recognized that Major League Baseball was a "unique organization" and that Rose's dispute was properly against Commissioner Giamatti insofar as Major League Baseball had no control over Giamatti's disciplinary proceedings.

10. Its name was changed to Major League Baseball Properties, Inc. in March 1989. See https://www.bloomberg.com/research/stocks/private/snapshot.asp?privcapId=7960445.

11. New York State incorporation filings searched online via https://www.dos.ny.gov/corps/bus_entity_search.html.

12. And these 11 don't include the various entities that MLB has brought into being since 1999, including cable television station MLB Network (launched January 1, 2009), nor Major League Baseball Advanced Media (MLBAM), the limited partnership launched in June 2000 and jointly owned by all 30 MLB teams. MLBAM not only runs MLB.com (and all 30 team websites), they have spun off into providing web and mobile streaming services to other major sports leagues like the NHL, as well as WWE and HBO. See for example Eric Fisher, "Deal with MLBAM a game changer for League's approach to digital," *Sports Business Daily*, January 23, 2017, https://www.sportsbusinessdaily.com/Journal/Issues/2017/01/23/Media/MLBAM.aspx.

13. In addition, there were two applications filed on August 31, 1973 depicting the silhouette batter logo with the letters MLB. The earlier one of the two was registered on December 18, 1976, but both are currently showing as "dead."

14. "Legal Notices," MLB.com, accessed September 8, 2019, https://www.mlb.com/official-information/legalnotices.

15. And please note, no "the" before MLB.

Setting the Record Straight on Major League Team Nicknames

Ed Coen

Of the major league teams that trace their history before 1960, most started out with several short-term unofficial nicknames or even no nickname at all. Although several reputable sources provide a history of these nicknames, there are numerous contradictions between the available sources, and sometimes even when these sources agree, they conflict with the original sources. In other words, they do not reflect what the team was actually known as at the time. The purpose of this study is to identify the nicknames, based on contemporary newspapers, that each existing team has been known as throughout its history. This article can then be used as a reference to avoid such discrepancies in the future.

THE NEED FOR THIS STUDY

To illustrate the need for such a source, I examined two of the most reliable sources to which researchers often turn. David Nemec's *The Great Encyclopedia of 19th Century Major League Baseball—Second Edition* is a useful book for that period in baseball history and provides a nickname for each major league team in each year from 1876 through 1900 as well as National Association teams 1871–75.[1] The teams page on Baseball-Reference.com is another popular source for nicknames by year for each team from 1871 to the present.[2] Two other sources deserving mention are *Total Ballclubs: The Ultimate Book of Baseball Franchises*, by Donald Dewey and Nicholas Acocella and *Baseball Team Names: A Worldwide Dictionary, 1869-2011*.[3,4] *Total Ballclubs* provides a history of all current and former major league teams, including a list of nicknames used, but does not provide a detailed description of what names were used in what years. *Baseball Team Names* provides a wealth of information about the origin of official, unofficial, and alternate names of various teams throughout the world, but since it does not consider frequency of use, it is not germane to this study.

Nemec and Baseball-Reference.com agree that the Boston National League team was known as the Beaneaters from 1883 to 1900. But would the fans in Boston have referred to their favorite team as the Beaneaters? An electronic search of "beaneaters" or "bean eaters" in the *Boston Globe* during the 1883 baseball season yielded one hit, and that one was a dispatch from New York, likely written by a New Yorker. A similar search for the 1891 National League championship season in both the *Boston Globe* and the *Boston Post* yielded five hits for the *Globe* and none at all for the *Post*. Of these five, two were in headlines, indicating that they were likely not written by a sportswriter, but by someone less familiar with the team. One was a direct quotation from Cap Anson, manager of the rival Chicago Colts. One was referring to Boston's American Association team. The final quotation was in a column in which a writer surveyed various quotations heard from the crowd. A manual search of the other Boston papers found no mention of Beaneaters in this time period. Beaneaters was not a nickname for a specific team, but a nickname for someone from Boston used by outsiders. This is illustrated by the fact that Boston's Union Association, Players League, American Association, and American League teams were also occasionally called the Beaneaters by reporters from other cities. Other similar examples are the New York Gothams and the Philadelphia Quakers. These nicknames are found in multiple modern sources, but they do not represent what the teams were known as at the time they played. Although it sounds strange to a modern ear to hear a team called simply the "Bostons," that is exactly how the Boston National League club was most commonly known to its own fans from 1878 through 1900.

Another example in which both sources agree is the St. Louis National League club in 1899. They all say the team was known as the Perfectos. But how often did the St. Louis writers use that moniker? In a search of the *St. Louis Post-Dispatch* and the *St. Louis Globe Democrat*, of the 38 hits, 11 were unrelated to the St. Louis baseball team. Of the remaining 27, four were in headlines, which were not necessarily written by sportswriters, and eight were either in descriptions of road games, often written by out-of-town reporters, or direct quotations from a paper outside of St. Louis. This leaves 15 hits or approximately 1 per month per paper. Of these 15, most were either a list of upcoming games or a short discussion of various facets of the team. Only one hit, out of two newspapers' coverage of 87 home games, was in an account of a home game. A manual search of the *St. Louis Star* yielded similar results. Although this strictly conforms to Nemec's stated criterion of "the nickname, if any, that was used most often in our primary sources," it again appears that by far the most common way to identify the team was no nickname at all.[5] Nemec also uses Perfectos as the nickname for the 1900 team, while Baseball-Reference.com and a look at the all of the St. Louis papers show that they were regularly called the Cardinals then.

Others have previously raised the issue of modern sources not conforming to original sources. In the 1998 *Baseball Research Journal*, Marc Okkonen used his experience poring through newspapers to compile a list of the common nicknames used by teams from 1900 through 1910.[6] Although I disagree with him on a few things, this current study is essentially an expansion of Okkonen's work to include the entire history of all current teams.[7] In articles in the 2003 and 2006 *National Pastime*, Bill Nowlin provided enough information on the nickname of the club now known as the Boston Red Sox to allow Baseball-Reference.com to correct its entry for that team.[8,9] This study aims to correct the record for all teams and all years.

DEFINITION OF THE TERMS

Although in most contexts, the word "nickname" implies something informal, the general practice with sports teams is to use "nickname" whether it's official or not. For the purpose of this study, "nickname" refers to the identifier other than the city for any team.

In this study I refer to "official" and "accepted" nicknames. An *official nickname* is a nickname given by the club itself. In some cases, the name is part of the club's corporate name, or an official statement was made from the club's front office. In others, the recognition was tacit, such as the use of the name on the team's uniform or in official publications. An *accepted nickname*, on the other hand, is an unofficial nickname made up by the fans or the press that has become widespread. In this study, I define an accepted nickname as any of two or three nicknames that were regularly used in at least two local newspapers in accounts of home games.

As for the definition of "regularly," that is where subjectivity comes in. Since it is not practical to count all mentions of a name for an entire season for all newspapers in a given city, I looked through the accounts of several home games for several different homestands throughout the season. If I found more than about three or four mentions, I considered it a regularly used nickname in that paper. A typical sample size was about ten games, but when it was not obvious if a name was regularly used, I looked at more games until satisfactorily determining that a nickname was accepted. As a general rule of thumb, if a nickname was used in more than a third of the home game accounts in a newspaper, I considered it regularly used in that paper. Although this method is admittedly subjective, in the majority of cases it was obvious one way or the other. In general, most papers tended to pick a name and stick with it throughout the season. If any two papers in a team's city were deemed to use a certain name regularly, as defined by this process, it was considered an accepted nickname.

In many cases an unofficial accepted nickname evolved into an official nickname. No attempt was made in this study to determine the exact date of that transition.

GROUND RULES

The first rule is that I relied only on contemporary local sources, primarily newspapers. As described above, sources written after the fact tend to be unreliable. When nicknames are unofficial, newspapers in other cities tend to lag behind the hometown newspapers. Since the foremost authorities on the nickname of a given city's team are the people in that city at that time, I relied solely on several newspapers from the team's home town. Furthermore, I only looked at accounts of home games, since accounts of road games were often written by local writers who sold them to the papers in the road team's city. Finally, only the text of the article was considered, since headlines are often written by people such as copy editors, who might be less familiar with the team or more prone to hyperbole.

The second rule is that official names take priority. Once an official name has been discerned, no attempt is made to search for an accepted nickname. One example of the application of this rule is the 1905 to 1956 Washington Nationals. For the latter part of that period, Senators was used at least as often as Nationals, but since the team has declared itself the Nationals, I call them the Nationals. Likewise, the Oakland A's of the 1970s were hardly ever called the Athletics, but that was still their official nickname.

The third rule is that no attempt was made to force one and only one accepted nickname on a team. Some teams simply had no nicknames. The above example of the Boston National League club in the nineteenth century is an application of this rule. Once Red Stockings and Reds fell out of use, they are identified simply as the Bostons, since in general teams with no accepted nickname were identified by the city. On the other hand, the New York American League club from 1906 through 1912 was called the Yankees and the Highlanders almost equally. To choose one over the other would be arbitrary. They were both accepted nicknames. It would not be wrong to refer to them as the New York Yankees or the New York Highlanders.

ORIGIN AND TYPES OF NICKNAMES

The first team names were simply the names of the group that sponsored the team. The Philadelphia Athletic Club became the Athletics. The Atlantic Base Ball Club of Brooklyn became the Atlantics. This style of nickname still exists today in the Oakland Athletics and the New York Mets. In the 1870s and 1880s, the team name (e.g., Atlantic, Athletic) generally appeared in standings and box scores instead of the city (e.g., Brooklyn, Philadelphia).

Another common source of nicknames was the color of the uniform. In early uniforms, it was the color of the socks that identified the team. Thus, in the 1870s nicknames included the Chicago White Stockings, the Boston Red Stockings, and the St. Louis Brown Stockings, often shortened to Whites, Reds, and Browns. This pattern continues today in the Boston Red Sox, the Chicago White Sox, the Cincinnati Reds, and the St. Louis Cardinals (originally named after the color, not the bird).

In the nineteenth century, it was also common for teams to have no nickname at all and to be identified by city name only. Newspapers of that era are full of accounts of the Bostons, the Chicagos, and the Brooklyns. Newspapers in cities with two teams tended to identify one by the city and one by another name. Philadelphia had the Philadelphias and the Athletics. New York had the New Yorks and the Metropolitans. Philadelphias, because of its length, was often shortened to Phillies. What is now the team nickname started out as just shorthand for the city name.

Nicknames in the 1890s and early 1900s were often inventions of sportswriters that caught on with the public. The club itself had little part in it. Some nicknames, such as the Brooklyn Dodgers, arose gradually, while others, such as the Chicago Colts arose suddenly. If it arose gradually, I give a year that the nickname became accepted by my methodology, but it is a judgment call. If it came about suddenly, I identify it as such.

In the 1910s official nicknames became more common. In these cases, an exact year, and sometimes even an exact date, can be discerned. Washington was ahead of their time in 1905 when they likely became the first major league team to hold a contest to determine a new team nickname: the Nationals.

By 1915 each team had the nickname it carried into the 1950s, although Brooklyn had three accepted nicknames, Dodgers, Robins, and Superbas. The latter two dropped out of use over the next 17 years. Three National League teams subsequently changed their name, only to change it back. The Braves became the Bees, Phillies was shortened to Phils and Reds was lengthened to Redlegs for short times in the 1930s, '40s, and '50s respectively.

RESULTS

Since nicknames have been stable since 1961, the teams that began in 1961 or later are not included in this study. The only nickname changes after 1961, other than as a result of a move, were on December 1, 1964, when the Houston Colt .45s became the Astros and on November 8, 2007, when the Tampa Bay Devil Rays became the Rays.[10,11] Below, in alphabetical order of the city they occupied in the 1903–52 era, National League first, are the complete histories of each pre-expansion era team's nickname.

NATIONAL LEAGUE
Boston[12]

When Harry Wright brought the nucleus of his Cincinnati Red Stockings to Boston in 1871, the obvious choice for a nickname was the Red Stockings. This name was accepted through 1874. In 1875, Reds was in use as often as Red Stockings, so both were accepted. In 1876, Red Stockings fell out of use, so Reds was the only accepted nickname. From 1877 through 1900 they had no nickname; they were simply the Bostons. As discussed above, the name Beaneaters was hardly ever used locally and was more of a nickname for the city than the team.

From 1901 to 1907 they were called the Boston Nationals to distinguish them from the Boston Americans. At that time, referring to a National League team as the Nationals or an American League team as the Americans was common, so every National League team was sometimes called the Nationals. Because this practice was much more common in Boston than elsewhere, Nationals is considered an accepted nickname for the Boston club. In 1907, newspapers began calling them the Doves, after owners John and George Dovey. Both Nationals and Doves appeared in multiple papers,

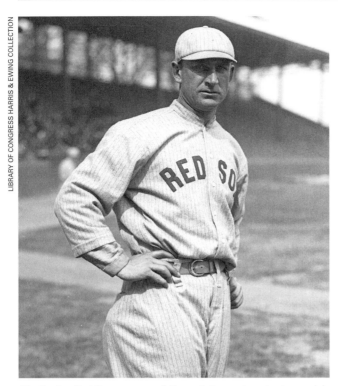

The Boston Red Sox were one of the early teams to put a team nickname (rather than city name, logo, or initial) across their jerseys. Pictured here is Jake Stahl in 1912.

making them both accepted nicknames. In 1908, Doves emerged as the single accepted nickname. When John Dovey sold his share of the team in December of 1910, George having died the previous year, the name Doves became obsolete.

In 1911, the Boston media tried to come up with a name based on the new owner, William Hepburn Russell. Heps, Hapes, Hopes, and Rustlers were all used, but none stands out as an accepted nickname. For 1911 then, they had no accepted nickname. This lasted only one year as Russell died in November of 1911.

Then James Gaffney bought the team and hired John Montgomery Ward as the president. On December 20, 1911, Ward suggested to reporters that the club be known as the Braves and the newspapers obliged.[13] This name was an allusion to Gaffney's involvement in New York's Tammany Hall political machine. The organization was symbolized by an Indian, and its lower ranking members were called braves. Although the Braves started out well—the 1914 Braves staged one of the greatest late-season comebacks in history—the 1920s and '30s were a time of futility for a city that until then was used to winning. In an attempt to reverse the Braves' losing habit, the team had a contest to choose a new nickname. On January 30, 1936, the name Bees was chosen.[14] Unfortunately, the Bees were

no more successful than the Braves. A new syndicate agreed to buy the team prior to the 1941 season and on April 29, 1941, just a couple of weeks into the season, announced that they would henceforth be the Braves again.[15] This name has continued in Boston, Milwaukee, and Atlanta to this day.

Brooklyn[16]

When Brooklyn entered the American Association in 1884, they had no nickname. This continued until 1888, when several of the Brooklyn players got married within a short span of time. Writers began to call the team the Bridegrooms, but not often enough to be an accepted nickname. The pennant winning teams of 1889 (their last year in the AA) and 1890 (their first year in the NL) were called the Bridegrooms on a regular basis. In 1891 however, the name died out and Brooklyn was left without a nickname. In 1895 through 1898 they were called the Grooms, a shortened form of the previous nickname. The name Trolley Dodgers, an allusion to the large number of trolleys that had to be dodged in Brooklyn, first appeared about this time. It was only used a few times, so it is not considered accepted.

In 1899 when Ned Hanlon took over the managerial helm, a new nickname was born. During the 1890s, a well-known show called "Superba," known for its groundbreaking special effects, had been produced by the Hanlon brothers, no close relation to Ned.[17] The show was commonly known as Hanlon's Superba, making the Superbas a natural nickname for Ned Hanlon's Brooklyn club. Superbas continued as the sole accepted nickname through 1909, even though Hanlon himself left after the 1905 season.

In 1910, the use of Dodgers increased enough to make it a second accepted nickname. In 1914, they hired Wilbert Robinson as their manager and in 1916, Robins joined Dodgers and Superbas as accepted nicknames. From 1916 through 1920, Brooklyn used all of these names, the only time any team had three accepted nicknames. In 1921, Superbas ceased to be used enough to be considered accepted, although the *Brooklyn Eagle* continued to use it until 1925. They continued to be known as both the Dodgers and the Robins (and sometimes alternatively as the Flock) until January 22, 1932. On that date, management made Dodgers official.[18] That name has stuck ever since, even though the team moved across the continent to Los Angeles.

Chicago[19]

When Chicago entered the National Association in 1874, they were the White Stockings, which was the accepted name in the NA and in the National League through 1887. In 1888 they switched to black stockings, but they were only called the Black Sox by one paper, the *Chicago Tribune*. In 1888 and 1889 the team was known primarily as just the Chicagos. In 1890 the core of the Chicago team left for Charlie Comiskey's Chicago White Stockings of the Players League. Chicago manager Cap Anson signed a group of young players who due to their youth became known as the Colts. Colts continued as the accepted nickname throughout Anson's tenure in Chicago. After the 1897 season, Anson was fired from the team after 19 years at the helm. Thus, the team became known as the Orphans in 1898. Orphans continued as the accepted nickname through 1901.

In 1902 and 1903 the Chicago newspapers used a dizzying array of nicknames. Colts, Cubs, Recruits, Remnants, Orphans, and even Microbes were all common names used by at least one newspaper. They had no accepted nickname for these two years. In 1904, the list was down to two as the papers were almost equally divided between Colts and Cubs (both referring to the relatively young team) so both were accepted nicknames. In 1905 Cubs became the single accepted nickname, used by all papers except the *Chicago Tribune*. The *Tribune* was the last holdout, preferring Zephyrs in 1905 and Spuds in 1906. By 1908, Cubs was definitely official because their uniform featured a cub holding a bat.[20]

Cincinnati[21]

When Cincinnati became a charter member of the American Association in 1882, they had no nickname. The Cincinnati papers just called them the Cincinnatis for their first five years. Then in 1887 every newspaper in Cincinnati identified the local team as the Reds. Reds was the accepted nickname both in the AA and, starting in 1890, in the NL. In the ensuing years they were sometimes called the Red Stockings, Redlegs, and even Red Sox, but Reds was by far the most common. This continued until April 9, 1953, when the official name was changed to Redlegs because "Reds" had been associated with communism.[22] Redlegs was the official nickname from 1953 through 1958 and on February 11, 1959, they became the Reds again.[23]

New York[24]

When New York entered the National League in 1883, they had no nickname. They were identified as New York and the American Association club was called the Metropolitans or Mets for short. In 1884, some newspapers called 6-foot 3-inch 220-pound third baseman

Roger Connor "the giant of the team."[25] Gradually the word Giants came to refer to the entire team even though a look at the roster shows that no other player was particularly large. In 1885, Giants was the common nickname in most New York papers, making it accepted. Although they abandoned New York for greener pastures in California 71 years later, they never abandoned the name Giants. At 135 years and counting, Giants is the longest continuous nickname in the major leagues.

Philadelphia[26]

When Philadelphia entered the National League in 1883, they had no nickname. They were just called the Philadelphias to distinguish them from the Athletics of the American Association. Philadelphias proved to be a mouthful and tough to fit in headlines, so it became Phillies. From 1886, Phillies was the most common way to identify the team and it gradually evolved into the team nickname through the 1941 season. Then on February 7, 1942, Phillies publicist Bill Phillips announced that it would be changed to Phils, apparently to avoid confusion with a cigar of the same name.[27] That only lasted a year however, as the team was sold and the new owner, William Cox, did not share the same concern and on March 8, 1943, announced that the team would be the Phillies again.[28]

A word should be added here about what some have erroneously called an alternate nickname: The Blue Jays. From 1944 through 1949, the team used a blue jay as a symbol, but never dropped Phillies from their uniform or official publications. The intent of this change is best illustrated by the headline in the March 5, 1944, article about the change in the *Philadelphia Inquirer*: "Phillies Accept Blue Jays as Team Emblem."[29] The designer of the emblem is shown holding up a drawing of a blue jay with the word "Phillies" under it. Clearly, the team was never meant to be called the Blue Jays and the bird was intended to be symbol, like the white elephant for the Philadelphia Athletics.

Pittsburgh[30]

One of the charter members of the American Association in 1882 was the Alleghenys. They represented Allegheny City, Pennsylvania, a suburb of Pittsburgh with a population of about 80,000, half the size of Pittsburgh. North of the Ohio River and west of the Allegheny River, it became part of Pittsburgh in 1907. This team is now often referred to as the Pittsburgh Alleghenys, but during its 5-year tenure in the AA, it was rarely if ever referred to as Pittsburgh in any Pittsburgh paper. They were simply the Alleghenys with no nickname. In 1887 they moved to the National League and the newspapers were divided as to whether to identify them as Allegheny or Pittsburgh. During this period, they couldn't even agree on how to spell Pittsburgh. The *Commercial Gazette*, *Daily Post*, and *Chronicle Telegraph* spelled it the current way and the *Dispatch* and *Press* spelled it without the final "h." All agreed that there was no nickname, although some papers occasionally called them the Allies in headlines. In 1890, the Players League formed and placed a team in Exposition Park, just across the Allegheny River from downtown Pittsburgh, very close to the site of the current PNC Park. Although technically also in Allegheny, the Players League club was known as Pittsburgh, and the National League club was known as Allegheny in all of the papers. Some modern sources use Innocents and Infants as the nickname for the team in 1890 only, alluding to their young players, but these names were very rare in all Pittsburgh newspapers. In fact, the team was called the Alleghenys much more often in 1890 than in the previous three years.

After the Players League folded, the National League team moved to Exposition Park and became the Pittsburghs. At the same time, other cities' newspapers began calling them the Pirates, as a derogatory nickname. This was an allusion to events that occurred after the collapse of the Players League. An agreement was made among National League and American Association clubs that all players who jumped to the Players League would return to their 1889 teams. When the Athletics inadvertently left second baseman Lou Bierbauer off their reserve list and Pittsburgh claimed him, they were derisively called "pirates." The name did not catch on at first with the Pittsburgh papers who from 1891 through 1894 just called them the Pittsburghs. In 1895 the Pittsburgh papers used Pirates enough that it can be called the accepted nickname. This continued until 1898, when as a result of the patriotic fervor sweeping the country during the Spanish American War, at least two Pittsburgh papers referred to the locals as the Patriots as often as the Pirates. The double nickname only lasted one year, and from 1899 to the present, they remained the Pirates. Finally, in 1911 the US Postal Service added the final "h" which had always been in the city's official name and all papers called them the Pittsburgh Pirates.[31]

St. Louis[32]

St. Louis was a member of the American Association for its entire existence, 1882–91. In 1882, they were called the Browns, after the color of the uniform socks. In 1883, they changed this color to red and had no nickname.

In 1884, they went back to being the Browns, which continued after their 1892 move to the National League, to 1898. In 1899 they had no accepted nickname. In some accounts, they were called Patsy's Perfectos, after Manager Patsy Tebeau. This was a reaction to Brooklyn's new nickname, Superbas and Perfectos both being popular Cuban cigars.[33] The appearance of Perfectos was too rare for it to be considered accepted. The following year they became known in all papers as the Cardinals, due to the red trim on their uniforms.

AMERICAN LEAGUE

Boston[34]

From their 1901 inception through 1906, the Boston American League club was called the Boston Americans to distinguish themselves from the Boston Nationals. In 1907, both Americans and a new nickname, Pilgrims, were primary names used in several Boston newspapers, so both were accepted nicknames that year. After the season, team president John I. Taylor decided he didn't care for the newspapers' choices and on December 18, 1907, he announced that henceforth the team would be known as the Red Sox.[35]

Chicago[36]

In 1901 and 1902 the Chicago American League club was called the White Stockings and White Sox about equally. In 1903 White Sox took over as the single accepted nickname and by the end of the decade, use of White Stockings disappeared altogether.

Cleveland[37]

In 1901 the Cleveland American League club had no nickname. In 1902 they were regularly known as the Blues. In 1903 and 1904 they were known as both the Blues and the Napoleons, for their star second baseman Nap Lajoie. In 1905, Lajoie became the manager and they were exclusively the Napoleons, although it was shortened to Naps on occasion. In 1906, Naps became accepted and continued through 1914. When Lajoie left after the 1914 season, the club ownership and newspapers got together and on January 16, 1915, chose Indians, which they have retained ever since.[38] This name was based on a former nickname of the old National League club, which was sometimes called the Indians in 1897 and 1898 because of outfielder Lou Sockalexis.

Detroit

Detroit's American League entry was always known as the Tigers, although during Ty Cobb's tenure as manager (1921–26) it was sometimes spelled Tygers.[39]

New York[40]

The first two years of this franchise, they were the Baltimore Orioles.[41] From 1903 to 1905, Highlanders was the accepted name, due to their location, Washington Heights in Manhattan. Yankees was used occasionally in 1904 and 1905, but not enough to be considered accepted. From 1906 through 1912 Highlanders and Yankees were both accepted. In 1913, when they abandoned American League Park and began sharing the Polo Grounds with the Giants, Highlanders almost disappeared as a nickname. Yankees has been the accepted nickname ever since.

Philadelphia

There is no question here. Whether in Philadelphia, Kansas City, or Oakland, the official nickname has always been the Athletics, although A's, as an alternate nickname, dates back to at least 1915.[42]

St. Louis[43]

In 1901, the franchise was in Milwaukee and called the Brewers.[44] In 1902 they moved to St. Louis and adopted the discarded name of the National League club: Browns. This continued through 1953, although in 1905 there was a vain attempt by the *St. Louis Post-Dispatch* to change the name to Ravens. From the move to Baltimore for the 1954 season to the present, the team has been the Orioles.

Washington[45]

Upon entering the American League, Washington chose the nickname from the 1892-1899 National League club: Senators. After four losing seasons, they decided to hold a fan contest to come up with a new nickname, hoping it would change their luck. On March 25, 1905, the winner was announced.[46] Going back to the great Washington teams of the 1860s and 1870s and the Eastern League pennant winners in the 1880s, they chose Nationals. These Nationals were no more successful than the Senators and Senators gradually re-emerged as alternate but unofficial name. Although Senators was used more often than Nationals in the rest of the country, Nationals remained the official name through 1956 and was used often in the Washington papers. The shortened form Nats was quite common in headlines even after Senators became the official name. Long-time owner Clark Griffith stubbornly clung to Nationals because he felt that using the name Senators for a usually losing team detracted from the dignity of the United States Senate.[46] When Calvin Griffith took over after the death of his father, he decided to make the preferred nickname official.

On October 30, 1956, he announced that Senators would now be the official name.[47] This only lasted four years, as in 1961 they became the Minnesota Twins.

SUMMARY

Table 1 on page 77 shows the accepted nicknames used by each club by season. ■

Notes

1. David Nemec, *The Great Encyclopedia of 19th Century Major League Baseball—Second Edition* (Tuscaloosa, AL: University of Alabama Press, 2006).
2. Baseball-Reference.com, https://www.Baseball-Reference.com/teams.
3. Donald Dewey, Nicholas Acocella, *Total Ballclubs: The Ultimate Book of Baseball Teams,*(Toronto: Sport Media Publishing, Inc., 2005).
4. Richard Worth, *Baseball Team Names: A Worldwide Dictionary* (Jefferson, NC: McFarland & Company, Inc., 2013).
5. Nemec, 523.
6. Marc Okkonen, "Team Nicknames," *The Baseball Research Journal* 27 (1998): 37–39.
7. Okkonen dismisses Pilgrims altogether as a nickname for the Boston AL club but my research shows it was used as often as Americans in 1907 in all Boston papers except the Post so I consider both Pilgrims and Americans to be accepted for that year. Okkonen refers to the 1911 Boston NL club as the Rustlers, but since only the Globe called them that, I do not consider it an accepted nickname. Okkonen wrote that the Chicago AL club was identified as the White Stockings only in 1900 through 1902, but I found both White Stockings and White Sox to be used regularly in 1900-1902. Okkonen considers Blues to be Cleveland's nickname in 1901, but I did not find it, or any other nickname, in any newspapers that year. Okkonen states that the press was not involved in the change of Washington's nickname from Senators to Nationals, but it was actually a committee of sportswriters that organized the contest to come up with a new name.
8. Bill Nowlin, "The Boston Pilgrims Never Existed," *The National Pastime* 23 (2003): 71–76.
9. Bill Nowlin, "About the Boston Pilgrims," *The National Pastime* 26 (2006): 40.
10. Mickey Herskowitz. "Houston 'Astros' To Play Beneath Big Dome in '65," *Houston Post*, December 2, 1964.
11. "Time to shine: Rays introduce new name, new icon, new team colors and new uniforms," raysbaseball.com, November 8, 2007.
12. Newspapers used in this analysis: *Boston Herald* (1871–1912), *Boston Globe* (1872–1911), *Boston Post* (1872–1911), *Boston Journal* (1871–1911), *Boston Record* (1907).
13. T. H. Murnane, "Found—A Name for Those South End Fence-Breakers, 'Boston Braves,' " *Boston Daily Globe*, December 21, 1911.
14. James C. O'Leary, "Braves Are to Be Called Bees," *The Boston Globe*, January 31, 1936.
15. "Bees Win Last Game; They're Braves Again," *Boston Herald*, April 30, 1941.
16. Newspapers used in this analysis, *Brooklyn Eagle* (1884–1932), *Brooklyn Union* (1884), *Brooklyn Standard Union* (1887–1931), *Brooklyn Citizen* (1888–1932), *Brooklyn Daily Times* (1886–1932).
17. "Theaters and Music," *Brooklyn Eagle*, November 23, 1890.
18. Thomas Holmes, "Brooklyn Baseball Club Will Officially Nickname Them 'Dodgers'," *Brooklyn Eagle*, January 23, 1932.
19. Newspapers used in this analysis: *Chicago Tribune* (1874–1907), *Chicago Times Herald* (1898), *Chicago Record Herald* (1901–1907), *Chicago Daily News* (1902–1907), *Chicago Inter Ocean* (1878–1907), *Chicago Journal* (1893–1905), *Chicago Times* (1877–1888), *Chicago Post* (1903–1904), *Chicago American* (1901–1904), *Chicago Chronicle*, (1901–1905).
20. Marc Okkonen, *Baseball Uniforms of the 20th Century*, 105. (New York: Sterling Publishing Company. 1991).

21. Newspapers used in this analysis: *Cincinnati Commercial* (1882), *Cincinnati Commercial Gazette* (1886-1887), *Cincinnati Enquirer* (1882–1890), *Cincinnati Times Star* (1882–1887), *Cincinnati Post* (1886–1887).

22. "Red Stockings Become Redlegs in Cincinnati," *The New York Times*, April 10, 1953.

23. "The 'Reds' Are Back in Cincinnati," *The Washington Post and Times Herald*, February 12, 1959.

24. Newspapers used in this analysis: *The New York Times* (1883–1912), *New York Herald* (1884–1907), *New York Post* (1909–1911), *New York World* (1884–1885), *New York Tribune* (1885).

25. "The New-Yorks lose a game to the Champions," *The New York Times*, August 16, 1884.

26. Newspapers used in this analysis: *Philadelphia Press* (1883–1886), *Philadelphia Record* (1886), *Philadelphia Inquirer* (1884–1886, 1944).

27. "Phils, not Phillies," *York* (PA) *Gazette and Daily*, February 9, 1942.

28. "Phillies Again," *Greenville, (PA) Record-Argus*, March 9, 1943

29. "Phillies Accept Blue Jays as Team Emblem," *Philadelphia Inquirer*, March 5, 1944.

30. Newspapers used in this analysis: *Pittsburgh Commercial Gazette* (1882–1899), *Pittsburgh Daily Post* (1882–1899), *Pittsburg Dispatch* (1889–1890), *Pittsburg Penny Press* (1884–1886), *Pittsburg Press* (1888–1898), *Pittsburg Chronicle Telegraph* (1885–1898).

31. "Now it is 'Pittsburgh,'" *The Washington Post*, August 9, 1911.

32. Newspapers used in this analysis: *St. Louis Globe Democrat* (1882–1905), *St. Louis Post-Dispatch* (1882–1900), *Missouri Republican* (1882–1884), *St. Louis Star* (1899).

33. "The Brooklyns Here," *St. Louis Post-Dispatch*, May 25, 1899.

34. Newspapers used in this analysis: *Boston Herald* (1901–1907), *Boston Globe* (1901–1907), *Boston Post* (1907), *Boston Journal* (1904–1907), *Boston Record* (1907).

35. "To Be Known as Red Sox," *The Boston Globe*, December 19, 1907.

36. Newspapers used in this analysis: *Chicago Tribune* (1901–1907), *Chicago Record Herald* (1901–1903), *Chicago Daily News* (1902), *Chicago Inter Ocean* (1902), *Chicago Journal* (1903), *Chicago Post* (1903), *Chicago American* (1901–1903), *Chicago Chronicle*, (1901–1903).

37. Newspapers used in this analysis: *Cleveland Plain Dealer* (1901–1915), *Cleveland Leader* (1901–1906), *Cleveland News* (1906), *Cleveland Press* (1901–1906), *Cleveland World* (1902–1904).

38. "Baseball Writers Select "Indians" as the Best Name to Apply to the Former Naps," *Cleveland Plain Dealer*, January 17, 1915.

39. "Announcement," *Detroit Free Press*, July 23, 1922.

40. Newspapers used in this analysis: *The New York Times* (1903–1912), *New York Herald* (1906–1909), *New York Post* (1909–1912).

41. *Baltimore Sun*, 1901–1902.

42. Jim Nasium, "Three Lone Singles Best Macks Made," *Philadelphia Inquirer*, September 2, 1915.

43. Newspaper used in this analysis: *St. Louis Globe Democrat* (1905).

44. *Milwaukee Journal* and *Milwaukee Sentinel*, 1901.

45. Newspaper used in this analysis: *The Washington Times* (1901–1904), *Evening Star* (1901–1904).

45. "Senators New Name," *The Washington Post*, March 16, 1905.

46. Bob Addie, "Bob Addie's Column…" *The Washington Post*, October 31, 1956.

47. Addie column.

Table 1. Accepted Team Nicknames by Team and year

NATIONAL LEAGUE			AMERICAN LEAGUE		
City	**Years**	**Nickname**	**City**	**Years**	**Nickname**
Boston	1871–1875	Red Stockings	Boston	1901–1907	Americans
Milwaukee	1875–1876	Reds		1907	Pilgrims
Atlanta	1877–1900	None		1908–	Red Sox
	1901–1907	Nationals			
	1907–1910	Doves			
	1911	None	Chicago	1901–1902	White Stockings
	1912–1935	Braves		1901–	White Sox
	1936–1941	Bees			
	1941–	Braves			
Brooklyn	1884–1888	None	Cleveland	1901	None
Los Angeles	1889–1890	Bridegrooms		1902–1904	Blues
	1891–1894	None		1903–1905	Napoleons
	1895–1898	Grooms		1906–1914	Naps
	1899–1920	Superbas		1915–	Indians
	1910–	Dodgers			
	1916–1932	Robins			
Chicago	1874–1887	White Stockings	Detroit	1901–	Tigers
	1888–1889	None			
	1890–1897	Colts			
	1898–1901	Orphans	Baltimore	1901–1902	Orioles
	1902–1903	None	New York	1903–1912	Highlanders
	1904	Colts		1906–	Yankees
	1904–	Cubs			
Cincinnati	1882–86	None			
	1887–1952	Reds	Philadelphia	1901–	Athletics
	1953–1958	Redlegs	Kansas City		
	1959–	Reds	Oakland		
New York	1883–1884	None			
San Francisco	1885–	Giants			
Philadelphia	1883–1885	None	Milwaukee	1901	Brewers
	1886–1941	Phillies	St. Louis	1902–1953	Browns
	1942	Phils	Baltimore	1954–	Orioles
	1943–	Phillies			
Allegheny	1882–1894	None			
Pittsburgh	1895–	Pirates	Washington	1901–1904	Senators
	1898	Patriots	Minnesota	1905–1956	Nationals
St. Louis	1882	Browns		1957–1960	Senators
	1883	None		1961–	Twins
	1884–1898	Browns			
	1899	None			
	1900–	Cardinals			

"Our Lady Reporter"

Introducing Some Women Baseball Writers, 1900–30

Donna L. Halper, PhD

In 1763, literary critic Dr. Samuel Johnson said about women preachers, "Sir, a woman's preaching is like a dog's walking on his hind legs. It is not done well; but you are surprised to find it done at all."[1] In the early 1900s, that same attitude prevailed when it came to women sports journalists: male editors and readers did not expect it to be done well and were surprised to find it being done at all.

Stereotypical beliefs about women permeated American popular culture. Newspaper articles claimed that women "autoists" (drivers) were a danger on the road.[2] As one magistrate stated in 1915, "In my opinion, no woman should be allowed to operate an automobile."[3] Another common belief was that women would be horrified by hearing even the mildest profanity. This was the rationale for discouraging women from entering law, because they might hear bad language in the court room.[4] Women were supposedly driven by unhealthy curiosity, like Eve in the Bible and Pandora in Greek mythology. And it was widely believed that the female brain was not equipped for understanding complex subjects like mathematics or politics; psychologist Gustave Le Bon, writing in 1895, compared women's intellectual capacity with that of children.[5] Women's allegedly limited brainpower, and their lack of common sense, was a staple of comedy: one of the most common roles reserved for female comics in vaudeville was the "Dumb Dora," a woman who was scatter-brained, vapid, and frequently illogical.[6]

One other common stereotype was that women hated sports. If they attended a game, it was only to make their boyfriend or husband happy, and if they were single, they would only come to the ballpark because they hoped to get a date with a player. A popular 1911 cartoon by Gene Carr called "Flirting Flora" reflected this belief. It depicted a stylish young woman who flirted with several ballplayers simultaneously, getting them to compete for her affection.[7] Meanwhile, the idea that women were not intelligent enough to comprehend the rules of baseball was promulgated by numerous anecdotes in newspapers, telling of an unnamed female reporter who covered a ball game though she had no idea what an umpire was, or the one who asked incredibly stupid questions of the players, or the society woman who sat through a game despite having no idea who the teams were.

Of course, there might be the occasional woman who knew something about baseball, of course because her husband had taught her: for example, L.W. Bloom, editor of the *Concordia* (KS) *Empire*, wrote a 1910 opinion piece praising Gertrude (Mrs. Earl) Brown, Concordia's biggest female fan, for her thorough knowledge of the game; she could even use a scorecard as well as her husband did. But such a woman was considered unique in Bloom's estimation, because "Most women do not understand a hit from a foul ball."[8]

But in many cities, reporters were noticing a growing number of "lady baseball fans." One New Brunswick (NJ) newspaper wrote in 1910 that there were as many female fans in that city as male ones, and that young women were so interested in baseball that the local high school was organizing an all-female team.[9] In Buffalo, the sports editor commented that in 1900 hardly any women attended the games, but only five years later, thousands of women were in attendance, many of whom could score the games and were joining in debates about whether a certain play should be a hit or an error.[10] And in Oakland, a woman reporter who observed an increase in female fans at the ballpark wrote they had become "a distinct factor in the summing up of the gate receipts for the season."[11] It is also worth noting that the song "Take Me Out to the Ball Game," which centers on the persona of a female fan, was written in 1908.[12]

However, while the evidence points to the number of female fans increasing, most of the fans were male, and not all were happy about women coming out to the ballpark. Some owners believed that the presence of women would be "civilizing" and result in less cursing or bad behavior from the athletes.[13] But baseball was presented as a pastime for men and boys, and though female fans might be tolerated (often with some amusement), the sport "provided male audiences with empowering images of manhood."[14] The ballpark

SPECIAL WORLD'S SERIES FEATURE

The Heroes of the Coming Big Baseball Games Personally Sized Up and Interviewed BY A WOMAN.

was thus a masculine domain where male fans and masculine behaviors were the norm. Perhaps as a reaction to more female fans attending games, stories began to appear in the newspapers about the (allegedly) strange behavior of these women, such as the nameless young lady who got so upset when the boy sitting next to her made a negative comment about her team that she jabbed him with her hatpin.[15]

Nearly all news and sports reporters of the early 1900s were male, as were their editors, who geared their coverage to the male reader. As such, sending a woman who usually wrote about fashion and homemaking to cover a ball game from the "feminine point of view" was considered a jolly gimmick. The headline would often mention the "lady reporter." Readers might see headlines like this one, promoting some unique interviews about the 1912 World Series: "The heroes of the coming big baseball game personally sized up and interviewed BY A WOMAN."[16] (And no, I did not add the capital letters.) Since women were presumed to know little about the game itself, a female reporter was expected to write a human interest story—this headline, also from 1912, was typical: "She's Going to Write About the Personality of Five Baseball Heroes."[17] Both headlines topped syndicated articles by Idah McGlone Gibson, an experienced female columnist who absolutely *did* know something about baseball, but perhaps the headline writers assumed she was just another "Dumb Dora."

Despite stereotyping, a few young women of that era had successful careers that involved baseball. From about 1905 to 1911, Amanda Clement umpired college and semi-pro games in South Dakota and several neighboring states. She was widely respected and praised for her accuracy; one reporter noted that "she knows her business…" and that she "seldom makes a mistake."[18] In 1911, Helene Hathaway Robison Britton became the owner of the St. Louis Cardinals, the first woman to own a professional sports team; she remained owner for seven years.[19] And the earliest female sportswriter we know about goes back to 1890—the possibly pseudonymous Ella Black, a Pittsburgh reporter who covered baseball for *Sporting Life*.[20] A few other pioneering women were soon to follow.

In Trinidad, Colorado, from about 1905 to 1910, Ina Eloise Young wrote about baseball for her local newspaper, the *Trinidad Chronicle-News*. She even became the newspaper's sports editor, highly unusual for a woman of that era. And after marrying in 1910, she and her husband settled in Denver where—using her married name, Ina Young Kelley—she covered sports for the *Denver Post* for another year and a half. Like umpire Amanda Clement, Ina's work was not seen as a gimmick and she was taken seriously by her male colleagues.[21]

Ina's first beat was current events—she covered everything from forest fires to labor strikes to the Fourth of July parade. Trinidad had no minor league team, but semi-pro baseball was very popular, and the newspaper covered it faithfully. The local nine was called the Trinidad Big Six (named for a bar-and-grill that was one of the team's sponsors), and until the 1905 season, a male reporter wrote about their games. But when he left, the *Chronicle-News* had no baseball expert, no one who even knew how to keep score. Luckily, Ina's dad and her youngest brother were big fans, and her brother showed her how to use a scorecard.[22] That was enough to land a job in the sports department.

Ina became a bylined reporter in 1907—unusual for anyone, male or female back then, when only a newspaper's biggest names got a byline. She was also promoted to "sporting editor," as sports editors were then known. She covered Denver Grizzlies minor league baseball as well as local games in the Trinidad area, and in 1908 she covered the World Series.[23] When profiling her, journalism magazine The *Editor and Publisher* said she was the only female sporting editor in the United States.[24] Ina's in-depth knowledge of baseball helped her to win over even the most skeptical of her male colleagues—one of whom, the *Boston Globe*'s Tim Murnane, was a former pro baseball player and among the best-known sportswriters of that era. He was so impressed with her reporting skills that he praised her in one of his syndicated columns, noting that "Miss Young proved an excellent scorer, was familiar with every inside play, and surprised me with [her] knowledge of the game."[25] Murnane nominated her for an honorary membership in the newly formed Baseball Writers Association in 1908.[26]

By accounts from the newspapers of her day, Ina was treated like any other reporter during her seven years of covering baseball: she sat in the press box, she interviewed players and managers, and once the initial surprise at seeing a "lady reporter" wore off, her male colleagues seemed to accept her, as did the players.[27] We may never know why she was such an exception, however. Few, if any, women of that time became reporters on the sports beat. Decades later, women sportswriters were treated as either curiosities or interlopers. For example, in 1941, Pearl Kroll—then a sportswriter for *Time*—found herself excluded from the press box; she was also expected to pay her own way when attending the spring training games she was covering.[28]

But despite the acceptance and praise Ina received, she sometimes had to fend off editors who wanted her to write articles for the society page. She also had to remind male sportswriters at other newspapers that not all fans (nor all readers of that publication) were male, as she did in a 1908 letter to the editor of *Sporting Life*.[29] And while Ina had been in the right place with the right expertise, a major limitation for other women of her era was that women reporters were rarely trained to cover sports—not even women's sports, which were neither as common nor as popular as they are today. Women were discouraged from participating in athletics, ostensibly because it was too strenuous, and because of the cultural belief that girls who took part in sports would become masculinized.[30] Women journalists were expected to focus on "feminine" topics like cooking, fashion, music, and the comings and goings of members of high society. Women could become editors, but only of the "women's page."[31] Some journalism schools even refused to admit them, including the Pulitzer School of Journalism at Columbia University.[32]

When a few women tried to write about sports, the reaction they got was often negative. As far back as 1901, certain male baseball writers expressed their annoyance about women who wanted to be taken seriously as reporters. Pseudonymous Buffalo sportswriter "Hotspur" (real name: Edward McBride) referred to them as the "squaws of the pencil." As an example of why women sports reporters deserved such derision, he told the story of an unnamed woman reporter who got an interview with then-college pitcher Chris (Christy) Mathewson. While Hotspur seemed to feel the woman asked foolish questions and wasted Mathewson's time, the young pitcher seemed pleased with their conversation; in fact, the questions she asked got him talking about himself in a way that gave readers more insight into Mathewson as a person. Readers learned his favorite subject in college was natural history, he never drank anything stronger than milk,

and would not play on the Sabbath. In the interview Mathewson admitted he was embarrassed by the adulation he was receiving—especially from female fans.[33] The interview was reprinted by the *Denver Post* a few days later, which mocked the player as much as the interviewer: while noting that Mathewson had "allowed" a "lady reporter" to interview him, sports editor Otto C. Floto observed that if the young man's answers were truthful, he was a perfect human being who belonged in heaven, since he was much too good for this world.[34]

Some of the women reporters seemed to accept the negative reaction they received and the jests that came their way. Some admitted they were not baseball experts (even if, as it turned out, they really did know a lot about the game), and apologized for any mistakes they might make. But women sports reporters developed their own strategies for winning over readers in that era. For some, using humor was effective—they showed they could not only take a joke but make some jokes of their own.

One good example of trying the humorous approach was Vella (Alberta) Winner, a women's page reporter for the *Portland* (OR) *Daily Journal*. In April 1915, she wrote a piece about her impressions of the Portland Beavers' home opener. She first reassured readers that she *did* know what a pitcher was, and she even knew the names of the players—and in the course of her article, she mocked some of the baseball clichés that men sportswriters overused. She then moved directly into commenting on some of the plays, as any male sportswriter would. But she also commented on who was at the ballpark; despite the rainy day, about 10,000 people were in attendance. And she observed that team owner Walter McCredie and his wife were watching the game; she talked to Mrs. McCredie, who seemed to be quite a fan, telling the reporter, "I never miss a game…I can keep just as good a box score as my husband." Vella also noted that all the Portland fans sincerely believed the home team would have won, if only the weather had been better.[35]

Another woman who used humor when covering a game was Bertha "Bee" Hempstead, a women's page, education, and features writer for the *Topeka* (KS) *State Journal*, who offered her observations about a minor league contest between Topeka and Denver in July 1915. While noting that the game itself didn't give hometown fans much to cheer about, Hempstead employed the style that Vella Winner and other society writers used, commenting on the sights, sounds, and interesting people in the crowd: a local merchant who never missed a game, a group of salesmen for the

Ina Eloise Young (top), Amanda Clement (middle), and Idah McGlone Gibson (bottom) were female pioneers in the masculine dominated world of early twentieth century baseball. Like Clement, who umpired college and semi-pro games in South Dakota, Young and Gibson earned the respect of their male peers as writers, despite the newspaper practice of promoting women writing about sports as some kind of gimmick.

Curtis Publishing Company who had won a contest and several female fans who were remarking on which players were the cutest. She also noted with dismay that Denver's first baseman was wearing torn stockings.[36]

A tactic used by well-known *St. Louis Republic* society and gossip columnist "Serena Lamb" (a pseudonym for Lucy Stoughton) was self-effacement. When talking to a ballplayer, she would claim to know very little about the game, and then ask questions that any good interviewer, male or female, would ask. In July 1900, she interviewed several Cardinals' ballplayers: outfielder Emmet Heidrick, who was recovering from a leg injury, and third-baseman John "Muggsy" McGraw. (Newspapers then spelled his nickname with two g's; years later, it was spelled with only one.) To open the interviews, she acknowledged—perhaps with some sarcasm—that she was a "mere woman" and that those seeking in-depth analysis of yesterday's game should seek out the "sporting columns."[37] Lamb's goal was to provide her readers with personal insights into the players. Her style was conversational, and in both interviews, readers learned some interesting "fun facts" about the players—for example, Heidrick's favorite color was blue, he had a large collection of silk ties, and he didn't seem to have a girlfriend (at least not one that he would talk about).[38] McGraw said he hated the nickname "Muggsy" and refused to answer to it, and he was also a world traveler who had visited Cuba, South America, and parts of Europe.[39]

Male sports writers were not expected to write about the emotions or personality quirks of players. The sports pages focused on box scores and statistics, and the story was about who won, who lost, who played well, and who did not. Unlike the aforementioned Ina Eloise Young who typically wrote the way the men did—discussing the game's most impressive plays or questioning a decision the manager made[40]—societal expectations left fertile ground to be tilled by female reporters.

And that brings us back to Idah McGlone Gibson. Of all the women who ventured from the women's page into sports reporting, she seems to have gotten the most respect, and with good reason: she was a nationally-known reporter and syndicated columnist, whose work appeared in both newspapers and magazines during the 1910s and 1920s. While she is all but forgotten today, a quick database search for her name on Newspapers.com gives more than 1,800 results in hundreds of old newspapers. Her career began in Toledo, Ohio, where she was a theater critic and then the society editor for the *Toledo Blade*. She later moved to Chicago, where she wrote about celebrities, dispensed household and relationship tips, and (as was often expected of female journalists) offered a "women's perspective" on current events in her syndicated columns for *The Day Book* and other newspapers. Idah was among the first to profile the wives of presidents. While today we take this for granted, in her era, a president's wife (the term "First Lady" was not yet in common use) was expected to stay in the background—in fact, there was an unofficial rule that she could not be quoted directly.[41] Idah visited with four presidents' wives, learning about their day-to-day activities. Her focus was always on what made each woman unique, rather than their status as wives of famous men. Given her ability to get interviews with a wide range of famous people, it is not surprising that the editor of *The Day Book* asked Idah to provide readers with the so-called "woman's perspective" on the 1912 World Series—to discuss the personalities of the players and show these men "in a new light— as a woman sees a popular hero."[43] Because the women's page writers did not have to observe the same parameters as the male baseball writers did, their profiles of players often brought out entirely different information because these profiles were aimed at female readers.

Not all newspapers that carried Idah's work ran the interviews in the same order, but they appeared in publications from coast to coast, and some newspapers did place them on the sports page.[44] In her interview with Red Sox manager Jake Stahl, they discussed, among other things, why he wasn't called Garland (his real first name); how he got his nickname; his off-season job in banking, and of course, what his predictions were for the Series. When she talked to the Giants' Christy Mathewson, he praised baseball as a great career for any college graduate, and Idah was impressed with his cultured and articulate way of communicating. They also talked about his approach to pitching, and how he had maintained his success for such a long time. (But he refused to make any predictions about the Series.) When she spoke to Red Sox star pitcher Joe Wood, her impression was that he was very level-headed and mature for someone only twenty-two; he asserted that he never drank liquor, nor even coffee or tea during the season, and he said he also tried to be careful about not eating too much, as he had seen other players have their careers shortened by not taking care of themselves. Several of Wood's teammates jokingly wanted Idah to ask him about all the love letters he got from female fans; when she did, Wood expressed puzzlement that female fans had crushes on ballplayers, and he said he didn't

respond to the letters, which undoubtedly disappointed the young women who sent them.[45]

She had a brief interview with John "Muggsy" McGraw, who had been the Giants' manager since 1902; McGraw evidently was willing to talk to female reporters—as you may recall, 'Serena Lamb" had sat down with him back in 1900. Now, twelve years later, Idah noted that he seemed very serious; he told her he seldom liked to smile, not even when being photographed. While courteous, he did not appear very happy to be interviewed that day. Since she was a society columnist, Idah asked him about the rumors that pitcher Rube Marquard was set to marry vaudeville star Shirley Kellogg (some sources said he had already married), but McGraw demurred, saying he never commented on players' personal lives. He did express satisfaction with his pitching staff over all. (Idah had her doubts and predicted Boston to win the World Series.[46] She would be right.)

She also had a brief but cordial meeting with Charles "Jeff" Tesreau. An up-and-coming pitcher on the Giants, he was already very popular with the fans, many of whom hung around the Polo Grounds after the games, hoping to meet him and get an autograph. His key pitch, he told Idah, was the spitter (which was still legal in 1912) that McGraw and Mathewson had encouraged him to use.[47] Given the number of big-name players who agreed to talk with her, we may assume that Idah's presence at the ballpark was not treated like a stunt.

In 1916, Idah did some additional baseball interviews, beginning with Wilbert Robinson, manager of the Brooklyn Dodgers. The article started off with an amusing anecdote: when she came to the ballpark, Idah was stopped by someone who told her no ladies were permitted to watch the team practicing. But someone else said she could go in, because "She ain't no lady. She's a newspaper reporter."[48] She also interviewed Philadelphia pitching star Grover Cleveland Alexander (who wasn't in the World Series, but she wished he were), and then chatted with Brooklyn outfielder Zack "Buck" Wheat. Unlike some players, Wheat seemed very shy about being interviewed, even when Idah asked him baseball questions. He did tell her that his wife had never seen a ball game till they married, and now she was a big fan; he also spoke about the positive effect marriage had on him and surprised Idah when he stated that "a ball player never amounts to much until he marries."[49]

In October 1917, she revisited John McGraw, who didn't seem any more eager to be interviewed by Idah than he had been in 1912. They discussed how a manager handles temperamental players. While he didn't want to name his most temperamental player, McGraw did single out the player he considered the *least* temperamental: Christy Mathewson.[50] But in nearly every story, the fact that Idah was a "woman reporter" or a "lady reporter" was still somewhere in the headline.[51]

Society changed for women in many ways during the 1920s. Women got the right to vote, and radio made its debut; by the end of the decade, Lou Henry (Mrs. Herbert) Hoover became the first First Lady to give a radio talk (and yes, the term "first lady" had come into common use).[52] More middle-class women were attending college, and there were more career opportunities open to them. And yet, some things did not change. The belief persisted that women were not knowledgeable about baseball and that women only attended games either because a male family member dragged them along or because they hoped to date a ballplayer. Novelist and reporter Katharine Brush, who wasn't seeking a husband (she already had one) and who did know something about baseball, became a correspondent for her local newspaper, the *Liverpool* (OH) *Review-Tribune*. She covered the 1925 World Series between the Pittsburgh Pirates and the Washington Nationals.

In Pittsburgh, she noted that she was the only woman reporter in the press headquarters, which caused most of the men to look at her as if she had wandered into the wrong place.[53] She also commented that many men she knew were not pleased when they met a woman fan who wanted to talk baseball; they were certain she couldn't possibly know what she was talking about…proving dismissive attitudes from 1900 were still around in 1925. Brush was undaunted and proceeded to cover the Series again in 1926; in both years, she wrote about the games, but also discussed the wives of the players, chatted with interesting fans, and even talked to a couple of the men covering the game for their newspapers. And she often observed an unspoken attitude from her male colleagues that she would be better off sticking to the women's page. (In fact, her editor told her to only write human interest pieces and not discuss what happened during the games.[54])

Whether they were sent by male editors who thought a "woman's perspective" on baseball might be entertaining, or they just wanted to prove they could cover baseball as well as a man, the female reporters of the early 1900s found different ways to navigate the obstacles put in their path. Baseball researchers have seldom examined their work, and few baseball history books have even acknowledged their existence until recently. (Also making it difficult to evaluate their efforts: some male reporters criticized them but did not tell us their names.[55]) Even though they were not beat reporters, there is still much more to learn about how these women (and those in the 1930s and 1940s) tried to redefine a woman's place in sports journalism, long before the Women's Movement made it easier for women to have non-traditional careers. I hope I have made a good start in introducing you to a few women who were determined to write about baseball, despite living in an era when they were discouraged from doing so. ■

Notes

1. Quoted in James Boswell's 1844 edition of The Life of Samuel Johnson, 205–06.
2. "Women Autoists Being Watched by Police," *Lincoln* (NE) *Star*, August 12, 1913, 1.
3. "Against Women Autoists," *The New York Times*, September 3, 1915, 9.
4. Mary Jane Mossman, *The First Women Lawyers: A Comparative Study of Gender, Law and the Legal Professions*, Bloomsbury, 2006, 48–49.
5. Quoted in Gina Rippon, *The Gendered Brain*, Pantheon, 2019, 3.
6. Horowitz, Susan, *Queens of Comedy: Lucille Ball, Phyllis Diller, Carol Burnett, Joan Rivers, and the New Generation of Funny Women*, (New York, Routledge, 1997), 110–12.
7. Gene Carr, "Flirting Flora: Shortstop Shorty Gets a Jolt," *Denver Post*, July 1, 1911, 6.
8. L.W. Bloom, "A Real Fan," *Concordia* (KS) *Empire*, July 7, 1910, 2.
9. "High School Girls Practice Baseball," (New Brunswick) *Central New Jersey Home News*, April 7, 1910, 6.
10. "The Anvil Chorus," *Buffalo Enquirer*, January 25, 1905, 10.
11. Lynn Ethel Wilson, "She Is A Peculiar Species, The Female Baseball Fan." *Oakland Tribune*, May 29, 1910, B7.
12. Jennifer Ring, *Stolen Bases: Why American Girls Don't Play Baseball*, University of Illinois Press, 2009, 28.
13. John Thorn, *Baseball in the Garden of Eden*, Simon & Schuster, 2011, 88.
14. Michael Kimmel, qtd in John Bloom, *A House of Cards: Baseball Card Collecting and Popular Culture*, University of Minnesota Press, 1997, 101.
15. "Female Baseball Fan Jabs Boy With Hatpin," *Sioux Falls* (SD) *Argus-Leader*, July 15, 1910, 1.
16. Advertisement in the *Pittsburgh Press*, October 2, 1912, 18.
17. Advertisement in (Chicago, IL) *The Day Book*, October 2, 1912, 9.
18. "S. Dakota Has Woman Umpire," *Buffalo Times*, June 2, 1906, 8.
19. Joan Thomas, *Baseball's First Lady*, Reedy Press, 2010.
20. Scod D. Peterson, *Reporting Baseball's Sensational Season of 1890*, McFarland, 2015, 38.
21. "Woman Sport Editor at the World Series," *Pittsburgh Press*, October 14, 1908, 8.
22. "She's Sporting Editor," *The Editor and Publisher*, December 21, 1907, 11.
23. "This Colorado Girl is an Authority on All Sports," *Brownwood* (TX) *Daily Bulletin*, January 6, 1910, 2.
24. "She's Sporting Editor," *The Editor and Publisher*, December 21, 1907, 11.
25. "How Miss Young Looked to Tim." *Trinidad* (CO) *Chronicle-News*, October 20, 1908, 6.
26. Ina Eloise Young, "Sporting Writer of this Paper Tells of Final Game," *Trinidad* (CO) *Chronicle-News*, October 17, 1908, 1, 9.
27. Ina Eloise Young, interviewed by A.H.C. Mitchell, quoted in "Women Should Be Editors of Sport," *Trinidad* (CO) *Chronicle-News*, November 7, 1908, 3.

28. Bob Considine, "Blank Contract Sent Grove by Tom Yawkey," (Scranton PA) *The Scrantonian*, March 9, 1941, 26.

29. Ina Eloise Young, "A Feminine Tribute," *Sporting Life*, March 28, 1908, 6.

30. June A. Kennard, "The History of Physical Education," *Signs*, (Vol. 2, No. 4, Summer, 1977), 841.

31. "Women in Journalism," *Brooklyn* (NY) *Daily Eagle*, May 5, 1911, P4.

32. "No Women in the School for Journalism," *Vicksburg* (MS) *Evening Post*, March 21, 1912, 4.

33. Hotspur, "Too Nice for his Little Job," *Buffalo Enquirer*, May 16, 1901, 4.

34. Odo C. Floto, "Denver Team Loses—The Same Old Story," *Denver Post*, May 19, 1901, 18.

35. Vella Winner, "Lady Reporter Takes in the Opener and is Impressed with What's Going On," *Portland* (OR) *Daily Journal*, April 14, 1915, 11.

36. Bertha Hempstead, "Thru Female Eyes," *Topeka* (KS) *State Journal*, July 24, 1915, 4.

37. Serena Lamb, "Muggsy McGraw, Ball-Player and Actor," *St. Louis Republic*, June 15, 1900, 30.

38. Serena Lamb, "Mr. Emmet Heidrick and His Necktie Fad: A Visit to a Baseball Favorite," *St. Louis Republic*, July 29, 1900, 31.

39. Serena Lamb, "Muggsy McGraw, Ball-Player and Actor," *St. Louis Republic*, June 15, 1900, 30.

40. At times, Ina did note something interesting from the crowd: during her World Series coverage in 1908, she remarked that the wives of the Cubs players were especially enthusiastic—they carried large Cubs banners and sometimes tooted horns in support of their team. Ina Eloise Young. "Miss Young Tells of Scenes and Incidents in Detroit Game," *Trinidad* (CO) *Chronicle-News*, October 16, 1908, 3.

41. Idah McGlone Gibson, "The President's Wife—Mrs. Tai As A Woman Sees Her," *Wilkes-Barre* (PA) *Times-Leader*, October 29, 1912, 10.

42. For example, Idah McGlone Gibson, "The Real Mrs. Roosevelt At Home And Her Personality," *Santa Fe New Mexican*, October 21, 1912, 7.

43. Ad promoting Idah McGlone Gibson's series of interviews, (Chicago) *The Day Book*, October 2, 1912, 9.

44. "Special World's Series Feature," *Pittsburgh Press*, October 2, 1912, 18.

45. Idah McGlone Gibson, "Why Pitcher Joe Wood Pays No Attention To 'Mash' Epistles," *Pittsburgh Press*, October 7, 1912, 14.

46. Idah McGlone Gibson, "The Mighty Muggsy McGraw As A Woman Sees Him," (Chicago) *The Day Book*, October 3, 1912, 21.

47. Idah McGlone Gibson, "Tesreau Gets More Stage Door Adulation Than a Chorus Girl," *Pittsburgh Press*, October 9, 1912: 14.

48. Idah McGlone Gibson, "Woman Reporter Pries Into Secrets Of Dodgers," (Madison) *Wisconsin State Journal*, October 4, 1916, 11.

49. Idah McGlone Gibson, "Ball Player Never Amounts to Much Until Married, Buck Wheat Tells Woman Reporter," (Salt Lake City) *Salt Lake Telegram*, October 8, 1916, 11.

50. Idah McGlone Gibson, "Author of 'Confessions of a Wife' Interviews John M'Graw," *Pittsburgh Press*, September 29, 1917, 10.

51. "Season End Worst Time for Title Team M'Graw Tells Woman Writer," (Madison) *Wisconsin State Journal*, October 2, 1917, 11.

52. "Mrs. Hoover In Talk Over Radio," *South Bend* (IN) *Tribune*, April 20, 1929, 2.

53. Katharine Brush, "Baseball is Man's Game, But Fans' Eyes Are On Washington Senators' Wives As They Are Tendered Keys Of City Of Pittsburgh," *East Liverpool* (OH) *Review-Tribune*, October 7, 1925, 1.

54. Katharine Brush, "Baby Alice Russell Is Youngest Rooter, While Eddie Moore Is Handsomest Player In Series," *East Liverpool* (OH) *Review-Tribune*, October 8, 1925, 1.

55. For example, John E. Wray discussing a nameless female reporter in "Wallie Schang Made Worst And Most Costly Mistake of the Series, Wray Writes." *St. Louis Post-Dispatch*, October 10, 1922, 15.

Correction

Joan Wendl Thomas reports an error in her article "All The Duckys…" in the Spring 2019 *Baseball Research Journal*. Regarding John McGraw on page 30, it was Detroit left fielder Dick Harley who spiked McGraw in 1902, not Ducky Holmes. Harley's grandson Bob Harley, a SABR member, graciously provided four newspaper stories and the actual date of the incident (May 24, 1902). Both Harley and Holmes were in the game, but Holmes did not reach base.

The erroneous information was gleaned from a widely reported story related by Detroit pitcher George Mullin. He went into detail about the spiking, but his account printed in 1907 did not provide the date of the game in question. Thomas searched in vain to determine if Holmes spiked McGraw at some other time. Mullin may have remembered remarks made by Holmes and McGraw correctly, as well as details of the play, but misidentified the player responsible for McGraw's injury—possibly because both names begin with an "H" and because of Ducky's reputation as a brawler.

Baseball and the Great Movie Comedians

Ron Backer

While Charlie Chaplin went into the boxing ring in *City Lights* (1931), the Marx Brothers played football in *Horse Feathers* (1932), Curly Howard wrestled his opponent to the mat in *Grips, Grunts and Groans* (1937), and W.C. Fields almost played golf in *The Golf Specialist* (1930), the true sport of the great movie comedians is baseball. From silent films to sound films, from short films to full-length features, and from black and white films to color movies, the comics of the cinema have often demonstrated that there is much humor to be derived from our national pastime. Here are some examples of the great movie comedians and their take on the game of baseball.

ABBOTT AND COSTELLO

Even though there are no baseball scenes in any of their movies, Abbott and Costello are the movie comedians most associated with baseball. The reason, of course, is their signature routine, "Who's On First," which the duo performed for many years for stage, radio, television, and movie audiences. Though the routine is now associated solely with Abbott and Costello, it has its origins in similar wordplay routines that were performed in vaudeville by other comics.

Abbott and Costello started their joint act in burlesque, moved to vaudeville, appeared on Broadway, and then became successful radio comedians, first appearing on shows of others and then starring throughout the 1940s in their own series. Abbott and Costello also appeared in thirty-six movies together, from their first one in 1940 to their last one in 1956, just before the break-up of their act. In the early 1940s, they were among the top box office stars in Hollywood. Their success in the movies and radio transferred to television in the 1950s, where they became one of the alternating hosts of the popular *The Colgate Comedy Hour*, along with such stars as Bob Hope, Martin and Lewis, and Eddie Cantor. They also had their own television show from 1952 to 1954.[1]

Abbott and Costello's big break in show business came in February 1938 when they appeared as guests on the popular Kate Smith radio show. They returned to the show the following month and performed "Who's On First" before a national audience for the first time. It was a smash hit. The duo became regulars on the Kate Smith program, with their contract requiring them to perform "Who's on First" on a monthly basis. Eventually, Hollywood beckoned.[2]

Their first film was *One Night in the Tropics* (1940), a musical comedy starring Allan Jones and Robert Cummings. While Abbott and Costello only have supporting roles, the film did provide movie audiences with their first chance to see the comedy duo perform "Who's On First." In this rare instance, Bud and Lou perform the routine in character, not on stage or in a radio studio. The two are running down a street when they hear a ball game on a car radio, causing them to stop to perform "Who's On First" for no apparent reason. Surprisingly, the duo never finishes the routine. The movie audience never learns the name of the pitcher, the catcher, the left fielder, the center fielder, or the shortstop.

The most famous film performance of "Who's On First" occurs in *The Naughty Nineties* (1945). The movie is a costume picture set on a showboat in the 1890s, giving Abbott and Costello the chance to perform their most famous routine on the riverboat's stage. This may be the duo's best performance of "Who's On First." Bud and Lou performed the routine differently every time they staged it, and this version seems to contain all of the many variations in the sketch that have been seen over the years. Most importantly, the routine is incredibly funny, so much so that if the movie audience strains to listen, it can actually hear the film crew laughing in the background.

Film of the comedy duo performing "Who's On First" from *The Naughty Nineties* plays almost continuously at the National Baseball Hall of Fame and Museum in Cooperstown, New York. It is still one of the museum's most popular attractions. In 1956, a gold record of Abbott and Costello performing "Who's On First" was placed on permanent exhibit there.[3] It is therefore no wonder that Abbott and Costello are so associated with baseball, even though there are no baseball scenes in any of their movies.

BUSTER KEATON

While Abbott and Costello are the movie comedians most associated with baseball, Buster Keaton may be the movie comedian who most loved the game. Keaton is a rare Hollywood star who enjoyed playing baseball, having started the sport at a young age. During breaks between filming, Keaton often arranged baseball games with the crew and the actors. Keaton also organized and appeared in a number of charity baseball games, sometimes with fellow movie comedian Joe E. Brown.[4]

When not playing baseball, Keaton was one of the most successful comedians of the silent film era, probably second only to Charlie Chaplin in fame. Keaton made his film debut in 1917 and by the early 1920s had his own production unit, producing silent short comedies and then full-length features, many of which are still famous today, including *Sherlock, Jr.* (1924), about a projectionist who dreams that he is a movie detective and *The General* (1926), a chase movie set on a locomotive during the Civil War. Keaton became known for his deadpan face and the hats he wore. Acrobat and athlete, Keaton performed all of the stunts in his films and used his knowledge of baseball in several of his movies.

In the film *College* (1927) Keaton plays a young man with a distinct antipathy towards sports who graduates from high school as the top scholar in his class. He enrolls at Clayton College because the most popular girl in high school enrolls there and in order to impress her, he takes up collegiate sports. At the tryouts for the baseball team, he dons the catcher's equipment to play third base, a batted ball goes through his legs and another flies right past his head, a thrown ball knocks his glove off, and a base runner sliding into third knocks Keaton to the ground. Batting does not go much better. Keaton hits himself in the head with four bats while taking practice swings, is hit by a pitch in the rear end, and once on base, trips when taking a lead off first when his foot gets caught underneath the bag. Needless to say, he does not make the team.

In *The Cameraman* (1928), Keaton's character, who aspires to be a newsreel cameraman, arrives at Yankee Stadium to film a game. Unfortunately, while the Yankees are playing baseball that day, the game is in St. Louis. Keaton ingeniously takes the opportunity to fulfill a childhood dream. He plays a pantomime game of baseball with himself at a real major league

Jim Thorpe has a bit part as a second baseman throwing a ball to home plate in Buster Keaton's One Run Elmer *(1935).*

ballpark. He steps on the mound, shakes off a sign from the invisible catcher, checks the bases which are apparently loaded, pretends to pick a runner off third, and when he pitches, gets the nonexistent batter to hit into a double play. At bat, Keaton takes a brush back pitch before hitting an inside the park home run, capped off by a head-first slide into the plate.

In *One Run Elmer* (1935), a sound comedy short but with very little dialogue, Elmer (Keaton) plays in a sandlot baseball game (with a prairie outfield) between the Bear Cats, Elmer's team, and the Rattlers, his rival's team, with the winning manager obtaining a date with a pretty young woman. About one-third of the nineteen-minute film concerns the baseball game, which contains a number of amusing moments. When Elmer, playing catcher, is upset with two of the umpire's calls, he signals the pitcher to throw one high. Elmer deliberately misses the pitch, which knocks down the umpire. Later, Elmer accidentally pitches a popcorn ball to a batter, requiring him and his teammates to collect all the pieces and then push them together, so that the runner can be tagged out at home plate. There is even a repeat of a gag from *College*, when Elmer, while batting, turns to complain to the umpire and the next pitch hits him in the rear end.

One Run Elmer is filled with fantastic moments, such as a ball being thrown about three feet off of first base and the bag jumping on its own to the first baseman's foot, Keaton taking a super-sized bat to the plate and knocking down the catcher and the umpire, and Keaton sliding under first base and then making second safely. The baseball game ends with a moment that previously could only be imagined for a cartoon. Elmer inserts two bullets into the barrel of his bat and when he hits, the ball literally explodes off the bat, resulting in a game-winning inside-the-park grand slam, although the play at the plate is close, with Elmer having to drop kick the catcher out of the way so that Elmer can land safely on home plate.

For sports fans, there is a special moment in *One Run Elmer*. Jim Thorpe, often considered the greatest athlete of the twentieth century, plays the second baseman for the Rattlers. Thorpe was an Olympic gold medalist, a Hall of Fame college and professional football player, and a professional baseball player.[5] Thorpe's sports career ended in 1928. He then went on to appear in about seventy Hollywood films, usually uncredited and having no lines (just as in *One Run Elmer*) and often in Westerns. Thorpe, with his long hair flowing out of his baseball cap, is easy to spot in *One Run Elmer*. Thorpe receives one tight shot, as he is the cut-off man on Keaton's inside-the-park home run that ends the game, providing baseball fans with a rare opportunity to see Jim Thorpe play the game.

HAROLD LLOYD

Harold Lloyd was another popular silent film comedian with a significant baseball-related scene in one of his movies. The scene occurred in *Speedy* (1928), the last of his eleven solely silent film features. Although Lloyd appeared in over 150 short silent comedies, it is his feature films which are best remembered today. They also put him in rare company. Lloyd, Keaton, Charlie Chaplin, and Harry Langdon were the only four silent film comedians who made successful and popular feature films during the 1920s. Most other silent film comics, such as Charley Chase and Laurel and Hardy, continued to make short subjects during the last decade of the silent era. At the height of his career, Lloyd was one of the most popular and highest-paid stars of his time.[6]

Lou Gehrig, far right, sneaks into a scene with Harold Lloyd (left) and Babe Ruth (center), in Lloyd's Speedy (1928).

Lloyd's usual comic character was an everyman, inept in many ways but determined to succeed, which he always somehow managed to do by the end of a film. Lloyd was famous for his trademark glasses, which he wore in all but the earliest of his films, even when his character was playing football, fighting, or sleeping in bed. Lloyd was also known for the physical stunts he performed, such as climbing a tall building and then hanging from a clock high above the street in *Safety Last!* (1923).[7] In addition to *Speedy*, Lloyd's interest in sports can be seen in *The Freshman* (1925), a college football comedy.

Speedy concerns the title character, a man who cannot seem to hold a job, trying to protect the last horse-drawn streetcar operating in New York City. There are a number of subplots set in and around New York City, including a short segment with Lloyd, as a taxi driver, taking the real Babe Ruth on a terrifyingly fast ride to Yankee Stadium. This may be the best segment in the movie, as Speedy talks to Ruth in the back seat, without looking at the road, causing many near collisions, and the Babe freaking out, yelling directions at Speedy, and even closing his eyes at one point. Even though *Speedy* is a silent film, there is funny dialogue in the inter-titles. Speedy lauds Ruth's hitting, saying, "Even when you strike out, you miss 'em close," to which Babe responds, commenting on Speedy's driving, "I don't miss 'em half as close as you do."

Babe Ruth appeared in ten films in his long film career, silent and talking, shorts and features. He always played himself. Ruth usually gave good performances, but his best may be in *Speedy*. Ruth's reactions to Speedy's reckless driving are hilarious.

In addition to the very funny car ride on the real streets of New York City, there are shots of Ruth giving out signed baseballs at a real orphanage in midtown Manhattan and a long shot of Yankee Stadium from the Macombs Dam Bridge. After they arrive at the Stadium, Ruth gives Speedy a free ticket to the game, giving Speedy the opportunity to personally see Ruth hit a home run. The home run is archive footage of a home run Ruth hit in the third inning of the seventh game of the 1926 World Series, which the Yankees lost to the Cardinals in seven games.[8] Lou Gehrig also makes an appearance in the background as Ruth and Lloyd talk outside Lloyd's cab in front of the Stadium.

CHARLEY CHASE

Although Mack Sennett was the most famous producer of silent comedies (Charlie Chaplin, the Keystone Kops, and others), Hal Roach (Our Gang, Laurel and Hardy, and others) was not far behind. In the 1920s, however,

Charley Chase was probably the most important and popular star at Roach. The comedian with the twitching nose, pursing mouth, and dancing mustache usually portrayed an average guy caught up in ordinary but exasperating situations. Chase appeared in about ninety silent shorts for Roach, plus numerous shorts for other studios, in addition to supervising and directing many other short comedies.

Chase was no longer a star comedian in the sound era, but he still made many appearances in the movies in featured roles. His most famous sound performance is probably as the drunken practical joker in the great Laurel and Hardy feature, *Sons of the Desert* (1933). In 1937, Chase left Hal Roach studios and began working at Columbia, where he continued appearing in short comedies, as well as directing the films of other comics, such as those of The Three Stooges, often using his real name, Charles Parrott.[9]

One of the last films in which Chase appeared was *The Heckler* (1940), produced just before his death that year at the age of 46. This baseball short commences at a tennis match with the Heckler (Chase) shouting disparaging comments at a tennis player and then laughing aloud at his own jokes. When he causes the tennis star to miss the ball because of his caustic comments, the Heckler shouts his catchphrase, "Boy, can I call them?" At the conclusion of the match, a baseball player with the strange name of "Ole Margarine" is introduced. He is playing for the Green Sox in the upcoming World Series. The Heckler starts to rattle Margarine, causing him to drop the tennis trophy. Once again, the Heckler shouts, "Can I call them?"

The scene switches to the World Series and the Heckler is in fine form again, shouting and laughing loudly, smoking his cigar, and disturbing the fans at the game as well as the players on the field. He is particularly hard on Ole Margarine, causing him to look bad both at bat and in the field, resulting in the Green Sox losing the first game. Some gamblers believe that the Heckler is the main reason for the Sox's loss and they therefore agree to share some of their winnings with the Heckler if he heckles the Green Sox in the next game. The Green Sox recognize the problem also. They put ice down the Heckler's pajamas while he is sleeping, causing him to lose his voice. The Heckler tries at the next game, but his taunting of Margarine is unsuccessful, leading to a surprise ending.

As to the film's humor, the Heckler spouts off lots of silly jokes, such as the moment in which he accidentally hits a fan with a bottle of soda pop and says that it didn't hurt the fan because it is only a "soft drink," or when the soft drink starts spraying soda, asking the umpire not to call the game because it's only a little shower. Then there are the slapstick jokes, such as a piece of sticky candy getting caught on a man's hair, resulting in a toupee being pulled off, a man ordering an ice cream cone from a vendor and getting it in his face when the Heckler accidentally hits his arm, and Chase grabbing another fan's straw hat to try to catch a foul ball, resulting in the ball going through the hat and ruining it.

Charley Chase is as obnoxious as anyone can be at a baseball game, but he is consistently amusing. Also, it is hard not to like a movie in which an outfielder gets hit in the head with a fly ball, a staple of baseball comedies.

While there are no real baseball players in the short, *The Heckler* has a legitimate star athlete in its cast. In real life, Bruce Bennett (Ole Margarine), under his given name Herman Brix, won the silver medal for the shot put in the 1928 Olympic games. Bennett's early movie career was forgettable, except for an appearance as Tarzan in a movie serial. After *The Heckler*, Bruce Bennett would go on to have significant supporting roles in major films, such as *Mildred Pierce* (1945) and *The Treasure of the Sierra Madre* (1948). He is remembered today by baseball fans for his role as aging pitcher Saul Hellman in *Angels in the Outfield* (1951).

SHEMP HOWARD

Shemp Howard is best remembered today as one of The Three Stooges, rejoining the team in 1947 after his brother Curley Howard suffered a debilitating stroke the year before. Shemp then appeared in seventy-three new comedy shorts as one of the Stooges until his death in 1955. Shemp, however, was a reluctant Stooge. In the 1920s, the original Three Stooges came together, consisting of Moe Howard and Larry Fine along with Shemp, but Shemp left the act in the early 1930s to start a solo career. Curly Howard then took Shemp Howard's vacated spot in the act. Shemp only returned to The Three Stooges after Curly's stroke because he believed that Moe and Larry would be out of work if the act were not reconstituted. Shemp intended to return on a temporary basis only, but his association with the Stooges became permanent when Curly never recovered sufficiently to return to the act.

Shemp's successful solo film career is often overlooked. He appeared in full-length features with W.C. Fields and Abbott and Costello, in mainstream movies such as *Pittsburgh* (1942), starring John Wayne and Marlene Dietrich, and in comedy shorts such as those he did for Vitaphone in the 1930s and for Columbia in the 1940s. In all, Shemp appeared in about fifty feature films, usually in bit parts or supporting roles, and another fifty comedy shorts, usually in supporting roles or as the star, all without any of the other Stooges.[10]

Shemp Howard's foray into the comedy of baseball occurred in his Vitaphone period, with the release of *Dizzy and Daffy* (1934). His co-stars in the comedy short and the only actors with their names above the title were Jerome and Paul Dean, better known to baseball fans as Dizzy and Daffy. The short was produced and released just after the 1934 World Series, in which the Dean brothers led the St. Louis Cardinals to a World Series win over the Detroit Tigers.

Shemp plays a pitcher named Lefty Howard, who has come down from the big leagues to pitch for the Farmer White Sox in their game against the Shanty Town No Sox. While Lefty talks a big game about his major league career, his near blindness—a particular difficulty for a baseball pitcher—is the cause of his trip to the low minors. In this game, Lefty is also plagued by the world's worst umpire, "Call 'Em Wrong Jones," who, in addition to his lack of skill in calling balls and strikes, has a severe stuttering problem.

This sets the scene for a very funny segment with Lefty pitching for the White Sox. It includes Lefty holding out his hand and catching a popup he never sees, eight Farmers' players surrounding a base runner in a rundown, allowing the base runner to squeeze out between them and almost score, Lefty getting hit in the head with a thrown baseball, and Lefty getting turned around and pitching the ball to second base. (All of that may not seem that funny in print but there are lots of laughs when actually viewing it.) Lefty is eventually removed from the game and Jerome, as he is referred to in the short, goes in as the relief pitcher. Jerome has a much more fluid and practical pitching motion than Lefty, striking out most of the batters he faces. One of Jerome's pitches is so fast that when the catcher catches it, his mitt starts to smoke.

The St. Louis Cardinals take both Deans up to the majors for the 1934 season and for some reason, they bring Lefty Howard along as their pitching coach. When Dizzy is injured running the bases in the eighth inning of the seventh game of the World Series, Lefty goes in to run for him. Unfortunately, Lefty's base running skills are not much better than his pitching. Daffy comes in to pitch the ninth inning, striking out the side and winning the World Championship for St. Louis.

The Dean Brothers barely appear in *Dizzy and Daffy* as actors, although each gets a chance to show off his pitching abilities. The revelation of the film is Shemp Howard, who is very funny as the nearly blind Lefty Howard. It is one of his best performances in films. He even gets a chance to give the umpire an eye poke, foreshadowing his later career as one of the Three Stooges.

In his Columbia period, Shemp Howard starred in a remake of the Charley Chase classic *The Heckler*, titled *Mr. Noisy* (1946), about a man who heckles a baseball player during the World Series. The remake is almost an exact duplicate of the original, and many people believe that Shemp Howard's performance in *Mr. Noisy* is better than the one by Charley Chase in *The Heckler*. *Mr. Noisy* was one of the last films in which Shemp appeared before he rejoined The Three Stooges in 1947.

RED SKELTON

Red Skelton was one of the top comedians on television for over twenty years. His comedy-variety program, aptly named *The Red Skelton Show*, debuted on NBC on September 30, 1951, moved to CBS two years later, and remained on the air until 1971 when it returned to NBC for a final season. With Skelton's weekly monologue, pantomime segments, and coterie of sketch characters such as Clem Kaddiddlehopper, a country bumpkin; the Mean Widdle Kid, an impish prankster; and Freddie the Freeloader, a silent tramp, *The Red Skelton Show* was one of television's top-rated programs throughout its entire run on CBS. It is also one of the longest-running television variety shows of all time.

Skelton's television program had its origins in his successful radio show, which debuted in 1941 and

Leo Durocher has a few lines in Red Skelton's Whistling in Brooklyn *(1943).*

continued into the 1950s, meaning that for several years, Skelton had shows on both radio and television. Many of the characters from Skelton's television show made their debuts on his radio program.[11]

Red Skelton also had success at the cinema, with roles in over thirty-five films, the most significant ones produced by MGM in the 1940s and 1950s. Skelton provided comic relief in some of those movies and starred in others. In those films, Skelton was known for his impish personality and clown persona. Skelton's films at MGM included a popular mystery-comedy trilogy that is sometimes known as the "Whistling" series, because of the titles of the three films. In all of the films, Skelton portrays actor Wally Benton, the star of a popular mystery series on the radio, whose detective character, "The Fox," always solves the crime. The first film in the series, *Whistling in the Dark* (1941), was one of the best mystery-comedies of the 1940s.

Near the end of the last film in the series, *Whistling in Brooklyn* (1943), the police chase Benton to Ebbets Field, believing he is a serial killer known as Constant Reader. In order to escape, Benton disguises himself as the bearded pitcher for the Battling Beavers and then pitches one inning of exhibition baseball against the real Brooklyn Dodgers while at the same time trying to prevent Inspector Holcomb, a police inspector from New York, from becoming the next murder victim of the real Constant Reader.

During the game, Benton tries to throw a ball with a warning message into the field box where Holcomb is sitting, accidentally picking a runner off first base when the first baseman intercepts the ball. He has trouble seeing the signals from the catcher and has to walk almost to home plate to see them. He catches a ball in his long, thick beard for the third out in an inning. When he comes to bat, he takes several very close pitches, one breaking a button on his shirt (which comes open) and another splitting the belt on his pants (which come loose).[12]

The scenes with Benton on the field in *Whistling in Brooklyn* generate the most laughs in the film. Of special interest to baseball fans are the location shooting at Ebbets Field and the real players who appear in the film. As to the latter, Wally Benton is not much of a pitcher and he hits the first three Brooklyn Dodgers he faces. All three batters are played by real Brooklyn Dodgers who, despite appearing in this film, were subsequently elected to the National Baseball Hall of Fame in Cooperstown: Billy Herman, who was then the second baseman for the Dodgers but who spent most of his career with the Chicago Cubs; Arky Vaughan, who was then the shortstop for the Dodgers but who is best-known for his years with the Pittsburgh Pirates; and Ducky Medwick, who was then the left fielder for the Dodgers but who had most of his success with the St. Louis Cardinals. The catcher is Mickey Owen, still known today for a third strike getting by him in the ninth inning of the fourth game of the 1941 World Series, leading to a Yankees win over the Dodgers in that Series. Another Hall-of-Famer, player-manager Leo Durocher, has a few lines.

DORIS DAY

Known today primarily for her series of popular romantic comedies of the late 1950s and early 1960s, Doris Day started her career in show business as a band singer for several bandleaders, including Les Brown, with whom she recorded her first hit record, "Sentimental Journey," in 1945. Day moved to the movies and appeared in a number of successful musicals at Warner Bros., beginning with *Romance on the High Seas* (1948). In the early 1950s, she began appearing in dramatic films, such as Alfred Hitchcock's *The Man Who Knew Too Much* (1956). For baseball fans, she played Aimee Alexander, the wife of famed pitcher Grover Cleveland Alexander (played by Ronald Reagan), in *The Winning Team* (1952). Even though there is no indication that Aimee Alexander was an accomplished singer in real life, Day, as Aimee, sings a song in the movie.

In 1959, Day appeared in *Pillow Talk*, a romantic comedy with Rock Hudson. The film was a huge success, leading to a series of similar romantic comedies with leading men James Garner, Cary Grant, and two more with Hudson. These movies were so popular that Day, in the early 1960s, was often the annual top box office star in Hollywood.

That Touch of Mink (1962) is a typical Doris Day romantic comedy. Wealthy businessman Philip Shayne (Cary Grant) pursues a younger, unemployed woman, Cathy Timberlake (Day). After Cathy indicates an interest in baseball, Philip takes Cathy to see "a local team," the Yankees, and for reasons never explained, they are allowed to watch the game from the Yankees dugout. That may not have been a good idea on the part of the Yankees, as Cathy constantly berates the home plate umpire, leading to a confrontation between the two of them when the umpire calls a strike on a Yankees batter, which Cathy believes was a ball. When Mickey Mantle and Roger Maris tell the umpire they agree with Cathy, he throws them out of the game. When Cathy asks for additional support from Yogi Berra, he is more judicious, saying, "It's a perfect strike. The ump was right." Berra still gets ejected from the game, with the umpire explaining, "I don't like sarcasm, Berra. You're out of the game, too."

The baseball scene in *That Touch of Mink* was probably more about box office than baseball. There was a time in Hollywood when it was believed that the inclusion of famous athletes in a film translated into higher box office receipts. Mantle and Maris were surely the most famous athletes in America at the time, because of their concurrent pursuit of Babe Ruth's home run record the previous year. Other examples just from this article are Babe Ruth, the year after he set the home run record, appearing with Harold Lloyd in *Speedy* (1928) and the Dean brothers appearing in *Dizzy and Daffy* (1934) shortly after their Cardinals won the World Series.

The umpire in *That Touch of Mink* is played by Art Passarella, a character actor who worked primarily in television starting in the 1950s. Interestingly, from 1941 to 1953 (with two years off for military service), Passarella was an American League umpire. He umpired in three World Series and two All Star Games. Throughout his career he ejected twenty-three players, managers, and coaches from games, so ejecting three more from *That Touch of Mink* was not much of an acting stretch for him.[13]

LESLIE NIELSEN

By far, the funniest baseball sequence ever filmed stars a man who came late to the world of comedy, Leslie Nielsen. For most of his career, Nielsen was known as a serious actor, in film roles such as the spaceship commander in the science fiction classic *Forbidden Planet* (1956) and the ship's captain in the popular disaster movie, *The Poseidon Adventure* (1972), and on television, particularly as a guest star on many television series, such as *The Fugitive, Columbo,* and *The Streets of San Francisco*. Nielsen's career took an unexpected turn after he received the role of the doctor in comedy classic *Airplane!* (1980). ("I *am* serious and don't call me Shirley.") Nielsen stood out among the other dramatic actors in the film—Robert Stack, Lloyd Bridges, and Peter Graves—leading to Nielsen starring in *Police Squad!,* a 1982 television comedy series written and shot in the style of *Airplane!* Nielsen played Detective Frank Drebin in the series and although the show is now considered a cult classic, only six episodes were produced.

That seemed to be the end of *Police Squad!* until the makers of *Police Squad!* and *Airplane!* decided to revive the character of Lieutenant Frank Drebin for *The Naked Gun: From the Files of Police Squad!* (1988).

Reggie Jackson and Jeanette Charles (as Queen Elizabeth) in Leslie Nielsen's The Naked Gun: From the Files of Police Squad! *(1988).*

Late in the film, Drebin gets a tip that during the seventh inning stretch of a game between the California Angels and the Seattle Mariners at Anaheim Stadium, a crime boss is going to have an unnamed, brainwashed baseball player assassinate Queen Elizabeth, who is visiting Los Angeles and attending the game. Drebin is determined to get down on the field and search each of the players for a weapon. To do so, he knocks out the home plate umpire and takes his place on the field.

The big game is announced on television by famed broadcaster Curt Gowdy, along with his color announcers, Jim Palmer, the Hall-of-Fame pitching star of the Baltimore Orioles, All-Star catcher Tim McCarver, and Dick Vitale, Mel Allen, Dick Enberg, and Dr. Joyce Brothers, all played by themselves.

Baseball-related comedy is rife and plentiful in *The Naked Gun* sequence. As everyone knows, there is a lot of spitting in baseball, but in this game, some even comes from the players' wives sitting in their special seats. Signals to the base runners come from the dugout via signal flags and a ship's signal lamp. Queen Elizabeth has to pass a hot dog down her row and even participates in The Wave. At one point, the *umpires* get a base runner into a rundown! All Mel Allen can do is employ one of his catchphrases, "How about that?"

Drebin makes for an unusual home-plate umpire. When he receives some positive fan reaction to a strike call he makes, he starts making more and more outrageous gestures during his strike calls, including a little bit of a moon walk at one point. At first, Drebin cleans home plate with the traditional brush but later he uses a hand vacuum and then a full size vacuum cleaner.

While all of this is going on, Drebin is searching the players, trying to find a potential murder weapon.

At one point, he searches the pitcher and although he finds sandpaper, an electric sander, and a full container of Vaseline, Drebin does not care because there is no hidden weapon. Drebin fails to search the right fielder, however, and when the seventh inning stretch arrives, it turns out that the killer is none other than Reggie Jackson, the Hall of Fame slugger and right fielder who played for the Angels 1982–86. What a neat twist!

The Naked Gun was so successful that Leslie Nielsen reprised his character in two sequels and also starred in several other movies with *Airplane!*-style humor. He is the most recent, but surely not the last, of the great movie comedians with a baseball scene in their films.

OTHER EXAMPLES

In the early 1930s, comedian Joe E. Brown, who once had a tryout with the New York Yankees,[14] starred in three baseball movies: *Fireman, Save My Child* (1932), *Elmer the Great* (1933), and *Alibi Ike* (1935). Richard Pryor played a baseball player in two films, *The Bingo Long Traveling All-Stars and Motor Kings* (1976), as a ballplayer in the Negro Leagues who hopes to make it to the white major leagues, first by posing as a Cuban and later as an American Indian, and *Brewster's Millions* (1985), playing a minor league ballplayer who inherits a fortune.

Other screen comedians had brief moments with the game of baseball. In *A Night at the Opera* (1935), the Marx Brothers substitute sheet music of "Take Me Out to the Ball Game" for opera music during a performance of *Il Travatore* and when the orchestra switches to the baseball melody, Chico and Harpo play catch in the orchestra pit. In *Zelig* (1983), Woody Allen inserts his title character into some archive footage of the Yankees at spring training, which includes some shots of Babe Ruth. Jerry Lewis attends a Dodgers exhibition game in Japan in *The Geisha Boy* (1958) and riles up the pitcher for the Japanese team, causing Lewis to end up with a baseball in his mouth. Clearly, baseball is not just our national pastime; it is also the pastime of the great movie comedians. ∎

Notes

1. Jim Mulholland, *The Abbott and Costello Book*, New York, NY: Popular Library, 1977.
2. Jeffrey S. Miller, *The Horror Spoofs of Abbott and Costello*, Jefferson, NC: Mcfarland & Company, Inc., 2000, pp. 5–12; Cary O'Dell, " 'Who's on First'—Abbott and Costello (Earliest existing radio broadcast version (October 6,1938)," http://www.loc.gov/static/programs/nationalrecording-preservation-board/documents/WhosOnFirst.pdf.
3. Bill Francis, "Who's On First Joined the Hall 60 Years Ago," Baseball Hall of Fame Website, https://baseballhall.org/discover/short-stops/whos-on-first (June 2, 2016).
4. Rob Edelman, "Buster Keaton, Baseball Player," SABR Website, https://sabr.org/research/buster-keaton-baseball-player.
5. An outfielder, Thorpe played for four full and two part seasons for the New York Giants. He also played part seasons for the Cincinnati Reds and the Boston Braves. He had a career batting average of .252, with just seven career homeruns. Jim Thorpe, Baseball Reference, https://www.baseball-reference.com/players/t/thorpji01.shtml.
6. "Harold Lloyd: The Third Genius," *American Masters*, PBS website, http://www.pbs.org/wnet/americanmasters/harold-lloyd-about-harold-lloyd/647.
7. Gerald Mast, *The Comic Mind: Comedy and the Movies* (Second edition), Chicago, Il: The University of Chicago Press, 1979, p150–55.
8. Goldstein, Bruce & McGee Scott (2015). *Speedy* commentary track (DVD). Criterion Collection.
9. Mast, pages 187–90; Charles Parrot aka Charley Chase Filmography, http://theluckycorner.com/crew/chase.html.
10. Filmography, Shemphoward.com, http://www.shemphoward.com/filmography.html.
11. "Lovable Clown Red Skelton Dies," *The Deseret News*, September 18, 1997, https://news.google.com/newspapers?id=F_RLAAAAIBAJ&sjid=2u0DAAAAIBAJ&pg=6805,971926&dq=red+skelton&hl=en; "Red Skelton, TV and Film's Quintessential Clown, Dies," *Los Angeles Times*, September 18, 1997, https://www.latimes.com/archives/la-xpm-1997-sep-18-mn-33654-story.html.
12. Actually, Benton should have been awarded first base on each of those pitches, because when a pitched ball touches the batter's uniform, it is the same as if the ball touches the batter's body, thereby becoming a hit-by-pitch. Major League Baseball Rules; definition of the word "Touch."
13. Retrosheet, https://www.retrosheet.org/boxesetc/P/Ppassa901.htm.
14. Joe E. Brown and Ralph Hancock. *Laughter Is a Wonderful Thing*. New York: A.S. Barnes and Company, 1956, 220.

Carl Lundgren

The Cubs' Cold-Weather King

Art Ahrens

All the poetry and folklore of "Tinker to Evers to Chance" notwithstanding, the great Chicago Cubs teams of 1906–10 won their four pennants and two World Series by way of outstanding pitching. The glories of Mordecai "Three Fingered" Brown, Ed Reulbach, Jack Pfiester, and Orval Overall have been widely recognized, and rightfully so. Sadly ignored, however, is right-hander Carl Lundgren, a major contributor to their first two league championship flags (1906–07) and their prior rebuilding period. Not to mention his later accomplishments at the college level.

Carl Leonard Lundgren was born February 16, 1880, in Marengo, Illinois—a quiet, picturesque hamlet roughly 55 miles west-northwest of Chicago and home to his mother, Delilah. His mother bore the Scottish surname Renwick, while his father, Pehr Hjalmer Lundgren, was a Swedish immigrant.[1] Unlike the Germans and the Irish, the Scandinavians would never take center stage in pre-World War I baseball, but they did play a sizable supporting role, which would be Lundgren's destiny as well.

After receiving his primary and secondary educations at local public schools, Lundgren entered the University of Illinois in Urbana in September 1898. By the following April he was pitching for the university baseball team, nicknamed the Illinis, under head coach George A. Huff, who would have a profound influence on Lundgren's future.

Lundgren established himself as an Illini star almost immediately. On April 22, 1899, on the team's first trip to Chicago, Lundgren defeated the University of Chicago Maroons, 4–2, on a frigid Saturday afternoon. This earned him his first major notice, as the *Chicago Tribune* commented: "Lundgren's pitching was a surprise to everyone. He did clever work, being steady at critical points, and in the last inning, in spite of the efforts of the rooters to rattle him, he steadied down and took things coolly, sending the ball over the plate as steadily as if he were throwing the first ball of the game."[2]

Lundgren was already displaying two earmarks of his future career, namely an ability to remain mentally

A two-sport athlete at University of Illinois, Carl Lundgren got his first exposure to major league competition when the Chicago Orphans (later called the Cubs) held their spring training on the Illini campus in 1902. He graduated a few months later and debuted with the Cubs on June 19.

NATIONAL BASEBALL HALL OF FAME AND LIBRARY, COOPERSTOWN, NY

calm and alert in pressure situations, and being especially strong in cold weather. Carl gained his first campus shutout on Memorial Day over Oberlin College, limiting his opponents to five hits. He aided his 5–0 win with a single, a double, and a run scored. The *Tribune* simply said, "Illinois played its best home game of the year."[3] Although the Illini came on strong at the end of the season, the University of Michigan won the championship of the Western College Conference (later to be nicknamed the Big Ten), while Huff's team finished second.[4]

That summer, Lundgren hurled for the amateur Marengo Athletics, who won 10 games with one tie and no defeats.[5] Then it was back to college, as Carl continued to excel both athletically and academically. He became a two-way halfback on the Illini football squad.[6] He played football through 1901 and was a member of the Kappa Sigma fraternity.[7]

Thanks in large part to Lundgren's pitching, the University of Illinois won the Western Conference pennant in 1900. That year, his catcher was Jake Stahl, who would go on to a career as a journeyman first baseman with several American League clubs and become a World Series winning manager. During this season, Lundgren enjoyed the easiest win of his college days, a 17–0 romp over Iowa on May 9, 1900.[8]

Perhaps the rarified championship air was too much for the college boys to handle, as the Illini slipped to fourth in 1901 while Michigan's Wolverines reclaimed the conference title. In addition to his pitching assignments, Lundgren appeared twice at second base and once in left field. At the season's close, the *Chicago Tribune* announced, "Pitcher Lundgren has been selected captain for next year."[9]

In Chicago, the city's befuddled National League team, called concurrently the Orphans (which replaced Colts as their nickname when longtime player-manager Pop Anson was fired in 1898) and the Remnants (due to player raids by the upstart American League), finished sixth in 1901, escaping the cellar by a mere game. Over the winter, the club hired Frank Selee, winner of five National League flags in Boston in the 1890s, in the 1890s, as the new field manager. One of Selee's friends happened to be Huff.[10]

By coincidence or otherwise, the Chicago Orphans held their 1902 spring training at the Illini campus, enabling Huff to showcase his youthful protégé as well as become an unofficial member of the team's scouting staff. The massive influx of young players at camp led to a new nickname for the team: the Cubs, though it would take another five years for the name to be used exclusively. Since Selee preferred the old name of Colts, that would be the dominant nickname during his tenure as manager.

As the spring session was winding down, the Colts played nine exhibition games with the Illini, winning five of them. Lundgren appeared in five contests, including a 6–1 complete game triumph over Chicago on April 15, the final game of the series.[11]

But Lundgren had to finish college first. He made his senior year a grand finale as he led the Illini to the Western Conference pennant once more. On May 12, he pitched his greatest college game, defeating archrival Michigan, 2–0, on four hits. Although not a power pitcher, he struck out 14 Wolverines in his complete-game performance.[12]

After the conference championship had been sewn up, the Illini headed to the east coast to challenge its prestigious teams. Starting and finishing all the games, Lundgren won against Princeton, 3–1, on May 24, Yale, 10–4, on June 4, and the University of Pennsylvania, 11–3, on June 7.[13,14,15] His only loss was to Harvard, 2–1, on May 30, in which he was simply outpitched.[16]

Following Lundgren's victory over Yale, the *Chicago Tribune* noted, "The Illini had accomplished a feat never before accomplished by a Western baseball team. It had defeated Yale on her own grounds. Never before at any kind of varsity sport has Yale been defeated by any Western college." The article also stated that the Illini were to report to New York's Polo Grounds on the morning of June 5 to practice with the

Colts before going to Pennsylvania, an indication that Lundgren might already have been signed.[17]

Lundgren graduated from the University of Illinois with honors, obtaining a degree in civil engineering, which he would never use.

The new graduate joined the Colts in Cincinnati, making his major league debut on June 19, 1902. Although it was far from a masterpiece, Lundgren managed to go the route in outlasting Reds ace Frank Hahn, with a final score of 7–5. He also singled and stole a base, which did not figure in the scoring. The *Chicago Tribune* summarized: "Lundgren. judging by his work, will certainly do. He was against a team on foreign grounds and with about as bad a bunch of rooters as has been seen at League park this season. Notwithstanding all the taunts hurled at him such as 'Back to college' and 'Make him tramp home' he stuck to his work and when hits were needed to score men he gathered himself together and pulled himself out of the hole.... During the first half of the game the youngster was wild, and gave two bases on balls, made two wild pitches and hit two batsmen. After that he settled down to his work, however, and the Reds found it difficult to single during the remainder of the contest."[18] Apparently, much of it was just a case of common rookie jitters.

Lundgren's first shutout came on July 8, as he blanked the Giants, 2–0, in a game called after seven innings due to both rain and darkness at Chicago's West Side Grounds. The *Chicago Tribune* remarked, "The way the visitors were playing, it would have taken them eighty-five innings to score off Lundgren."[19] At Boston on July 30, Carl went 13 innings to subdue the Beaneaters, 3–1, in what would remain the longest stint of his career. He had a whitewash going until the bottom of the ninth, when Boston tied it on an error by center fielder Davy Jones. Gaining a second wind, the rookie retired heavy hitters Duff Cooley, Fred Tenney, and Gene Demontreville in order in the last of the 13th to preserve a well-earned victory.[20]

The 1902 season had been one of experimentation, as no fewer than 38 players tried on a Colt jersey at various times. Lundgren was 9–9 for the year, but his 1.97 ERA (compiled retroactively) was fourth lowest in the National League and best among all rookies. While the team finished in fifth place at 68–69, it was a vast improvement over the previous campaign (which finished 53-86) and Selee felt confident about the future.

The manager's optimism was borne out as the Colts vaulted into contention with a strong third place finish in 1903. They boasted three 20-game winners in

Jack Taylor (21–14), Jake Weimer (20–8), and Bob Wicker (20–9). Lundgren, the fourth starter, finished with an 11–9 record.

The specter of scandal reared its head when club president and owner James Hart accused Taylor of throwing games to the White Sox during the crosstown City Series in October. Although the charges were never substantiated, the National League fined Taylor for misconduct. On December 12, 1903, Taylor and catcher Larry McLean were traded to the Cardinals for pitcher Mordecai "Three Fingered" Brown and receiver Jack O'Neill, in one of the best deals the club has ever made.

The departure of Taylor meant more pitching opportunities for Lundgren, as Brown was still an unknown quantity at this point. As Selee's Colts inched up to second place in 1904, Lundgren began living up to expectations with a 17–10 record. His win total tied him with Bob Wicker for third on the staff behind Weimer (20) and Herb Briggs (19). Lundgren's repertoire included a variety of curves, a sinker, and an occasional fastball. Streaks of wildness, however, would be a recurrent Achilles Heel.

In Johnny Evers's 1910 volume *Touching Second*, coauthored by sportswriter Hugh Fullerton, the following appeared: "Lundgren was quite studious and the 'Human Icicle,' one of the most careful observers of batters ever found. He was of the type that studies three aces and a pair of tens before calling—and studies a pair of deuces just as hard. When he calls, he wins, and he pitched wonderful ball for Chicago."[21]

The "Human Icicle" phrase referred to his uncanny effectiveness in wintry conditions; sometimes "Human Cucumber" would be substituted instead. He was also nicknamed "Lundy" for obvious reasons.

On September 1, 1904, Lundgren enjoyed his finest outing yet, a 3–0 four hitter over the Brooklyn Superbas (the once and future Dodgers) in Chicago. The *Chicago Chronicle* beamed, "Carl Lundgren had the Brooklyn baseball players in his inside pocket yesterday afternoon and fairly mopped up the diamond with them."[22] The *Chicago Inter-Ocean* lauded him as, "one of the best and at the same time one of the most reliable pitchers in the National League."[23]

Two days later, Lundgren came through with a perfect game in his personal life when he married Maude Cohoon in his native Marengo.[24] Although there would be no children, it was a lasting marriage and by all appearances a happy one. The bride was permitted to accompany her groom on the Colts' upcoming road trip and he responded with a 4–2 win over the Cardinals on September 5, the second game

Mordecai Brown joined the team in 1903, and by 1906 was the dominant pitcher on the Cubs staff.

of a doubleheader sweep. From August 28 to the end of the season, he won seven of his last 10 starts and finished with career highs in innings pitched (242) and strikeouts (106). It had been a satisfying year in more ways than one.

Another one of George Huff's college discoveries, Ed Reulbach, joined the team in 1905 and quickly became a star hurler. For Lundgren, it would be a bittersweet season. Although he had a 13–4 record, he spent nearly all of June and July on the bench. While he was generally brilliant in cold weather, the converse tended to apply as the temperatures rose. Consequently, he found himself on the sidelines for lengthy periods during the peak of summer. He had already sat out the entire month of August in 1903, save for two garbage-time relief appearances.

After Lundgren was shelled by way of eight hits and five runs on June 4, 1905, in a 5–4 loss to the Pirates in Chicago, in which he only lasted three innings,[25] Selee did not use him again until the second outing of an Independence Day twin bill on the home field, in which he edged the Cardinals, 3–2. He made two more appearances that month, both in relief of loser Bob Wicker.[26]

Major changes at the team's upper level occurred. As July became August, first baseman Frank Chance replaced the ailing Selee as manager. (Chance had already been virtually running the team as captain throughout July.) Selee retired to Colorado, where he died of tuberculosis four years later. On November 1, James Hart would sell the franchise to Charles W. Murphy, who was financed by Charles P. Taft, half-brother of the future US president William Howard Taft.

Lundgren resumed his spot in the rotation with a bang. Following a 2–1 victory over the Beaneaters on

August 4 at West Side Grounds, Carl found himself back on the diamond the next day in a new role. During the morning game of a doubleheader in which Chicago shut out Boston, 6–0, umpire James Johnstone was injured by a foul tip. This left him unable to officiate the nightcap, which caused a problem since he was the only ump assigned to the series. Lundgren and Irv Young of the visitors were recruited to do the umpiring in game two as the Colts won again, 5–1. The *Chicago Chronicle* observed that the square-off "was played without a kick or howl, the teams accepting every decision given by Young and Lundgren without a murmur."[27] And if this were not enough, Lundgren returned to the mound 24 hours later to slam Boston, 8–0, to complete a series sweep. Johnstone was still recuperating, so Sam Mertes of New York, on a day off, served as umpire. (The Giants had arrived to begin a four-game set the next day.)[28]

Now that Frank Chance was at the helm, the team became increasingly known as the Cubs, as that was the name he liked best. By the final month of the season, they had settled into third place as John McGraw's Giants copped their second straight flag.

On August 17, 1905, the Cubs purchased the contract of pitcher Jack Pfiester from Omaha of the Western League. The left-hander would become prominent in the years to come. But the headline story on September 27 was Lundgren coming within one out of a no-hitter over Brooklyn at the Cubs' home field. After walking two batters in the second inning, in which he fanned the other three, the Human Icicle set the Superbas down in order, with five more strikeouts along the way. Then, with two out in the top of the ninth, Jimmy Sheckard lifted a blooper which fell between second baseman Johnny Evers and center fielder Jimmy Slagle, rolling past them for a double. In the words of the *Chicago Chronicle*, "[Doc] Gessler followed it with a sharp clean drive to center, the only unquestionable hit of the game for Brooklyn," which scored Sheckard. Gessler then stole second and scored on right fielder Billy Maloney's two-base muff off the bat of Emil Batch. Batch, in turn, was forced out at second on Jack Hummel's grounder to end a 7–2 Chicago triumph.[29] All the newspaper accounts concurred that Gessler's single was Brooklyn's only legitimate hit of the game. If only Sheckard's Texas Leaguer had stayed in the air a few seconds longer…

The team that most personified the Cubs of the Tinker to Evers to Chance era coalesced into its definitive form starting in the winter of 1905–06. Third baseman Harry Steinfeldt was acquired from the Reds and outfielder Jimmy Sheckard from the Superbas. Sheckard

Ed Reulbach was another pitcher whose success would overshadow Lundgren.

would be stationed in left field as Frank Schulte was switched to right. They also obtained Pat Moran, who became a dependable back-up catcher to Johnny Kling. The already formidable pitching staff would be enhanced even further with the addition of Orval Overall from the Reds in June 1906 and the reacquisition of Jack Taylor from the Cardinals a month later.

The result was an unstoppable juggernaut that laid all opposition to waste in a record-setting season. And in early 1906, it was Carl Lundgren setting the pace by winning eight of his first nine decisions, highlighted by a seven-game winning streak from April 21 through May 20. Included were back-to-back three-hit shutouts— 8–0 over Brooklyn on May 12 and 1–0 atop Philadelphia in 10 innings on May 16, both at West Side Grounds. After the latter contest, the *Chicago Chronicle* commented, "Lundgren had everything in the calendar and as control is included in the list no further explanation of his three hit game is necessary."[30]

On July 4, 1906, for the first time in their history, the Cubs won both ends of a separate-admission doubleheader by scores of 1–0. The Pirates hosted Chicago as Three Fingered Brown blanked them in the morning game, the lone safety being pitcher Lefty Leifield's infield single in the third inning. Brown's act was a tough one to follow, but Lundgren came reasonably close, allowing the Bucs only five hits in the afternoon.

With these victories, the Cubs record stood at 49–21, with Lundgren their winningest pitcher at 13–3. Genuine stardom finally seemed within his grasp, as he was on a trajectory to win 27 or 28 games. At the very least, a 20-plus win season appeared to be a cinch. Fate, however, would decree otherwise.

As the rest of the staff got hotter along with the weather, Lundgren steadily lost his effectiveness. He continued to take his regular turn on the mound through the rest of July, but his offerings were hit hard and he displayed increasing wildness. He ended the month with a 5–2 complete game victory in Boston, despite giving up 12 hits and two walks, on July 30. On the same day, Chance announced that he would be using Taylor, Pfiester, and Brown as much as possible, itself an ominous sign.[31] Furthermore, since owner Murphy had coughed up money as well as good players to obtain Taylor and Overall, it would not have been wise for the manager to let them sit idle. Consequently, the Human Icicle was the odd man out, despite his 15–5 record.

Lundgren did not make another pitching appearance until August 15 in Chicago, when he almost blew a huge lead in relief. With the score a seemingly safe 10–0 over Brooklyn, Chance rested Brown after the seventh inning and sent Lundgren in to mop up. While the eighth inning was uneventful, the Superbas erupted for seven runs off Lundgren in the ninth on five hits, three walks, and a wild pitch. He walked in one run while another two plated on Evers's throwing error.[32] Although the Cubs hung on to win, 10–7, Lundgren's outing could not have inspired confidence.

Lundgren did not get a return assignment until the second game of an August 24 doubleheader with the Phillies, probably because Chance had no one else to pitch. His 7–3 victory was due more to Cub bat work than his own finesse, as Lundgren allowed nine hits and three free passes.[33] Again. no assurance builder…

In less than a week. Lundgren was back on the field for three straight games as a replacement umpire. With the Reds in town on Friday, August 31, scheduled umpire Robert Emslie was down with suspected food poisoning, so Lundgren shared the duties with Emslie's partner James Johnstone. Lundgren showed no bias in favor of his team but did not need to either, as Overall handled the Queen City by a score of 8–1. The next day, the Cardinals came to Chicago as Johnstone joined Emslie on the sick list. Now the Cub pitcher was joined in officiating by St. Louis receiver Peter Noonan in another 8–1 Chicago triumph behind the red-hot Brown. The regular umpires remained ill on September 2 as Lundgren worked with Cardinal hurler Ed Karger. The Cardinals won, 5–2, to halt the Cubs' winning streak at 14 games. To quote the *Chicago Chronicle*, "As usual, when pay players handle the game, there was little kicking."[34]

The Cubs' pennant clincher came on September 19 with a 3–1 Reulbach win at Boston for their 106th victory of the season, tying the record set by the Giants two years earlier. Five days later, in game one of a now-meaningless doubleheader at the Polo Grounds, Brown had to exit the game on account of muscle spasms with one out in the fifth inning and Giant runners at first and second. Chance called on Lundgren to relieve him and he came through with his best pitching job in over two months. Spike Shannon's single knocked home Bill Dahlen from second, but Lundgren slammed the door on New York thereafter, holding them scoreless and whiffing five to preserve a 6–2 win. Although Brown was credited with the victory, under today's rules Lundgren would have received it, as starter Brown did not finish the fifth inning. The *Chicago Daily News* beamed, "Lundgren showed yesterday that he had returned to form again and that he will be in shape to do a lot of hard work in the world's series. This cool weather has braced him up wonderfully."[35] On September 27 he received his first start since August 24, losing to the Superbas, 4–0, at Brooklyn. It was deceptive, as Brooklyn did all of its scoring in the first inning; from that point on, Lundgren hurled nothing but goose eggs.[36]

As the season drew to a close, Lundgren finished on a high note. In the morning game of a doubleheader at Philadelphia on October 1, the cold weather man gave what might have been the finest performance of his career. He allowed two singles, neither of which resulted in an advancement. There was neither a walk nor a hit batsman. The best description came from Charles Dryden in the *Chicago Tribune*: "So completely were the Phillies vanquished that not a gent was left on base. Spud [this is what the *Tribune* called the team in 1906] Lundgren was a human hurricane that swept them off the map. Gook [Sherry] Magee singled in the second and was caught stealing. [Paul] Sentell combed a safety in the seventh. 'Kitty' [Bill Bransfield] forced him and was thrown out stealing. The Spuds played a perfect game and Lundgren walked no one."[37]

As a result, Lundgren faced the minimum 27 batters in a 4-0 victory. In game two, Ed Reulbach edged the Quakers, 4–3, in a match called after six innings by mutual consent. It was Reulbach's 12th win in a row, hoisting his final record to 19–4 for a league-leading .826 average. The twin wins were the Cubs' 114th and 115th of the campaign.

Record victory number 116 (not matched until 2001 by the Seattle Mariners with a longer schedule) came in Pittsburgh on October 4 as Jack Pfiester got the 4–0 win against the Pirates for his 20th triumph. Lundgren contributed to this historic affair also, playing second base in place of Evers, who was filling in for the resting Harry Steinfeldt at third. In the ninth inning, Lundgren's double to center field sent Chance across the plate for Chicago's third run, after which Lundgren himself scored on Evers's infield hit and Joe Nealon's errant throw. Defensively, he made no errors, two assists, and three putouts.[38]

For the season. Lundgren was 17–6 with a 2.21 ERA and five shutouts. Although an enviable showing, it was a disappointment compared to his awesome start. Brown had emerged as the dominant man on the corps with a 26–6 ledger plus a league-leading ERA of 1.04 and nine shutouts. Taylor and Overall each checked in at 12–3 after donning Cub flannels.

In the meantime, the "Hitless Wonder" White Sox had captured the American League flag to give Chicago a crosstown World Series, which the city has not witnessed since. As their feeble .230 batting average was lowest in their league, they were three-to-one underdogs with the oddsmakers. Now it was time for Frank Chance to select his pitchers.

The "Peerless Leader" appears to have scratched Lundgren because the White Sox had roughed him up somewhat in the 1905 City Series, which the Cubs won in five games. As for Jack Taylor, Chance feared that if Taylor pitched and lost, the game-throwing charges would resurface.[39] Both would sit on the bench for the entire series, as Chance went with Brown, Reulbach, Pfiester, and Overall.

After the first four contests, the World Series was tied at two wins apiece. The Hitless Wonders suddenly became sluggers in the fifth game, belting Reulbach, Pfiester (credited with the loss), and Overall to outlast the Cubs, 8–6, despite committing six errors. In game six, Brown started his third game in six days, and on just one day's rest. Thoroughly exhausted, Brown surrendered seven runs in one-and-two-thirds innings before being sent to the showers. Overall managed to stop most of the bleeding in relief, but it was too late, as the Sox coasted to an 8–3 victory and a World Series title. The next day, the *Chicago Daily News* remarked, "Some criticism of Chance is heard for permitting Brown to remain in the box as long as he did yesterday, and also for not using Lundgren at any time in the series."[40] Giants manager John McGraw noted, "After Lundgren and Taylor had helped the Cubs win the pennant I believe Manager Chance should have used one or both of them in the world's series."[41] Doubtlessly, countless Cub fans echoed the same sentiments as they drowned their sorrows in neighborhood saloons. It should also be reiterated that in his last three appearances during the regular season, Lundgren had pitched brilliantly, except for one shaky inning. Furthermore, the first three games of the World Series had been played in temperatures which were far below normal—precisely the kind of weather that Lundgren thrived in. The atmospheric conditions for the final three contests, while seasonably pleasant for October, were still nowhere near a stifling heat wave. When these elements were factored into the equation, it would have made perfect sense for Chance to have given Lundgren at least one start, regardless of his showing in the previous year's City Series.

One thing is certain—Lundgren could hardly have fared any worse than the others had in the last two games. Chance's intransigence might have cost the Cubs the Series.

As any native Chicagoan can verify, springtime in the Windy City is nearly always a miserable, watered-down version of winter, and 1907 was a bad one even by those standards. After the Cubs and their fans shivered through a 6–1 opening day victory over the Cardinals on April 11, the next two games were snowed out. At game time on April 14, it was 34 degrees in Chicago with a frigid west wind that made it feel at least 10 degrees cooler. Patches of snow dotted the spacious outfield at West Side Grounds. It was in these Lundgren-friendly environs that the winter air wizard embarked on his finest season with a four-hit 2–0 win versus St. Louis. In referring to the day as "football weather," the *Chicago Chronicle* called Lundgren, "the government bonds as a chilly day pitcher."[42]

The bad weather followed the Cubs on their first trip east as Lundgren downed the Pirates on April 20 by a score of 5–1, in a game halted after eight innings because of the cold. Back in Chicago on May 4, conditions had moderated ever so slightly with a 40-degree day and a northeast wind in Old Man Winter's last, vengeful gasp. Although he gave up six hits and seven walks, Lundgren was able to blank the Pirates, 1–0. The Cubs managed but two hits, both by Artie Hofman, whose fourth-inning single drove in the solitary run. As the *Chicago Tribune* put it, "Tradition says Lundgren is at his best when the frost is on the pumpkin."[43]

Lundgren was even effective on days when he was not supposed to be. The temperature was 86 with a dense humidity on June 22 when he posted a 3–0 six-hitter over the Cardinals on his home turf. The *Chicago Inter-Ocean* kiddingly commented, "While it was not cold enough to please the arctic curver, he managed to get away with the better end of the argument."[44] He would eventually spend some time on the

Manager Frank Chance passed Lundgren over when it came to picking his World Series starters in 1906 and 1907.

sidelines during the heat, but not as much as during the previous two seasons.

In another runaway race, the Cubs took the flag with a 107–45 record, good for a 17-game margin above the second-place Pirates. Despite going winless between July 15 and August 27, Lundgren closed out with 18 wins against seven defeats. Two of his losses were by 1–0 scores and another by 2–1, so with a few timely hits his record could easily have been 21–4. His minuscule 1.17 ERA was a hairsbreadth behind Jack Pfiester's circuit-best 1.15, while his seven shutouts ranked third to Orval Overall's and Giant Christy Mathewson's league-best eight. Lundgren was the stingiest in the league in hits per nine innings (5.65) and opponent's batting average (.185). The sole area where one could find fault with his account was that his walks outnumbered strikeouts, 92 to 84, though obviously the damage done was minimal.

His stellar showing notwithstanding. Lundgren was again bypassed for the 1907 World Series against Detroit. On October 6, Chance announced that Overall, Pfiester, Reulbach, and Brown would be his starters.[45] Reulbach (17) and Pfiester (14) had both won fewer games than Lundgren. Even Brown looked like a question mark, having seen little action since he strained a muscle in his pitching arm in late August.[46] One can only guess that, for whatever reason, Chance did not have faith in Lundgren when it came to the "money games."

As it turned out, Lundgren's services were not needed. After the first game had been called as a tie when the sun went down after 12 innings, the Cubs skinned the Tigers in four straight to win the World Series. The question of whether or not Chance would have used Lundgren had the series extended any further remains one of baseball's unsolved mysteries.

The 1908 season seemed to begin well enough for Lundgren, as he won six of his first nine decisions. Ominously, however, he was having problems finding the plate even in the games he won. In his first start of the year, April 16, he went into the ninth inning at Cincinnati with a 7–1 lead, then promptly issued 11 straight balls to start the frame. Luckily, he was able to hold onto a 7–4 win.[47]

One of Lundgren's most sublime moments came nearly two months hence. On a cool day with intermittent rain at Brooklyn's Washington Park on June 11, Lundgren and Irvin "Kaiser" Wilhelm of the Trolley Dodgers, as they were once again being called, held each other to a 1–1 draw after 10 innings. In the top of the 11th, Cub catcher Johnny Kling singled, then took second on Joe Tinker's sacrifice bunt. Chance let Lundgren bat for himself and he "cracked out a beautiful biff [a long single] along the third base line and tallied J. Kling with the winning run."[48] He then retired all three Brooklynites on long fly balls in the bottom of the inning for a 2–1 triumph. For Lundgren, whose lifetime batting average was .157, it was the only time in the majors that he won his own game with his bat in the final round. Hopefully he savored it, for the glory would be ephemeral.

Seven days later the Cubs started Ed Reulbach in a game against the Giants at the Polo Grounds. But after Reulbach walked the first two batters in the third, Chance yanked him in favor of a half-warmed-up Lundgren, who didn't fare much better. Lundgren gave up three runs on seven hits and two walks in seven relief innings, but Chicago clung to a 7–5 win in which "the pitching kept the club in hot water all the time."[49] It would be Lundgren's last victory in the big time.

From that point on it was all downhill, as Lundgren lost his next six starts and had two decisionless relief appearances, all of which were ineffective in varying degrees. His control, never one of his strong areas to begin with, had now vanished completely. After an 8–3 home loss to the Phillies on August 18, in which Lundgren was knocked out of the box in the sixth inning,[50] he spent the remainder of the year as a dugout spectator.

When the Cubs began their final scheduled road trip on September 10, Lundgren, Chick Fraser, Kid Durbin, and the injured Jimmy Sheckard remained in Chicago.[51] Fraser and Sheckard rejoined the team in Cincinnati on September 29.[52]

After the most nail-biting and controversial pennant race in history, the Cubs met the Tigers again for the 1908 World Series. Once more, the Bruins tamed the Bengals in five games as Lundgren observed the proceedings from the sidelines. This time, Chance's decision not to use him was understandable.

Still, Chance was not ready to give up on Lundgren quite yet. He made two more token appearances in April 1909. The first was a relief stint for loser Zerah "Rip" Hagerman in a 3–1 loss to the Cardinals on April 16 at Chicago, and the second a start versus the same team in St. Louis on the 23rd. In the latter, he lasted three-and-one-third innings, allowing four runs on six hits and three walks before Hagerman relieved him. St. Louis went on to a 6–3 victory as Lundgren was tagged with the loss in his final bow as a major leaguer.[53] Four days later he was placed on waivers, exiting with a 91–55 record. In the generally cooler months of April, May, September, and October, he was a juicy 53–26. Eleven of his 19 shutouts occurred during these months as well.

While the release came as no surprise, his teammates were sad to see Lundgren leave, as he had always been popular. The news stories all agreed that there appeared to be nothing wrong with his arm, although some opined, "He seems to have lost confidence in himself."[54] How Lundgren lost his effectiveness so totally at such a young age will probably never be known after the passage of more than a century. And perhaps an occult-minded researcher will theorize that "the curse of Carl Lundgren" prevented the Cubs from winning a World Series for more than a century after he left the team.

On May 9, 1909, the *Chicago Tribune* reported: "Carl Lundgren, dean of the Cub pitching staff in point of continuous service, was disposed of to the Brooklyn club yesterday and President Ebbtts in making the purchase announced he would seek waivers on Carl immediately with a view to disposing of him to the Toronto club of the Eastern League…"[55] After briefly refusing to report, Lundgren joined the 1909 Toronto club and went 1–3 for the Maple Leafs before being suspended by manager Joe Kelley.[56] Several weeks later, Toronto sold Lundgren to Kansas City of the American Association, but rather than join the Blues, Lundgren apparently spent the remainder of 1909 pitching in semi-pro ball in the Chicago area although details of those exploits have yet to be uncovered.[57]

Lundgren rejoined Toronto in 1910, then over the next three years drifted to Hartford of the Connecticut League, then Troy of the New York State League. Mobile of the Southern Association nearly signed him but in the end did not because of his sore arm. However, in 1912 and 1913 he also served as pitching coach at Princeton University. This would be a turning point in his baseball life.

In August 1913, Branch Rickey resigned his post as head baseball coach at the University of Michigan to become field manager of the St. Louis Browns. On August 12, the school hired Lundgren as his successor, to report the following February.[58]

During Lundgren's first three years at Michigan, the Wolverines played as an independent team, having left the Western College Conference several years earlier. One of Lundgren's players in his first two seasons at the helm was future Hall of Famer George Sisler, then primarily a pitcher. On May 8, 1915, Sisler allowed five hits and fanned 20 batters in a game against Syracuse that was called as a 2–2 tie after 13 innings due to rain in Ann Arbor, Michigan.[59] Upon his graduation a month later Sisler would join the St. Louis Browns and become the greatest player in the St. Louis Browns annals, such as they were.

Michigan canceled its 1917 baseball season due to the Great War, then rejoined the Big Ten the following year. It was then that Lundgren's coaching career really took off, as his teams captured Western Conference titles in 1918, 1919, and 1920, with records of 9–1, 9–0, and 9–1. Ace pitcher Vernon "Slicker" Parks hurled a 7–0 no-hitter over Lundgren's alma mater, the Illini, on May 31, 1919, to clinch that year's pennant.[60] Parks would later enjoy a brief stay in the majors, as would shortstop Kenneth "Nike" Knode, who hit a home run in the second inning.[61]

Following the 1920 championship, Lundgren spent the summer as a pitching instructor for the Cardinals.[62] The Redbirds went from 54–83 in 1919 to 75–79 in 1920 to 87–66 in 1921. How much of the improvement was the result of Lundgren's pitching tips as opposed to the bats of Rogers Hornsby and others is open to debate.

George Huff, now the athletic director at the University of Illinois, had retired from active coaching. Impressed by Lundgren's success at Michigan, he persuaded his former pupil to return to his old school to run the baseball team. The results were immediate: Lundgren's Illini copped conference pennants in 1921 (10–1, with the only loss being the final game of the season) and 1922 (8–2). During a 7–3 win over Michigan on May 20, 1922, Lundgren's lineup boasted four future major leaguers: Otto Vogel, Harry McCurdy, Dick Reichle, and Wally Roettger.[63] Vogel would later be a varsity coach at Iowa.[64] McCurdy became a footnote in Phillies trivia by leading the National League in pinch hits with 15 in 1933. Roettger, after eight major league seasons as mainly a second-string outfielder, would succeed Lundgren as Illinois' baseball coach.

With five straight championships under his belt, Lundgren had emerged as college baseball's equivalent of fellow Scandinavian Knute Rockne, the legendary Notre Dame football coach. Huff called him "the greatest of all college baseball coaches."[65] In a fawning writeup entitled, "A Maker of Men" in the May 1923 *Sporting Life* (no relation to the paper which ceased publication in 1917), Gene Kessler praised Lundgren as, "the kind who says little and thinks a lot," "a self-repressing genius," "a man of the highest integrity," "especially noted for his ability to bring the fine qualities out in coaching the young pitchers," and "does not look a day older than when he was pitching winning baseball for the Chicago Cubs." Unfortunately, the piece did not delve into his strategies as a coach other than, "Lundgren is a baseball martinet but not a driver. He has strict discipline, but handles his men in a psychological manner."[66] This, of course, could have meant anything. Despite the syrupy tone of the article, at least some of the adulation had to have been deserved in light of Lundgren's record.

It also appears to have been an early precursor of the *"Sports Illustrated* jinx," as following the publication of that piece, Illinois lost two of its last three games to finish third in the Big Ten standings while Michigan took that season's pennant. Over the next three years. the Illini were competent but unexceptional, winding up fifth in 1924, sixth the following year, then up to fourth in 1926.

Not until 1927 did Illinois repeat as champions, and even then they had to share the title with Iowa, as the Hawkeyes won their final game on May 30 to tie the Illini at 7–3.[67] (At that time, there were no playoffs in college baseball, rainouts were not rescheduled, and ties were neither resumed nor replayed.) Lundgren's team then slipped to seventh in 1928 and fourth the year after.

Starting in 1930, Illinois became a perennial contender again as Lundgren, now the assistant athletic director as well as baseball coach, began his second-most productive period. In an exciting, heavy-hitting season, Wisconsin's Badgers won the Western Conference flag while Illinois finished a close second in the 1930 race. The juiced-up baseball employed by the majors apparently filtered its way down to varsity ball, as the Illini scored more than 10 runs in five of their eight conference wins, topped off by a 14–0 massacre of Northwestern on April 28.[68] And one of the Badgers' nine victories was a 16–12 slugfest, also versus Northwestern, on May 7.[69]

Illinois pulled in at 8–2 again in the Big Ten pennant drive in 1931, and this time it was good enough for the flag as they edged out Chicago, which finished at 8–3. One of the Illini victories was a 3–2 edging of Chicago on their turf on April 18, defeating Maroon ace Roy Henshaw.[70] Henshaw would have an eight-year stay in the majors, helping the Cubs win the 1935 pennant with a 13–5 record. Illini catcher Paul Chervinko went on to play as a third-stringer for the Dodgers in 1937–38.

Following the championship, Illinois finished second the next two seasons. In 1933, the Illini had the winningest record (8–2) in the Western Conference, but Minnesota came through with the best winning average (6–1, .857). Two Illinois victories were back-to-back blowouts on successive days: 15–4 against Northwestern on May 16, and 20–7 over Chicago on the 17th, both away from home.[71,72]

Lundgren would not be denied a pennant in 1934 as the Illini assembled a 9–1 finish for his fifth championship in Urbana. Their only loss came on May 5 at Ann Arbor, as old nemesis Michigan's Francis "Whitey" Wistert fanned 10 Illini in a 4–1 win.[73] Before the year was over, Wistert would have a barely visible fling in the majors with two mound trips for the Reds. Concurrently, Fred Frink, an Illini outfielder, experienced an equally microscopic career with the Phillies, appearing in two games as a late-inning replacement.

It had been Illinois' winningest season since 1921. In midsummer, Carl and Maude Lundgren vacationed in Canada. On August 21, 1934, they were attending a Kiwanis club picnic in their hometown of Marengo when the coach began suffering nausea and chest pains in the late afternoon. Taken to the nearby home of relatives, Lundgren died of heart failure at 9:15 PM.[74]

As he had apparently been in normal health, Lundgren's passing was a shock to all who knew him. Survived by his wife and two sisters, he was buried in Marengo City Cemetery following a brief service. In Big Ten competition from 1918 through 1934, Lundgren's teams had posted 126 wins against 46 losses (27–2 at Michigan and 99–44 at Illinois) for a .733 winning average. He never led a team to a losing record—his poorest showing in the Western Conference was 6–6 in 1928.

Still a well-known figure at the time of his death, Lundgren's role in the last great Cubs team was gradually forgotten. Three Fingered Brown's handicap helped enable him to win 20 games six straight years en route to 239 career victories and eventual enshrinement in Cooperstown. Ed Reulbach led the league in winning percentage for three consecutive seasons, and is the only pitcher in history to master a shutout doubleheader. Jack Pfiester, who won 20 fewer games than Lundgren in the majors, is remembered as the "Giant Killer" for winning 15 of 20 decisions against the New York team. Jack Taylor hurled an incredible 187 consecutive complete-game starts between 1901 and 1906. Orval Overall, a two-time 20-game winner, topped the National League in strikeouts in 1909. Lundgren, unfortunately, had no such eye-popping feathers in his cap. And as a quiet, scholarly individual, he was neither colorful nor controversial. Nevertheless, his achievements as a pitcher and varsity coach speak for themselves. In 35 years of baseball, Lundgren left a legacy to be proud of. As such, his memory deserves a better fate. ■

Notes

1. Bill Lamb, "Carl Lundgren," SABR BioProject, https://sabr.org/bioproj/person/acf35363.
2. *Chicago Tribune*, April 23, 1899.
3. *Chicago Tribune*, May 31, 1899.
4. *Chicago Tribune*, June 7, 1899.
5. *Marengo Beacon-News*, January 23, 1975.
6. Lamb, Lundgren SABR Bio.
7. Unidentified newspaper clipping, ca. 1906, in Lundgren's Hall of Fame file.
8. *Chicago Tribune*, May 10, 1990.
9. *Chicago Tribune*, June 17, 1901.
10. Gil Bogen, *Johnny Kling: A Baseball Biography* (Jefferson: McFarland & Co., 2006), 51.
11. *Chicago Tribune*, April 16, 1902.
12. *Chicago Tribune*, May 13, 1902.
13. *Chicago Tribune*, May 25, 1902.
14. *Chicago Tribune*, June 5, 1902.
15. *Chicago Tribune*, June 8, 1902.
16. *Chicago Tribune*, May 31, 1902.
17. *Chicago Tribune*, June 5, 1902.
18. *Chicago Tribune*, June 20, 1902.
19. *Chicago Tribune*, July 9, 1902.
20. *Chicago Tribune*, July 31, 1902.
21. John J. Evers and Hugh S. Fullerson, *Touching Second* (Jefferson: McFarland & Co., 2005), as quoted in Peter Golenbock, *Wrigleyville: A Magical History Tour of the Chicago Cubs* (New York: St. Martin's, 1996), 100.
22. *Chicago Chronicle*, September 2, 1904.
23. *Chicago Inter-Ocean*, September 2, 1904.
24. *Marengo Beacon-News*, op. cit.
25. *Chicago Chronicle*, June 5, 1905.
26. *Chicago Chronicle*, July 14, 1905 and July 21, 1905.
27. *Chicago Chronicle*, August 6, 1905.
28. *Chicago Chronicle*, August 7, 1905.
29. *Chicago Chronicle*, September 28, 1905.
30. *Chicago Chronicle*, May 17, 1906.
31. *Chicago Chronicle*, July 31, 1906.
32. *Chicago Inter-Ocean*, August 16, 1906.
33. *Chicago Inter-Ocean*, August 25, 1906.
34. *Chicago Chronicle*, September 3, 1906.
35. *Chicago Daily News*, September 25, 1906.
36. *Chicago Daily News*, September 27, 1906.
37. *Chicago Tribune*, October 2, 1906.
38. *Chicago Tribune*, October 5, 1906.
39. Lowell L. Blaisdell, "Trouble and Jack Taylor," *The National Pastime* (Phoenix: SABR, 1996), 135.
40. *Chicago Daily News*, October 15, 1906.
41. *Chicago Daily News* and *Chicago Journal*, October 15, 1906—both papers carried the same McGraw quote.
42. *Chicago Chronicle*, April 15, 1907.
43. *Chicago Tribune*, May 5, 1907.
44. *Chicago Inter-Ocean*, June 23, 1907.
45. *Chicago Daily News*, October 7, 1907.
46. Cindy Thomson and Scott Brown, *Three Finger* (Lincoln: University of Nebraska Press, 2006), 49.
47. George R. Matthews, *When the Cubs Won It All* (Jefferson: McFarland & Co., 2009), 33.
48. *Chicago Inter-Ocean*, June 12, 1908.
49. *Chicago Daily News*, June 18, 1908.
50. *Chicago Daily News*, August 18, 1908.
51. Matthews, 149.
52. Matthews, 171.
53. *Chicago Tribune*, April 24, 1909.
54. *Chicago American*, *Chicago Journal*, and *Chicago Record-Herald*, April 28, 1909—all three papers had the same quote.
55. *Chicago Tribune*, May 9, 1909.
56. *Sporting Life*, June 26, 1909; Lamb, "Carl Lundgren" SABR Bio.
57. Unidentified newspaper clipping in Lundgren's Hall of Fame file. The year appears to be 1909, as the wording is, "He is now pitching independent ball in and around Chicago."
58. Unidentified newspaper clipping in Lundgren's Hall of Fame file.
59. *Chicago Tribune*, May 9, 1915.
60. *Chicago Tribune*, June 1, 1919.
61. *Chicago Tribune*, June 1, 1919.
62. Gene Kessler, "A Maker of Men," *Sporting Life* (May 1923), 47.
63. *Chicago Tribune*, May 21, 1922.
64. Otto Vogel Obituary, *Chicago Tribune*, August 22, 1934. Mike Pearson, "Illini legends, lists, and lore: Otto Vogel," *The* (Champaign) *News-Gazette*, October 25, 2014.
65. Kessler, "A Maker of Men."
66. Kessler, "A Maker of Men."
67. *Chicago Tribune*, May 31, 1927.
68. *Chicago Tribune*, April 29, 1930
69. *Chicago Tribune*, May 8, 1930.
70. *Chicago Tribune*, April 19, 1931.
71. *Chicago Tribune*, May 17, 1933.
72. *Chicago Tribune*, May 18, 1933.
73. *Chicago Tribune*, May 6, 1934.
74. Lundgren's death certificate in his Hall of Fame file.

Beyond the Miracle

The Mets of the Early 1970s

Douglas Jordan, PhD

The year 1969 was eventful. Astronauts Neil Armstrong and Buzz Aldrin first set foot on the moon, President Nixon began troop withdrawals from Vietnam, and the Beatles released their classic album "Abbey Road." Two other major events took place in New York State. The Woodstock festival brought a generation together in musical celebration and, in arguably the most surprising event of the year, the New York Mets won the World Series. This was so unlikely that the team has been referred to as the Miracle Mets ever since.

Looking back, this baseball miracle seems to be the lone successful season in the first two decades of franchise existence. But this perception is wrong. The Mets' performance that year was surprising based on the seven seasons that preceded it, but 1969 was not the only successful year for the Mets. The team was competitive from 1969 to 1973. The purpose of this article is to refresh our memories of what actually happened during that time period. All of the data used in the article are from Baseball-Reference.com.

THE EARLY YEARS

As with most expansion teams, the franchise struggled in its early years. The inaugural 1962 campaign is legendary for ineptitude. The team won only 40 games (the fewest wins by any team in a 162-game season) while losing 120, and finished tenth out of ten teams in the NL. But that team's Pythagorean win total was 50, which indicates that the team should have won more games based on runs scored and runs allowed than its actual record. So Mets fans can argue that the 1962 team was not as abysmal as the 40-win season suggests.

The team's win/loss performance did not improve much between 1963 and 1968. Table 1 shows that the team finished in last place (tenth of ten) four of those six years, and in second-to-last place (ninth of ten) the other two years. All of those teams struggled offensively, finishing tenth or ninth in on-base plus slugging averages (OPS), batting average (BA), and runs scored per game (R/G) every year. The pitching and fielding were similarly poor. The team had the worst earned run average (ERA) and runs allowed per game (RA/G) in the league every year until 1965, with only slight

Table 1. NY Mets data from 1962–73

Season	Wins	Losses	Place	Games Behind	Pythagorean Wins	Pythagorean Losses	R/G	BA	OPS	ERA
1973	82	79	1 (6)	–	83	78	3.78 (11)	.246 (11)	.653 (11)	3.26 (3)
1972	83	73	3 (6)	14	72	84	3.38 (9)	.225 (12)	.639 (10)	3.26 (5)
1971	83	79	T3 (6)	14	86	76	3.63 (8)	.249 (6)	.669 (7)	2.99 (1)
1970	83	79	3 (6)	6	88	74	4.29 (9)	.249 (9)	.703 (9)	3.45 (1)
1969*	100	62	1 (6)	–	92	70	3.90 (9)	.242 (8)	.662 (11)	2.99 (2)
1968	73	89	9 (10)	24	77	85	2.90 (T9)	.228 (10)	.596 (10)	2.72 (4)
1967	61	101	10 (10)	41	59	103	3.07 (10)	.238 (9)	.613 (10)	3.73 (8)
1966	66	95	9 (10)	29	62	99	3.65 (9)	.239 (10)	.643 (10)	4.17 (9)
1965	50	112	10 (10)	47	51	111	3.02 (10)	.221 (10)	.604 (10)	4.06 (10)
1964	53	109	10 (10)	40	59	103	3.49 (9)	.246 (9)	.644 (9)	4.25 (10)
1963	51	111	10 (10)	48	50	112	3.09 (9)	.219 (10)	.600 (9)	4.12 (10)
1962**	40	120	10 (10)	61	50	110	3.83 (9)	.240 (10)	.679 (9)	5.04 (10)

T means tied for that position
*Starting in 1969, the place figure is of 6 in division but other data are of 12 in the NL.
**Starting in 1962, the place figure is of 10 in the NL and other data are of 10 in the NL

improvement in 1966 and 1967. In terms of fielding, performance during the early years was similarly awful. The Mets committed 210 errors in both 1962 and 1963. The 1963 error total is the last time any team committed more than 200 errors in a season (but the Cubs managed to commit 199 errors in 1974). The fielding improved only slightly over the following few years.

But the Mets' story changed significantly in 1968 under new manager Gil Hodges. Superficially, it didn't appear to be much of an improvement: the team won 73 games, came in ninth place, and still hit weakly. But buried in the minutiae of baseball data, we can see the pitching and fielding had improved significantly. The team's ERA of 2.72 was fourth-best in the league and the RA/G was second-best at 3.06. The 133 errors that the Mets committed were the fourth-fewest in the league. The stage was set for the drama to come the next year.

THE SURPRISING 1969 REGULAR SEASON

To the discerning observer, it didn't take long for the Mets to establish that the 1969 season was going to be different from the previous seven campaigns. The team went 9–11 in April, but seven of the 11 losses were by one or two runs. The 12–12 record they put up in May didn't seem impressive, but it was only the third time in franchise history that the team had a .500 record or better for a month. However, to the casual baseball fan, it looked like nothing had changed. The Mets were 5½ games behind the Cubs at the end of April, and trailed them by nine games by the end of May.

The Mets showed that they could be a factor in the pennant race when they had a franchise-best month in June with a record of 19–9. But after a 15–12 July, the team went 4–7 on an 11-game road trip. By August 13, they found themselves ten games behind the Cubs (the largest deficit of the season).

What happened next shows how quickly gaps can close in the standings when the trailing team gets hot, and the leading team goes cold. From August 14 to August 27, the Mets righted the ship with a 9–1 homestand, and went 12–1 over 13 games. During the same time period, the once historically hot Cubs went 5–9. The Cubs' lead over the Mets shrank to 2½ games on August 27. A laughingstock for seven seasons, the Mets were suddenly in their first pennant race. Could they handle that pressure? History shows the Mets were up to the challenge.

The Cubs came to Shea Stadium on September 8 for a crucial two-game series, holding a 2½ game lead. The Mets swept the short series, and then moved into first place on September 10. They stayed there the rest of the season, going 23–7 in September while the Cubs went 8–17 that month. The Mets concluded the season by going 9–1 over their last ten games, and finished 100–62 for the campaign. The Cubs were eight games back. The 100 games the Mets won were the best in the NL by seven games over the West Division champion Braves, who won 93.

How did the Mets accomplish this miracle? Table 1 shows the answer. As is not unusual in baseball history, pitching and fielding were the foundation upon which the team built the championship. The Mets' ERA of 2.99 and RA/G of 3.34 were second-best in the now 12-team league, both numbers just slightly higher than the league-leading Cardinals. The 122 errors they committed were the second-fewest in the league. The team's hitting improved modestly. Although the Mets' OPS of .662 was still second-lowest in the league, their .242 batting average was tied for seventh and wasn't too far below the league average of .250. The team scored 3.90 runs per game (ninth in the league) compared to the league average of 4.05 R/G. Excellent pitching and fielding, combined with slightly improved offense (and some luck; as their Pythagorean win total of 92 versus the 100 actual wins implies) led to a stellar, 100-win season.

THE FORGOTTEN COMPETITIVE YEARS, 1970–73

Fifty years makes the memory hazy. In retrospect, the 1969 World Series victory seems isolated because of the terrible seasons that preceded it and the fact that it took the Mets 17 years to win another world championship. But in fact, the Mets were competitive within the division between 1970 and 1973. The team even got to the World Series in 1973, but came up one victory short of winning. Had they managed to win that game, the team's nationwide reputation for this time period would be very different. In fact, a better question to ask is, why didn't the Mets win more than one title in this era? The answer: short stretches of uncharacteristically poor play each season in 1970 through 1972.

1970

A glance at the final East Division standings at the end of the 1970 season shows that the Mets' record was 83–79. They finished in third place, six games behind the Pirates. These numbers suggest that the Mets were not competitive that season. This suggestion is inaccurate: the Mets were very competitive all season, and had a good chance of winning the division into late September. But they came up just short in crucial games

The Mets were competitive from 1969 through 1973 because of a stellar pitching staff headed by Tom Seaver.

down the stretch, and failed to get into the postseason. Let's clear some of the haze away from a half-century of memory.

In 1970, the Mets went 10–9 in April and finished the month 3½ games behind the Cubs. They fell to five games out on June 11, but then went 10–2 over their next 12 games and moved into first place by 1½ games on June 25. At the end of July, the Mets had a 55–46 record and led the division by half a game. But even though they played poorly in August and compiled a 13–18 record that month, they were only 1½ games out of first place on August 31. They won six of seven games in early September and were tied for the division lead on September 10. The Mets were still tied for the lead on September 14, at 78–69, after a victory at Montreal.

But a crushing loss to the Expos the next day was the beginning of the end. They lost the next three games by scores of 4–2, 3–2, and 2–1 and fell 3½ games behind the Pirates on September 19, with just 11 games left to play. They went 5–6 and finished six games back. There was no miracle in 1970, but the team had been competitive throughout the season, thanks to pitching and fielding. Table 1 shows that the Mets had the best pitching staff in the league in terms of ERA and RA/G, with fielders who committed the second-fewest errors (124) in the league. But the strong pitching could not make up for the weak offense.[1]

1971

The story of the 1971 season is similar to the 1970 season. The team won 83 games again, but this time finished 14 games out of first place. Those numbers once again make it appear that the team was not competitive. However, a closer look at the 1971 season reveals a different narrative. The Mets went 12–7 in

April and finished the month in first place by one game. The team stayed in first place for the first half of May. About a month later, on June 9, the Mets owned a 32–20 record and were tied for the lead of the East Division. At the end of June, the team was 45–29 and two games behind the Pirates. The Mets were in, or close to, first place for half the season. They were clearly competitive to this point in the campaign.

But baseball teams can go through bad spells, and the Mets had one as the calendar turned to July in 1971. They went 3–16 over the next 19 games, and fell 13½ games behind the Pirates. The Mets lost just ½ game to the Bucs over the rest of the season, but July cost them the division. So as in 1970, the team was competitive but failed to reach the postseason. And as in 1970, pitching was the strength of the team. The Mets led the league in both ERA and RA/G with an error total that was third-best.

1972

The 1972 season was eerily similar to the previous year. The Mets started well, going 29–11 over the first two months in spite of the untimely passing of Gil Hodges about two weeks before the season began. They built a 6½ game lead over the second place Pirates on May 20. They didn't play as well in June (12–15), but were still tied for the division lead at the end of the month. However, just like 1971, they didn't play well in July. An 11–15 record that month left them seven games behind the Pirates, who went 20–10 over the same stretch. By the end of August, another sub-.500 month left them 13 games behind and they finished 13½ games out of first place. So, once again, the team was competitive for half the season before a stretch of poor play ruined their chance of winning the division.

Another way to look at the results for these seasons is to compare the Pythagorean win totals each year. (The numbers are given in Table 1, previous page.) The 1969 team won 27 more games than the '68 team but the Pythagorean win total for the '69 team was only 15 games higher. This suggests that at least some of the improvement in '69 was due to chance. Similarly, the '70 and '71 Pythagorean win totals were just four and six games less than the 92 Pythagorean wins the Mets had in '69. This suggests that those two teams were almost as good as the '69 version of the club, but they were not as lucky. The '72 team was luckier than expected with a win total that exceeded its Pythagorean win total by 11 games. But that was not enough to overcome a 13-game deficit that year.

THE COMEBACK IN 1973

In retrospect, it seems appropriate that the events of the 1973 season more closely resembled what happened in 1969 than the seasons in between. But unfortunately for Mets fans, the deliriously happy ending of 1969 was not to repeat. The Mets started the season well, going 12–8 in April, and were tied for the division lead at the end of month. But the team played poorly over the next two months, going 20–31 and landing at the end of June in last place, 11 games behind the Cubs.

The Mets then lost four of the first five games in July, and fell 12½ games behind. This was the biggest deficit of that season. The situation didn't change much over the rest of July and they finished the month in last place, 10½ games behind the Cardinals, making the postseason picture look bleak. But the team played better in August (18–14), while every other team in the division played poorly. The Mets finished the month in fifth place (out of six teams), but had shortened the distance between themselves and the Cardinals to 5½ games. This means that they were in the pennant race—on the fringe, to be sure, but not to be counted out with certainty.

The NL East division race in September 1973 deserves an article of its own. (And in fact, that race is part of the story in Matthew Silverman's *Swinging '73: Baseball's Wildest Season*.) The Mets, Pirates, and Cardinals battled down to the wire, with the three teams within two games of each other going into the final weekend of play. The Mets finally clinched the division on Monday, October 1, when they defeated the Cubs in a makeup game from earlier that season.

The Mets' reward for winning the East Division with 82 wins was a date with the mighty 99-win Cincinnati Reds in the NLCS. On paper the series was a mismatch, but Mets pitching put some sand in the gears of the Big Red Machine. The Reds scored only two runs in four of the five games (versus the Reds' average of 4.57 runs per game all season) and the Mets prevailed in the series with a 7–2 win in Game 5, behind the pitching of Tom Seaver. This victory earned the Mets a trip to their second World Series in five years.

Their opponent was the defending champion Oakland Athletics. Once again, the Mets appeared to be outmatched. And once again, the Mets' pitching kept them competitive. The first three games were very close affairs, and the teams alternated wins over the first four games of the series. Game 5 was the final home game for the Mets. Jerry Koosman and Tug McGraw combined to shut the A's out. With the 2–0 victory, the Mets were now one victory away from their second championship.

The prospect of earning that win seemed very favorable. The Mets had to win only one of the following two games, and 19-game winner Tom Seaver was slated to start the next game on short rest. Hindsight suggests Yogi Berra should have saved Seaver for Game 7 so he could have pitched on regular rest, but Berra argued that he was going for the win with his best pitcher in Game 6. Seaver pitched well in Game 6, giving up just two runs in seven innings. But Catfish Hunter was even better. He only allowed one run over his 7⅓ innings, and the A's won Game 6 by a score of 3–1 to force a Game 7.

The starting pitchers for Game 7 were 14-game winner Jon Matlack for the Mets, and 21-game winner Ken Holtzman for the A's. Game 7 was scoreless for the first two innings. But Bert Campaneris and Reggie Jackson each hit two-run home runs off Matlack in the bottom of the third, which gave the A's a 4–0 lead. That was all the run production that Holtzman needed, and the A's went on to win the game, and the World Series, by a score of 5–2. The Mets fell one victory short of their second championship.

CONCLUSION

The Mets' surprising World Series victory in 1969 is often perceived as the lone successful season in the first 20 years of franchise existence. But that perception is wrong. The Mets were competitive from 1969 through 1973 because of a stellar pitching staff headed by Tom Seaver, Jerry Koosman, and Tug McGraw for that whole time period. Nolan Ryan was part of the staff 1966–1971, although he was still learning his craft during his time with the Mets. Jon Matlack joined Seaver and Koosman as an important cog in the pitching staff during 1972 and 1973. The Mets came within one victory of a second championship in 1973. So even though the team won just one World Series before 1986, the Mets had a window of success in the early 1970s that is usually not recognized. ∎

Acknowledgment

My thanks to two peer reviewers for their input. Their comments improved the paper substantially.

Note

1. A statistical quirk from the 1970 season is interesting: The team won exactly 15 games in each of May, June, July, and September. So the team had the same number of wins in four of six months.

Philadelphia in the 1882 League Alliance

Robert D. Warrington

istories of the Philadelphia Phillies portray the club's admission to the National League (NL) as a straightforward and swift process. Late in 1882, League president Abraham G. Mills informed former star player and old friend Alfred J. Reach that the Worcester franchise was moving to Philadelphia. Mills asked Reach—now a successful business entrepreneur in the city—if he'd like to own the club. "I'm in," Reach told Mills, and the Philadelphia franchise was quickly organized to play during the 1883 season.[1] A simple story; indeed, too simple. The facts tell a different tale.

Philadelphia's journey to NL membership was complicated and protracted. The team's participation in the 1882 League Alliance was a crucial step toward major-league status, and Reach's enthusiasm for joining the league may not have been as unbridled as depicted by some authors. This article examines the club's entry into the Alliance, its 1882 season, and how the transition from the Alliance to the NL unfolded. It also investigates the genesis of the team's longstanding nickname "Phillies" and questions the accuracy of the oft-told tale of how it became associated with the franchise.

AL REACH CREATES HIS CLUB

Initial indications that Reach was interested in owning a professional baseball club appeared in October 1881. An article in the *New York Clipper* stated that "two first-class clubs in Philadelphia are promised" for the 1882 campaign. In addition to the existing Athletics club,

Star player and successful sports equipment manufacturer, Al Reach is the Founding Father of the Phillies, serving as the club's first president and part-owner.

"H.B. Phillips will act as manager of the new club now being organized...Al Reach, the veteran Athletic player, is to act as treasurer of the new club."[2]

Why Reach decided to return to professional baseball as an owner probably is attributable to several factors:[3]

- He missed being part of the game. As a former player, Reach longed to experience the excitement of a baseball season again; if not on the field, then in the front office.[4]
- Reach judged Philadelphia had a sufficient population to support two professional clubs as long as they fielded "first-class" teams.[5]
- He had the capital to finance a team. The sporting goods company Reach owned had made him wealthy.[6]
- Reach believed his club could be profitable.[7] Reviving major league baseball in Philadelphia—where it had been absent since 1876— would spark renewed interest in the game among the city's citizens.
- He relished the opportunity to challenge the Athletics—the city's premier baseball club.[8] The time had come to end that reign.[9]

NO ROOM IN THE AMERICAN ASSOCIATION

The timing of Reach's reentry into professional baseball was heavily influenced by the co-founder of his club, Horace B. Phillips. Manager of the Athletics during most of the 1881 campaign when that club was part of the Eastern Championship Association (ECA), Phillips saw an opportunity in Philadelphia and other large cities that did not have major league baseball teams. Seizing the initiative, he became one of the architects of the American Association (AA), which formed after the 1881 season to challenge the NL's monopoly on major league status.

In September 1881, while still managing the A's, Phillips invited baseball representatives in six cities—Cincinnati, Philadelphia, Pittsburgh, St. Louis, Louisville, and Brooklyn—to attend the inaugural meeting of the Association.[10] These cities were selected because they were not, for a variety of reasons, members of the NL, and because they represented a larger population base than the eight teams comprising that league.[11]

Phillips intended to have his Athletics club represent Philadelphia in the new organization. But fate intervened, and he was released as team manager in early October.[12] If the A's were going to join the association, it would not be with Phillips at the helm. Undaunted, he joined with Reach later that month to organize a second professional club in the city that would petition for admission to the AA.[13]

The association's initial organizational meeting was held in Cincinnati on November 2, 1881. Reach and Phillips attended the meeting at which Reach announced he had "collected a large sum of money for the new club and promised that a first-class team would be placed in the field."[14] But the team's membership posed problems for the association. Establishing franchises in Philadelphia and New York—neither city was represented in the league—was essential to the organization's challenge to the NL's major league baseball monopoly. Its leaders, however, wanted to enroll one club from each city, not two, and the Athletics had also applied to join the association.[15]

As noted, the Athletics had been the lead name in Philadelphia baseball since the 1860s. As John Shiffert has written in his study of the city's early baseball period:

> Although no less [sic] than six organizations would bear this name between 1860 and 1901, including a series of independent professional teams in the late 1870s and early 1880s and a minor league team in the 1890s, there should be no doubt that the best in baseball in Philadelphia in the nineteenth century usually meant Athletic baseball.[16]

For a new baseball organization determined to prove its legitimacy as a major-league alternative to the NL, the choice of which franchise to select was easy for association leaders. Phillips was pressured to combine his bid with the Athletics' application so the two groups would enter the AA as a single franchise.[17] But the amalgamation was purely a face-saving device for Phillips and Reach. Ownership and management of the Athletics had already been established under William Sharsig, Charles Mason, and Chick Fulmer.[18] They had no interest in sharing leadership of the club with Reach and Phillips, especially the latter, whom they had fired as team manager the previous month.

As the AA organized for the 1882 season, Phillips, Reach and their ballclub found themselves excluded from the organization.[19] As one history notes:

> And the City of Brotherly Love had split into two factions again with the Athletics the winner, leaving Horace Phillips, one of the prime movers to create a new major league, for the moment aced out of a spot in it.[20]

Undesirous of operating as an independent amateur club, Phillips and Reach needed to affiliate with another professional baseball organization, and the only one available was the National League. Yet, seemingly insurmountable problems existed with that union as well.

A CIRCUITOUS APPROACH TO NL MEMBERSHIP

The formation of the AA was a nightmare scenario for NL owners, who strived to maintain the league's monopoly on major-league status. Owners could hope the Association would fail, as had other upstart organizations seeking to be recognized as major leagues. But they also understood the disadvantages of having within its ranks teams from cities with smaller populations—Troy and Worcester—and were not about to cede the cities with the greatest populations—Philadelphia and New York—to the AA.[21] Clubs representing those metropolitan areas had been expelled from the league after the 1876 season when they refused to make their final western road trips believing they would lose money because they were out of pennant contention.[22] An embargo on Philadelphia- and New York-based teams remained in effect.[23] In a conversation with a newspaper reporter during the summer of 1881, league president William A. Hulbert explained his unwillingness to remove smaller teams from the NL to make room for clubs from larger cities. The conversation was prompted by a request from the Metropolitans of New York for admission to the league. The reporter wrote:

> President Hulbert has answered the application [from the Metropolitans] in a non-committal manner, saying that he will thoroughly investigate the matter. The chances the Metropolitans have for admission into the League if Hulbert alone is to be consulted may be deemed rather slim, judging from what he recently informed a Chicago reporter. He said that he would never consent to any course toward any member of the body, no matter how weak, looking for securing its withdrawal in order to let in any other

organization, however strong, or however much it might promise in the way of patronage of the game. The present members, who had helped to build up and make the League the success that it is has rights in it, and as long as they did not see fit to withdraw from it, he would vote to retain them to the exclusion of all others. Whether all the eight would elect to remain next year he did not know. If one of them, or two of them, should drop out, there would be so many places to be filled from the most available materials at hand; if not, he did see any chance for outside applicants.[24]

The Metropolitans' application was not approved when NL owners met on December 7, 1881, in part because none of the clubs that composed the NL in 1881 had chosen to leave the league, intending instead to continue as members during the 1882 season.[25] The league also remained bound by Hulbert's prejudices against New York and Philadelphia, whose ouster from the NL he had orchestrated in 1876.[26]

But Hulbert had become seriously ill by the time of the owners meeting in December. Despite his protest that he could no longer continue as league president, Hulbert was reelected to the position.[27] Owners realized retaining him as president would maintain the embargo, but Hulbert was absent from the December meeting because of his illness. This gave NL owners an opportunity to counter the threat posed by the AA's emergence. If they needed a reminder of the magnitude of that menace, it was provided by the *New York Clipper*:

> The six cities represented in the American Association contain over two million inhabitants, while the eight cities of the rival professional association foot up but little more than half that number.[28]

The owners chose an alternative structure to confront the twin challenges of rectifying the sizable population imbalance favoring cities represented in the AA while sustaining the embargo against Philadelphia and New York. This approach would keep clubs based there out of the AA, formally link them to the NL, allow games between teams in those cities and the league to be played during 1882, and position Philadelphia and New York to join the NL in 1883. That was the League Alliance.

THE LEAGUE ALLIANCE

The League Alliance was initially established by the NL in 1877 as a means to extend its control over independent teams across the country. It served several purposes for the league and its members:

- Discouraging contract-jumping and escalating salaries by forbidding clubs from luring players away from alliance teams with offers of more money.
- Allowing games against alliance members to be scheduled on off-days. Doing so would expose baseball to wider audiences and provide potentially lucrative paydays for clubs.
- Creating opportunities to assess alliance clubs and their players for possible future recruitment into the league.
- Dissuading teams that joined the alliance from banding together to organize a second major league that would compete with the NL.[29]

There were minimal requirements for admittance into the League Alliance. Clubs had to agree to play by NL rules and abide by decisions of the league regarding disputes. The league secretary was informed of players under contract to alliance teams so NL clubs would not attempt to sign them.[30]

Estimates of the size and composition of the 1877 alliance vary depending on the source.[31] Twenty-eight clubs were listed as members at various times during 1877, but many disbanded due to insolvency; only five played as many as 30 games against other alliance teams. The organization itself, while continuing to exist formally on paper, became largely dormant after 1877.[32]

At the December 1881 meeting, NL owners revised the league's constitution to resuscitate the League Alliance, make it more sustainable as a business operation, and smooth the way for teams from New York and Philadelphia to gain membership. The most important changes were:

- Any club could join by signing an agreement and paying $25.
- Only one club could join from any city.
- No NL clubs could play games against non-league clubs in any city in which an alliance team was located.
- There would be an alliance championship series.[33]

John B. Day, president of the New York club—formally named the Metropolitans of New York—attended the December meeting as a non-voting member and accepted the offer to join the alliance.[34] In addition, a letter from Reach, in which he agreed to have his Philadelphia club become a member of the alliance, was read to the assemblage.[35] NL owners approved the entry of both into the organization and limited membership to just those clubs.[36] This was done primarily for four reasons:

- It maximized the number of games New York and Philadelphia would play against league teams and each other in anticipation of the cities' admittance to the NL in 1883.
- Games held in the two cities with the largest populations would almost certainly draw the greatest number of fans and prove the most lucrative.
- Having NL clubs visit New York and Philadelphia would whet the appetite of fans eager to see the league return to their cities and play games on a regular basis.
- An alliance team in Philadelphia would deny the Athletics exclusive major league status in the city, and discourage support for the association from taking root there by providing a different professional club to follow.[37]

A newspaper report on Philadelphia's alliance membership noted the franchise had been snubbed by the AA, and identified the great challenge it faced in actually fielding a team:

The Philadelphia Club under the management of H.B. Phillips and Al Reach has been admitted to the League Alliance. This is the same club that the American Association declined admitting, and as yet exists only on paper.[38]

FINDING A HOME
Among the most pressing needs facing Reach in operating his team was finding a ballpark to call home. Fortunately, a location existed that had hosted baseball games since as early as 1860. Recreation Park, positioned at the intersection of 24th Street and Ridge Avenue in what was then an outer portion of Philadelphia, had been the site of home games for multiple amateur clubs and the Centennials of the 1875 National Association.[39] More recently, the Philadelphias ballclub of the 1881 ECA had called it home.[40]

Even before being accepted into the alliance, Reach and Phillips had focused on Recreation Park as the site for their ballclub's home games.[41] Reach sought to secure the facility, but discovered it had been leased for other purposes in 1882.[42] His search broadened, including negotiating for use of the circus lot at Broad

and Federal Streets[43]. Eventually, however, Recreation Park became available, and Reach immediately set about improving the grounds and grandstand, which had fallen into disrepair.[44] A contemporary newspaper account of the upgrades provides an excellent depiction of the ballpark at the start of its tenure as home to Reach's team:

The now handsome grounds of the Philadelphia Club located at Twenty-Fourth Street and Ridge Avenue present a striking contrast to the old rookery which existed there a couple of months ago…The changes effected involve the erection of a substantial fence, and also of a grandstand and four rows of free seats. The main stand has patent perforated folding numbered chairs. In the rear of these chairs are several handsome private boxes, capable of holding four to eight persons. The wings will be seated with regular chairs, the entire stand accommodating fully 1,500 persons. Along the left and right field fences seats with foot-rests will be provided sufficient for 2,000 people. The field has been plowed up, sodded and rolled, and is in splendid condition for ball playing…At the sides of the grandstand, dressing rooms for the players and offices for the managers have been erected. On top of the grandstand a handsome reporters' stand has been placed.[45]

THE ROSTER
With their club admitted to the League Alliance and their ballpark being readied for the upcoming season, Reach and Phillips had to move quickly to assemble a roster.[46] If their team did not play top-flight baseball, fans would desert it, especially given the alternative of watching the Athletics play at Oakdale Park.[47]

Unexpectedly, finding a new manager for the club became part of this challenge. In early January 1882, Phillips resigned as manager and "severed all official connection with the Philadelphia Baseball Club." This decision and its timing appear odd given the efforts Phillips had put into forming the club. According to a newspaper report on his decision:

[Phillips]) intends hereafter to devote his entire and strict attention to the superintendency of lacrosse, football, lawn-tennis, polo, bicycling and other kindred sports at Twenty-Fourth Street and Ridge Avenue, Philadelphia.[48]

With Phillips's departure, operation of the Philadelphia club came under the sole purview of Reach. It was apparent, however, he did not want to include field manager among his duties. His tenure in the role was characterized as "temporary" until a new manager could be found.[49] By Opening Day in early April, John Manning was performing as the team's player-manager.[50] Phillips returned soon thereafter as field manager, but he would resign the role a second time before the season had concluded (see below).

Reach assembled a group of players with considerable professional baseball experience, despite the limited time. Moreover, with the notable exception of catcher, the position players remained for the most part in their roles throughout the season, a remarkable achievement for a newly formed club.

A review of the lineups the Philadelphia club fielded in games during 1882 shows the seven position players comprising the regular starting lineup in June still were part of it in October.[51] A review of their baseball careers reveals the majority had prior NL experience before joining Reach's team:[52]

John "Pop" Corkhill, 1B[53]	No prior experience
Tim Manning, 2B	Providence, 1882
Arlie Latham, 3B	Buffalo, 1880
William McClellan, SS	Chicago, 1878; Providence, 1881
Mike Moynahan, LF	Buffalo, 1880; Detroit, 1881; Cleveland, 1881
Fred Lewis, CF	Boston, 1881
John Manning, RF	Boston, 1876, 1878; Cincinnati, 1877, 1880; Buffalo, 1881

Three of these players—McClellan, Lewis, and John Manning—would go on to play for the Philadelphia Club when it joined the NL in 1883, while Moynahan would sign with the Athletics in 1883. The others would also continue their careers in professional baseball after 1882 with various NL and AA clubs.[54]

The position that proved most vexing for Reach to fill was catcher. The club experimented with nine different players at the position during the season, all of whom displayed various shortcomings. Joe Straub was the regular catcher during the first months of the season, but the team's dissatisfaction with him was evident in its periodic audition of other players at the position.[55] None of the potential replacements lasted very long, and the club eventually dismissed Straub himself because, according to one newspaper report, of his "inability to throw."[56]

The peripatetic Phillips furnished a partial, short-term remedy. Having resigned his position as manager before the season started, Phillips did so again in July 1882, announcing he would organize a team to represent Indianapolis in the AA for the 1883 season.[57]

William Barnie, who had been managing the independent Atlantics of Brooklyn club, was hired to manage the Philadelphia club after Phillips resigned, a position Barnie would hold for the rest of the season.[58] Barnie also happened to be an accomplished catcher, having played for teams in the National Association.[59] When the club finally tired of Straub's erratic throwing and released him, Barnie occasionally stepped in as catcher. He wanted to manage, not catch, however, and the club continued to audition catchers during games in September and October. None proved to be the answer; Reach's team never found a long-term solution to its catching conundrum during the season.[60]

There were eight players on the team who appeared in almost 67 percent of Philadelphia's games in 1882. Only one player, John Manning, appeared in every game.[61] The roster fluctuated despite the stability these players provided to the lineup throughout the season. Reach, Phillips, and Barnie had to contend with player turnover while maintaining the team's cohesion and improving its performance on the field.[62] Players who appeared briefly for the club and then disappeared included infielder Frank Fennelly and outfielder Elmer Foster.[63]

Other players, such as Joe Battin and Frank Gardner, stayed longer with the Philadelphias but were still gone before the season ended. Released by the club in June, Battin signed to play with the independent Atlantics. After a few weeks with that team, Battin became something of a nomad. He umpired some games in the AA, but also played for various independent clubs during the rest of the season.[64] Gardner played outfield and occasionally pitched for the Philadelphias during the first part of the season, but suffered an ignoble end with the team. He was suspended in early August for what was termed, "indifferent play." Another account of the incident attributed Gardner's suspension to "alleged dissipation."[65]

Philadelphia's pitching staff in 1882 was astonishingly constant because two men started over 86 percent of the games. The first incredible iron man in the box was Jack Neagle.[66] He started 68 games, 49 percent of the total the team played that year.[67] As amazing, he finished all but two games he started.[68] Neagle's record at the end of the season was 23 wins, 42 losses, and three ties.[69] Hardly a commendable won-lost total, but a remarkable feat of endurance in terms of a single-season load for one pitcher.[70]

Neagle was out for ten days in May after being injured in a game, which undoubtedly cost him two or three starts[71] Moreover, when not hurling the ball, Neagle could be found patrolling the outfield in games, mostly in right field, but occasionally in left.[72]

That Neagle was a prized pitcher—as much for his endurance as his skill—was evident in the fact the Eclipse club tried to sign him for the 1883 season before the 1882 season concluded. The first report that talks were underway appeared in August, but they ultimately proved unfruitful. According to a newspaper article, "It is said that Neagle wanted $100 advance money, and that negotiations dropped right there."[73] The pitcher opened 1883 with Philadelphia, but shifted to Baltimore and then Allegheny—both in the AA—before the season concluded.[74]

The other iron man pitcher was Hardie Henderson. He had no professional baseball experience before 1882, but proved almost as durable as Neagle and ended the season with a winning record.[75] Henderson started 52 games for Philadelphia in 1882, 37 percent of the games the team played that year. By the end of the season, he compiled a record of 28 wins, 21 losses, and three ties.[76] With the exception of one game, furthermore, he finished them all.[77] Like Neagle, Henderson could be found playing the outfield, mostly right field, in some games when he wasn't in the box.[78]

Henderson joined Neagle in staying with Philadelphia when the team transitioned to the NL in 1883, but only for a single game. In it, he gave up 24 runs over nine innings and was gone from the roster. Henderson migrated to the Baltimore club of the AA later in the season and lost 105 games with that team 1883–86. He concluded his big-league career by pitching for the AA's Brooklyns in 1887 and the NL's Pittsburgh club in 1888.[79]

A few other pitchers made cameo appearances for Philadelphia in 1882. One with the last name of "Buffington" [sic] started two games early in the season.[80] Philadelphia played its second game on the schedule on April 11, and he was trotted out against the NL's Providence Grays, a formidable team that had finished in second place in 1881. Offering up a rookie pitcher against such a tough opponent didn't turn out well:

The home team presented Buffington in the pitcher's position, and he proved to be the weakest point, his wild delivery materially assisting the boys from Providence in running up their score…The experiment of placing such an inexperienced man as Buffington in the pitcher's

position against such a nine as Providence will not bear repetition.[81]

Suffering a 19–6 drubbing in that contest, the team remedied the situation by assigning Buffington to make his second start against a local amateur club, Young America, on April 22 at Recreation Park. He rose to the occasion by throwing the first no-hitter in the Philadelphia club's history. One member of the opposing team reached first base on an error, and two others received free passes on walks.[82]

Norm Baker was another rookie pitcher who had a two-game stint with Philadelphia. He started consecutive games on September 6 and 7, competing against amateur teams. Philadelphia won both games by the scores of 13–3 and 5–2, respectively.[83] Baker did not return to Philadelphia the next year, but instead, played for Allegheny in the AA. He spent the rest of his brief professional career in the association, pitching for Louisville in 1885 and Baltimore in 1890.[84]

THE 1882 SEASON
Philadelphia's opponents during the 1882 season can be divided into three groups: the League Alliance Championship Series against the Metropolitans; NL and AA teams; and amateur clubs. Research done for this paper unveiled 139 games played by the Philadelphias that year. Overall, the team finished the season with a 67–66–6 record. Appendix A lists the dates, opponents, final scores, decisions, attendance, and home/away venue for the games.

LEAGUE ALLIANCE CHAMPIONSHIP SERIES
When the Metropolitan and Philadelphia clubs joined the League Alliance in December 1881, a provision was enacted that the two clubs would play a championship series,[86] which would comprise 24 games.[87] New York demonstrated its superiority, as the Metropolitans won their thirteenth game of the series on July 26, and claimed the League Alliance Championship.[88] At that point, the Philadelphias had gained only five wins with one game tied. The games were mostly competitive, however, and drew sizable crowds at the Polo Grounds and Recreation Park, much to the delight of club owners.

One game of the series is exceptional because it illustrates vividly how much baseball has evolved—at least in one important regard—since 1882. Played at Recreation Park on May 17, the Metropolitans won, 12–6. But what caught the attention of a sportswriter who reported the results was the number of balls used during the game:

That the contest was no ordinary one is proved by the fact that it took three balls to finish it. The first ball Corkhill hit foul over the fence, and it was rendered useless by being run over by a Ridge Avenue [trolley] car. The second the same player hit foul through a [trolley] window, and cut the covering.[89]

Although estimates vary, a generally accepted, frequently cited figure is that eight to ten dozen baseballs are used on average in a nine-inning baseball game now.[90]

With the League Alliance championship decided—despite five games remaining between Philadelphia and the Metropolitans—and almost half the baseball season still to play, a dilemma arose of how to sustain fan interest in the rivalry.[91] To the rescue came a Philadelphia "gentleman who admires the sport." He offered as a prize "a valuable silver punch bowl" to the winner of a new 12-game series between the Metropolitans and Philadelphia.[92] Both clubs accepted and revised their schedules to allow for the extra games. The battle for the trophy began on August 31.[93]

The new series started auspiciously for Philadelphia, winning the first four games. But the Mets stormed back to win five in a row and take a one-game lead in the race for the punch bowl. Reach's team tied the series by winning the tenth game in what was proving to be a very exciting competition. (See Appendix A for the dates and scores of these games.) The outcome of the 11th game, however, was mired in controversy that marred the series conclusion.

The contest was played in Philadelphia on October 24. In what turned out to be a regrettable decision, Reach was selected to umpire the match. At the end of the sixth inning, the Philadelphias led, 1–0, and claimed darkness had made the ball almost impossible to see. The Metropolitans, however, insisted on continuing play, and scored two runs in the top of the seventh inning to take the lead. Philadelphia had two outs in the bottom of the seventh when Reach suddenly called the game on account of darkness. With his decision, the score reverted back to the last completed inning, and Philadelphia won the game 1–0, taking a 6–5 lead in the series. New York players howled in anger at what they regarded as Reach's biased decision to keep his team from losing the game.[94]

The Metropolitans were in a foul mood when they took the field at Recreation Park on October 25 to play the final game of the series, believing they had been cheated the day before. According to one newspaper account of the contest, "The 'Mets' disputed every decision made by the umpire [Charles Fulmer] that was not in their favor, and in return, were hooted and jeered by the crowd." The visitors won the game, 9–4, thereby tying the series again, 6–6.[95]

Reach offered what were described as "extra inducements" to the Mets to play a tie-breaking game on October 26, but they refused to stay over "on account of dissatisfaction at Reach's action in calling the game on October 24."[96] Thus, the New York-Philadelphia rivalry ended indecisively. While the series served its purpose in attracting good-sized crowds, the trophy went unclaimed.

GAMES AGAINST NATIONAL LEAGUE AND AMERICAN ASSOCIATION CLUBS
National League

It was up to Philadelphia and the Metropolitans to schedule their games against NL and AA opponents during the latter's off-days. Financially, both teams had every incentive to maximize the number of games against professional competition because they would draw the largest crowds. Reach wasted no time trying to arrange matches.

At the March 7, 1882, NL owners meeting in Rochester, New York, Reach attended as a non-voting delegate representing his Philadelphia club, as did John B. Day for the Metropolitans. The 1882 NL schedule was approved at the meeting, and with its adoption, open dates were identified when NL teams would be available to play alliance clubs. Despite his best efforts, Reach secured only one date—a game against the Detroit Wolverines in Philadelphia on May 29.[97]

Undaunted, Reach continued his efforts and a month later had scheduled 30 games involving all NL clubs except Worcester.[98] More games would be added as time passed, including against Worcester, and by the time the season ended, Philadelphia had played 65 games against NL opposition.[99]

The Philadelphias played all of their games against NL clubs at home, contributing significantly to a major imbalance in the number of home versus away games Reach's club played in 1882. At season's end, the final tally was 111 home games and 28 games on the road.[100] (See Appendix A)

NL owners had compelling reasons to allow Reach's team to host all the games their clubs played against Philadelphia:

- They were eager to discover if enough fans would go to games throughout the season to warrant, from a financial perspective, adding the city to the league's ranks. This was especially important given the presence of another major-league franchise in Philadelphia and the NL's goal of adding "big market" clubs to its structure while shedding "small market" teams.

- Games in Philadelphia would likely draw bigger crowds than if the Philadelphias traveled to NL ballparks to play. Fans in those cities wanted to see their teams play major-league caliber talent, not newly formed, adjunct alliance clubs of lesser ability.
- Limiting travel expenses for Philadelphia would alleviate costs associated with operating the franchise; in particular, during its inaugural season when the club was still organizing and establishing its financial foundation.

In addition to permitting their teams to be the visitors in all games against Philadelphia and the Metropolitans, NL owners pledged not to play any other clubs located in or near those cities.[101] Despite these generous terms, the owners also enacted provisions governing compensation to ensure they would not lose money in doing so. When NL clubs played each other, the home team was obliged to guarantee the visiting club $100 in compensation; if money received in gate receipts exceeded $200, then the visiting club would receive half of that amount.[102] The same arrangement would apply in games hosted by alliance clubs. Moreover, if an NL team traveled to a League Alliance city and the game was postponed due to inclement weather, the visiting club would still be guaranteed a $50 payment.[103] Although Reach and Day pleaded for more lenient treatment at the March League meeting, given their clubs were not full members of the NL, they were rebuffed and forced to accept the terms.[104] The potentially adverse consequences were noted in a newspaper article that opined, "The Philadelphias very unwisely have submitted to the league's demands, and consequently are in danger of being financially swamped."[105]

Given the NL's determination to run a "clean" sport, Philadelphia and the Metropolitans also were required to take steps to prohibit gambling at their ballparks—a scourge that had tainted professional baseball's reputation for honest games in the past. The Philadelphias announced no open betting would be allowed at Recreation Park during the season, nor would the club permit telegraph wires to be connected from the grounds to city pool rooms where off-site betting on sporting events was concentrated. This was intended to thwart game updates from being communicated almost instantly from the ballpark to the gambling dens.[106]

A concession Philadelphia and the Metropolitans were able to obtain from NL owners was to charge a 25-cent admission fee for their games, half the NL minimum of 50 cents.[107] Since neither club was actually in the NL, the reasoning was that people would be less willing to pay the league price to attend games. The arrangement worked out well for the NL and Philadelphia. In a revealing comparison of gate receipts for games against other league clubs versus those for games in Philadelphia, Detroit manager Frank Bancroft offered the following figures:

> On the Detroits' Eastern trip, recently closed, their share at Worcester for three games, at 50¢ admission, was $112; at Troy three games, $196; at Providence, three games, $496; at Boston, three games, $481; a total of $1,258 Against this, to prove that more money could be made at 25¢ admission, Bancroft gives his share of five games with the Philadelphia Club as follows: First game, $105; second, $217; third, $311; fourth, $223; fifth, $500; a total of $1,356, beating the League $98, with seven games to spare.[108]

Though enjoying home field advantage in every game against NL clubs, Reach's team compiled a woeful 15–45–5 record in those contests.[109] Collectively, the outcomes confirmed Philadelphia would have a long way to go to become competitive after joining the NL. Even with all the losing, however, robust crowds filled Recreation Park to watch their home team take on league opponents. Rarely did fewer than 1,000 fans sit in the stands, and attendance often exceeded that number.[110] (See Appendix A.) For this reason, the club's win-loss record was not the most important measure of success. The season demonstrated Philadelphia could support an NL franchise; that was the most significant and enduring outcome of the games Reach's team played against league clubs in 1882.

American Association

Reach longed to play the Athletics more than any other club. Pride played a role in his outlook; Reach wanted to dethrone the A's as the city's preeminent baseball club. He also needed to demonstrate to Philadelphia fans that his club could compete successfully at the professional level, and was not a second-class organization. In addition, dollar signs swirled in Reach's mind when he envisioned spectators pouring into Recreation Park to watch games against his team's intra-city rivals.

The evidence for such optimism was considerable as newspaper coverage stoked the city's interest in the upcoming series:

The chief topic in baseball circles in Philadelphia, Pa., is the inaugural contest between the Athletic and Philadelphia Clubs for the local championship…The attendance, it is estimated, will be about the largest ever chronicled in the annals of baseball in the Quaker City.[111]

The only hitch in arranging the first game was the location. Both clubs wanted it at their home ballpark, believing the inaugural game would draw the largest crowd of the series. Moreover, instead of dividing gate receipts evenly, the Athletics and Philadelphias wanted the entire receipts from games at their ballparks.[112] It was eventually decided the A's would host the first contest—not a surprise given the franchise's predominant stature in the city—and the Philadelphias would be the home team for the second game, which would follow two days later.

The initial game at Oakdale Park on May 20 attracted an estimated 10,000 fans—the largest crowd to witness the Philadelphias play in 1882.[113] The closely contested affair was followed with "almost breathless interest" by spectators who saw the visitors eke out a 7–6 victory by scoring a run in the ninth inning.[114]

The crowd that attended the second game played on May 22 at Recreation Park—while somewhat smaller in size—was treated to another tense match:

Never was there a more exciting game of baseball played than that yesterday between the Athletics and Philadelphia Clubs, which was won by the latter after ten innings had been played by a score of 6 to 5. Between seven and eight thousand people paid the admission fee to Recreation Park, while fully a thousand more witnessed the contest from the windows and roofs of surrounding houses. All the railways leading to Twenty-Fourth Street and Columbia Avenue ran loaded cars as early as two o'clock, and by three o'clock all the available seating capacity was crowded, while the people were still coming in droves. A portion of the right and left field was roped off to make room for the crowd, and when the game commenced there was not room for even one more.[115]

Amid the euphoria generated by the first two games, a third game was scheduled between the teams at Recreation Park on May 26. But the newspaper article describing the success of game two contained an ominous addendum that raised doubts the series would continue: "There is talk of trouble over playing the full series, as previously agreed upon."[116]

The trouble resulted from two factors. First, the NL's opposition to the AA becoming a second major league. The senior league chose to dismiss the association as a substandard enterprise, offering an inferior product on the field. Refusing to recognize the major league status of the AA led to considerable friction between it and the NL.[117] Second, the inclination of players to "jump" teams for better paychecks. NL clubs were prohibited from signing players who jumped from other league franchises. In addition, they could not play teams who had on their rosters players who had jumped from an NL club. Players who did so were blacklisted. Owners were not precluded, however, from signing players who jumped from clubs outside the league.[118]

John "Dasher" Troy signed to play with the Athletics for the 1882 season, but then altered course and signed with the NL's Detroit Wolverines. Association officials immediately protested Detroit's action and characterized the move as an attempt by the league to break up the AA.[119] They insisted Detroit rescind the signing and tell Troy to honor his contract with the Athletics. Detroit balked, however, and the association retaliated by declaring Troy its first blacklisted player. In addition, AA officials announced that not only would association teams decline to play the Wolverines, they would also refuse to schedule games against any clubs that played Detroit.[120]

The Philadelphias were scheduled to play their first game against the Wolverines on May 29, and the Athletics signaled their objections to Reach by "indefinitely postponing" the game scheduled for May 26. The ostensible reason given was that the A's had to play a makeup game against the St. Louis Browns that had been canceled due to inclement weather earlier in the season. But scheduling the makeup game at the last moment to deliberately conflict with the May 26 game, and leaving open-ended when the game against the Philadelphias would be rescheduled, were intended to send an unmistakable message to Reach. Don't play Detroit while Troy is on the team's roster, or there will be no more games with the Athletics.[121]

The Philadelphias-Wolverines game occurred despite the warning. Reach had little choice as a member of the League Alliance with aspirations to join the NL. To refuse to play Detroit because it had signed Troy was sure to rile league owners, who could inflict far greater punishment on the Philadelphias by ordering all NL clubs not to play games against them, and perhaps even expel the franchise from the alliance.

Front cover of Phillies' 1882 scorecard featuring an artist's depiction of Recreation Park and the various sports played at the site—baseball, bicycling, foot races, etc. The name of the visiting team would be changed each series.

As expected, the association exacted retribution by preventing its teams from playing any additional games against the Philadelphias. The two games in May against the Athletics were the only ones Reach's team would play against AA opponents in 1882.[122]

NL owners, realizing the financial drawbacks of the AA boycott, attempted to resolve the dispute over Dasher Troy in late June.[123] If the association would reinstate him, then Detroit would release Troy to return to the Athletics. In a move that must have aggravated Reach, NL owners sweetened the pot by offering the A's the opportunity to play all league clubs in Philadelphia after September 30. The Philadelphias would no longer have the exclusive right to play NL teams in the city for the last month of the season. The Athletics refused to consider the proposition.[124]

The breech between the NL and AA widened as the 1882 season progressed. One sportswriter assessed, "The prospect of an amicable adjustment of the difficulty is very dim."[125] The confrontation was aggravated by the continuing propensity of players to sign with a club in either the AA or NL, and then renege to sign at a higher salary with a team in the other organization. For example:

> (Charlie) Bennett of the Detroits, who had signed to play with the Allegheny Club next season for $1,700 and who had received a bonus of $500 now seeks to recede from his contract in order to play with a League nine. The Allegheny directors refuse to take the money back, and threaten to expel Bennett unless he lives up to his contract.[126]

President Denny McKnight of the AA "declared war to the knife" with the NL over the issue of signing players who had jumped their contracts with the AA, and "promises that the names of many prominent players of the League, and, perhaps, managers, will appear on the black list of his Association."[127] Peace would not come between the association and league until after the 1882 season had concluded.[128]

GAMES AGAINST AMATEUR CLUBS

Although not nearly as lucrative at the gate as games against major-league clubs, Reach was obliged to schedule numerous contests against amateur competition—independent and college clubs. Doing so avoided big gaps in the schedule—a failing of the original 1877 League Alliance—and gave his players additional experience individually and as a team.[129] While Reach had no illusions that matches against amateur players would be huge money-makers, he also realized a home game with a few hundred fans in the stands was more profitable than an empty ballpark with no game scheduled. His financial position also was strengthened by the fact that guaranteed minimum payments, and 50–50 sharing of gate receipts required for games against NL teams, did not apply when amateur clubs visited Recreation Park. Reach further maximized the potential profitability of these games by scheduling most of them against local/regional amateur competitors. This reduced transportation costs and encouraged fans of amateur teams to attend games at Recreation Park by minimizing the distance they had to travel.

The Philadelphias played 40 games against independent and college clubs in 1882, racking up an impressive tally of 38 wins and two losses. This lopsided victory total enabled Reach's team to squeeze out an overall winning average (.503) for the season. (See Appendix A.)

Despite almost always losing against the Philadelphias, most amateur clubs gained a big advantage in playing Reach's team by having some of the games played at their ballparks. While matches at Recreation Park would hopefully cover an amateur club's costs and perhaps even generate a small profit, games against Philadelphia at home held the prospect of a big payday because they would likely draw larger crowds than games against other amateur clubs.[130]

Variations in the number of times the Philadelphias visited the home ballparks of amateur teams were considerable. For example, Reach's team played the Merritts of Camden, New Jersey, three times at Recreation Park and once at the Merritts' ballpark. The Trenton, New Jersey, club was visited three times by the Philadelphias, while the Trentons played at Recreation Park only once. The Atlantic City, New Jersey, nine played in Philadelphia on four occasions, but never hosted Reach's team at home.[131]

With the exception of the series against the Metropolitans, the only away games the Philadelphias played in 1882 were against independent and college clubs. Most were located in New Jersey, but Reach's team traveled to New Haven, Connecticut, in May to play the Yale College team twice.[132] In addition, the Philadelphias made their only "western" road trip in September to play three games sequentially in the Pennsylvania cities of Reading, Pottsville, and Harrisburg.[133]

In addition to playing professional teams at their home ballparks, amateur franchises also were untrammeled by the squabbling that prevented NL and AA clubs from playing each other during most of the 1882 season. Amateur teams displayed no favoritism in arranging home and away games against members of both organizations, nor did league and association clubs seem to mind the crossover in scheduling. For example, the Brooklyn Atlantics traveled to Recreation Park to battle the Philadelphias on April 12, losing badly, 15–1. Then, the Atlantics took on the Athletics at Oakdale Park on April 15 and were again pummeled, 25–7.[134]

With some exceptions, games against amateur opponents at Recreation Park drew crowds in the low hundreds. There were, nevertheless, several noteworthy contests during the season that attracted a greater number of fans, and that constituted important "firsts" for the Philadelphia club as part of its inaugural campaign:

- As noted previously, a pitcher named "Buffington" [sic] threw the first no-hitter in club history on April 22. The second no-hitter occurred at home on May 1 when Hardie Henderson faced the Merritt nine "who did not make a base hit during the game." Only three of the visitors reached base—two on walks and one on an error. The Philadelphias coasted to an 8–0 victory.[135]

- In what was attributed to a "misunderstanding," Buffalo was supposed to play the Philadelphias on June 13—the Bisons' first visit to the city—but instead, played Worcester that day. An estimated 3,000-4,000 people were outside Recreation Park waiting for the gates to open when it was announced the game would not be held. To not disappoint the crowd, an impromptu game was hastily arranged that featured Reach's team against a "Picked Nine," consisting of Philadelphias and amateur players. Most people left, but around 1,000 of them paid to watch the game, which Philadelphia won, 12–5.[136] Manager Phillips displayed a letter from Buffalo manager Jim O'Rourke after the game accepting June 13 as a date to play the Philadelphias. O'Rourke was severely criticized within baseball circles for failing to keep the engagement.[137]

- The Philadelphias played the Orion Club of Philadelphia at Recreation Park on July 19, their first game against a "colored" team. In yet another no-hitter, Neagle struck out 14 batters, including striking out the side in the seventh and eighth innings. The home team won convincingly, 17–1 in a game that was witnessed by 2,000 spectators, "one third of them colored." It was the only game played by Reach's team against a "colored" club that season.[138]

- In another first for the Philadelphias, a team from a foreign country came to town to play a baseball game. The Atlantics of St. Thomas, Canada, visited for a two-game series on August 16 and 17. The Atlantics "were the championship baseball nine of Canada," and their roster was composed of "picked players from the Dominion." The initial contest ended with Reach's club on top, 7–4. The Canadians played a competitive game "but lacked the experience necessary to cope successfully against such a nine as their opponents." Neagle was in the box for the Philadelphias, and he tallied 11 strikeouts as Atlantic players were unable to overcome his "curved pitching."[139] In the second game, the Philadelphia nine again prevailed by a score of 2–0. Henderson handcuffed the

Canadians in the contest. Each game attracted 800 people to the ballpark.[140]

By the end of the 1882 season, scheduling games against amateur clubs had clearly served its intended purpose. It avoided long periods of idleness in the Philadelphias' schedule, crowd size was respectable—and sometimes more than that—at most games, and the contests helped Reach's team take a key developmental step in preparing for its ascension to the National League.

MOVING UP TO THE NATIONAL LEAGUE

There was never any doubt Philadelphia's and the Metropolitans' admittance to a resurrected League Alliance in 1882 was an interim step to facilitate their membership in the NL the following year. Their path was made that much easier when league president William Hulbert died on April 10, 1882. With his passing, resistance within the league's leadership to welcoming both cities into the fold ended. Arthur Soden, who favored dropping small market teams from the league's ranks and replacing them with clubs from large metropolitan areas, succeeded Hulbert as president.[141]

That the Troy and Worcester franchises were on the chopping block was no secret as the 1882 campaign progressed. As early as July, rumors were rife that Philadelphia would take Worcester's place in the league.[142] Confirmation of same came at the NL owners meeting in Philadelphia on September 22. It was announced that Troy and Worcester had resigned from the league effective at the end of the season, and that the Metropolitans and Philadelphias had filed applications for membership to replace them. The reason cited by the league for Troy's and Worcester's decision was that the clubs had "fared very badly during the last few seasons, both financially and in the race for the pennant…So by allowing the Empire and Quaker Cities to fill the places left vacant by the retirement of Troy and Worcester every other club in the association will benefit by it financially."[143]

When the applications for withdrawal were presented at the owners meeting, not a single delegate objected, according to one newspaper report. Confirmation that the resulting openings were reserved for New York and Philadelphia came when the league received and promptly rejected applications from several AA clubs to join.[144]

Officials of the Troy and Worcester franchises denied vehemently they had voluntarily resigned their memberships in the NL, claiming that a resolution forcing them out had been introduced at the meeting and passed 6–2 (Troy and Worcester voting in the negative). But the die was cast. League owners had determined neither city had a sufficient population to give visiting clubs a share of gate money adequate to pay their expenses. In one sportswriter's opinion, "It was simply a question of business whether two non-paying cities should be continued in the co-partnership when two paying cities could be secured to take their place."[145]

With Worcester's demise official, several players began leaving the team at the end of September to play out the season with other clubs. After Worcester's last game, Jackie Hayes, an able catcher, joined the Philadelphias. His acquisition held the prospect of solving the team's catching problem. Hayes's first game with his new club was on October 4 against the Buffalo Bisons. A game summary lauded his performance:

> Hayes, late of the Worcesters, made his first appearance with the home nine, and his playing behind the plate was the feature of the game. He put out two, assisted twice, had no errors and made two base hits and two runs.[146]

After the game, Hayes succeeded in getting a ten-dollar advance on his salary from Manager Barnie, and then skipped town with the Bisons to finish up the season with that club. The irony of Hayes jumping from Worcester to Philadelphia—the club that would replace Worcester in the NL—and then jumping after one game to another league team after he extracted an advance on his salary—presumably was not lost on Reach or Barnie.[147]

The applications from New York and Philadelphia would be decided at the December owners meeting, but in a surprising development—given all the work that had been done to facilitate their membership—the Metropolitans decided in October to join the AA in 1883.[148] Another New York-based club, the New Yorks, took its place in the league.[149]

At the December 7, 1882, NL owners meeting in Providence, Philadelphia and New York were admitted as members of the league.[150] Given how histories of the franchise portray Reach's eagerness to join the NL, this should have been a joyous moment for him.[151] But was it? The Metropolitans had already decided to abandon the league in favor of membership in the association, and there is evidence Reach was also reconsidering. A newspaper article revealed threats were necessary to convince him to follow through on the club's application to join the league:

The reason that the Philadelphia Club entered the League was because Al Reach was told that if he did not, a League club would be placed in Philadelphia which would throw out the League Alliance Club.[152]

Whatever doubts Reach harbored about becoming a member of the NL in 1883 were almost certainly attributable to the less favorable financial position his team would inhabit compared to participating in the League Alliance in 1882:

- The club would be compelled to charge the league minimum admittance fee of 50 cents, versus the 25 cents it charged while a member of the alliance. As Bancroft's figures, cited earlier, illustrate, a 100 percent increase in the admittance fee for a ticket might dissuade people from attending games.

- Reach's costs for operating the club would increase dramatically once a member of the NL. In 1882, Philadelphia was able to play 80 percent (111 of 139) of its games at home, including all of the matches against NL opponents. The balance would shift to a 50–50 split as Reach's team would be scheduled to play half its games at home and half on the road against league teams. The hike in away games meant travel costs—transportation, meals, and accommodations—would escalate dramatically for Philadelphia in 1883.

- As a member of the NL, games against amateur clubs dropped off the schedule.[153] In 1882, the Philadelphias played 30 percent (40 of 139) of their games against such teams, and of those, 70 percent (28 of 40) were played at home. Eliminating those matches also contributed to Reach's team spending much more time on the road in 1883, thereby increasing travel costs further.

- More games against NL opponents in 1883 (99) versus 1882 (65) would cause Reach to share a greater percentage of gate receipts with visiting teams, as league rules mandated. The more unfavorable split in ticket revenue was especially apparent with the simultaneous deletion of games against amateur clubs from the schedule. Reach got to keep a greater percentage of the admission fees from the latter matches.[154]

- Reach also recognized that despite his club having a year of experience and retaining some players from the 1882 roster, the 1883 Philadelphias were still going to have a difficult time competing against other NL clubs. He must have wondered if spectators would come to the ballpark to see his team lose many more games than it won, especially as the season continued. Reach's worst fears were realized when the club posted a 17–81 record. Over 135 years later, this remains the worst winning percentage in a season for the franchise.[155]

Operating the Philadelphias during their inaugural year in the NL was expensive, and Reach lost money.[156] Some believed he had erred, and suggested he cut his losses by bailing out of the enterprise.[157] It is doubtful they fully appreciated that Reach—faced with a threat from NL owners to place another franchise in Philadelphia if he did not join the league—had little choice but to acquiesce and persevere.[158] To his credit, moreover, Reach remained determined to make his club the premier baseball team in the city.

Whatever misgivings Reach may have held about the future, participating in the League Alliance was a crucial step in the emergence of the Philadelphia National League Baseball Club. It provided a necessary segue for his team to form, organize, and mature in preparation for becoming a major-league franchisee the next year. The alliance experience also proved to NL owners that Philadelphia's membership in the league was advantageous, and that the city could support two professional clubs simultaneously, even when the marquee Athletics belonged to a rival organization. The League Alliance experiment worked. Philadelphia remains a member of MLB, while the Athletics and AA have long since receded into baseball history.

THE NICKNAME CONUNDRUM

The Philadelphia National League Club's longstanding nickname of "Phillies" has been deliberately omitted from the text until this point to separately examine how this name emerged and became associated with Reach's club. Also requiring investigation is the commonly held belief the Philadelphia franchise had a nickname other than Phillies at its outset.

The corporate name of Reach's franchise in early 1882 was the Philadelphia Ball Club and Sporting Association. Later that year, it was changed to the Philadelphia Ball Club and Exhibition Company.[159] This author has been unable to discover any information from contemporary sources affirming the Philadelphia club officially adopted a specific nickname during this period.[160] The only evidence from a club official that Phillies was the preferred sobriquet comes from a quotation attributed to Reach that has been cited in some histories of the team. The moniker allegedly appealed to Reach because, "It tells you who we are and where we're from."[161] When it is used in secondary publications, however, no citation is provided referencing a primary source where the quotation first appeared. Moreover, research by this author has failed to discover the quotation in any source contemporary to the period. This author questions whether Reach actually uttered those words, and suspects the quotation was later attributed to him as a simple and convenient way to explain how the Philadelphia NL team got its nickname.

In addition, judgments that Reach originated Phillies as a creative yet sensible moniker for his team ignores the fact it predates his club. In 1881, two Philadelphia-based teams joined the newly-created Eastern Championship Association. One was the well-established Athletics, and the other was an embryonic club to which the sobriquet Phillies was attached in newspaper game reporting.[162] That represented the first application of the nickname to a Philadelphia baseball club. The team lasted only a month before folding—a fate that befell many franchises of that era. Nevertheless, Reach didn't invent the name Phillies for his club. Sportswriters simply transferred it from the previous year's Philadelphia team upon which the nickname had been bestowed.[163] Reach's Phillies were regarded as the successor to the ECA Phillies, and for that reason inherited the same nickname.

Some histories of the Philadelphia NL franchise date the Phillies nickname to 1883 when the club joined the NL.[164] This is erroneous. When used in reference to Reach's team, the sobriquet first appeared in the *Philadelphia Inquirer* on April 14, 1882, in a description of a game the Phillies played the previous day at Recreation Park against Princeton College.[165] The moniker continued to appear periodically in city newspapers throughout the rest of the Phillies' season in the League Alliance.[166] Newspapers published in other cities also identified the club as the Phillies in their reporting.[167]

If frequency of a nickname contained in newspaper coverage is the best indicator of validity, then there is no question Reach's club was called the "Philadelphias." That moniker appeared far more frequently in period newspaper reporting than any other referring to the ballclub. Additional terms used periodically to identify the team included "Philadelphia Club" and "Philadelphia nine."[168] But none was used as often as Philadelphias, and it continued to be the dominant nickname for the team in newspaper reporting for several years until Phillies eventually supplanted it.

Some histories of the Philadelphia NL Baseball Club state the team's first nickname was "Quakers," which was later superseded by Phillies. For example, David Nemec, in his book on nineteeth century baseball, identifies the franchise as the Philadelphia Quakers for 1883–84, and then updates the moniker for the 1885 season and beyond by replacing Quakers with Phillies.[169] Other team histories judge the nickname was Phillies from the beginning.[170]

Regarding the genesis of "Quakers," Lieb writes, "The nickname of the old National Association Philadelphias—the Quakers—persisted, and for years a number of Philadelphia dailies preferred to refer to the new club as the Quakers."[171] That is an odd explanation for Quakers being the first nickname since none of the Philadelphia-based members of the National Association (NA), which operated 1871–75, had that moniker.[172] While some newspapers may have used Quakers to refer to Reach's team, others did not. For example, the *Philadelphia Inquirer*—a major newspaper in the city—did not used it once in its reporting on the club over the 1882–83 seasons; nor did the *New York Clipper*, which provided extensive coverage of major league baseball over those years, including games played by Philadelphia teams. This author judges as dubious the proposition Quakers was the official—or even commonly-accepted—nickname of the team given its absence in major newspaper coverage of the club at the time.[173]

Moreover, it makes little sense that sports reporters would reach back eight years to the NA era to resurrect a nickname for the new Philadelphia club, especially when none of the Philadelphia-based teams in the NA actually used it. A more persuasive explanation is that they reached back only one year to the 1881 ECA Philadelphia club and applied its moniker to the 1882 League Alliance Philadelphia team.[174] In both years, Phillies was used to distinguish the team from the better-known Athletics, and to provide a shorthanded but still obvious way to identify the club in game accounts.

There will always be some vagueness about the nickname of the Philadelphia NL club during its earliest years because the franchise never embraced a particular name officially, and newspapers used a variety of monikers to refer to the team in their reporting. In this author's view, a more evidentially sound case can be made that Phillies was applied as the franchise's sobriquet from the outset rather than Quakers. It was simply transferred by sportswriters from the failed 1881 ECA club to the new 1882 League Alliance club.

Although several nicknames were used to refer to the Philadelphia NL club during its formative years, the use of others faded and Phillies emerged as the consensus choice for the team name. It is important to add, moreover, the adoption of Phillies evolved over time from multiple sources of reporting on the team, rather than at a specific time through a formal declaration by the club. Regardless of the ambiguity surrounding its origin, the Philadelphia NL and MLB franchise has been known as the Phillies for over 135 years, and the nickname will undoubtedly remain into the indefinite future. ■

Notes

1. Frederick Lieb and Stan Baumgartner, *The Philadelphia Phillies* (New York: G.P. Putnam's Sons, 1953), 11–13.
2. "Baseball in Philadelphia," *New York Clipper*, October 15, 1881.
3. For a biographic sketch of Al Reach as a player, businessman, and owner, see, Rich Westcott and Frank Bilovsky, *The Phillies Encyclopedia*, 3rd ed. (Philadelphia: Temple University Press, 2004), 365–67.
4. David M. Jordan, *Occasional Glory: A History of the Philadelphia Phillies* (Jefferson: McFarland & Company, Inc., 2002), 6. Jordan notes that Reach's "love of baseball" was one of the motivating factors in his decision to start a baseball club.
5. Ibid. Philadelphia's population had reached 847,000 by 1880.
6. Lieb and Baumgartner, 12.
7. One newspaper reporter commented, "There can be no doubt of the pecuniary success of Al Reach's new enterprise." "Opening the Season in Philadelphia," *New York Clipper*, April 15, 1882.
8. In 1882, the club was called the Athletic, just as the New York club was called the Metropolitan. These and other names have been pluralized in the text to reflect contemporary usage, and because the teams themselves began to pluralize them afer a few years.
9. David Shiffert, *Base Ball in Philadelphia* (Jefferson: McFarland & Company, Inc., 2006), 4. Shiffert writes that in 1865, Reach became the first ballplayer to change cities for a salary, jumping from Brooklyn to the Athletics of Philadelphia.
10. David Nemec, *The Beer and Whiskey League* (New York: Lyons & Burford), 20–21.
11. Nemec., 14–16.
12. "Baseball," *New York Clipper*, October 8, 1881.
13. *New York Clipper*, October 15, 1881.
14. "Baseball," *New York Clipper*, October 29, 1881. Nemec states that only Phillips represented the new Philadelphia club at the November 2 meeting. Nemec, *Beer and Whiskey*, 21–22.
15. According to Nemec, Chick Fulmer, manager of the Athletics, pledged his club "could put up $5,000 that very day" to underscore its financial solvency. Phillips, speaking for the new Philadelphia club, claimed his club had plenty of financial backing but did not specify a figure.
16. Shiffert, 4.
17. Nemec, 22.
18. *New York Clipper*, October 15, 1881.
19. The Metropolitans chose not to join the AA since doing so would mean foregoing potentially lucrative games against NL clubs during the 1882 season. Representatives from the club who attended the meeting, James Mutrie and W.S. Appleton, also doubted the long-term viability of the AA. Asked to leave the November 2 meeting and come back when they were ready to commit, the pair exited and never returned. Nemec, *Beer and Whiskey*, 21. Brock Helander, *The League Alliance*, https://sabr.org/bioproj/topic/league-alliance.
20. Nemec, 23.
21. Lieb and Baumgartner, 12. According to them, NL president Mills was later quoted as saying, "We've got to get these big cities back into our league. Both New York and Philadelphia have tremendous futures, and some day their populations will be in the millions. If we permit the American Association to entrench itself in these cities, the Association—not we—will be the real big league." Whether Mills uttered these words,

or they sprang from the author's fertile mind is unknown because Lieb and Baumgartner didn't source their history of the Phillies and were suspected of manufacturing quotations for their books to enliven the text and validate their analysis and conclusions.
22. David Nemec, *The Great Encyclopedia of 19th Century Major League Baseball* (New York: Donald I. Fine, 1997), 87.
23. Nemec, 173.
24. "A League Club," *New York Clipper*, July 16, 1881.
25. Nemec, *Great Encyclopedia*, 156, 176.
26. Nemec, 173.
27. Michael Haupert, William Hulbert, https://sabr.org/bioproj/person/d1d420b3.
28. "The American Association," *New York Clipper*, March 25, 1882.
29. Helander.
30. Helander.
31. Helander identifies 13 clubs as "generally recognized as members of the League Alliance." Baseball-Reference.com lists 16 more clubs as members of the Alliance. https://www.baseball-reference.com/register/league.cgi?id=a9132541.
32. Helander.
33. Helander.
34. Bill Lamb, John Day, http://sabr.org/bioproj/person/c281a493.
35. Helander.
36. A curious report appeared in the *New York Clipper* newspaper that offered an entirely different version of what occurred at the December 7 NL owners meeting, It reads: "The Metropolitan Club and the Philadelphia team said to be under the management of Al Reach and H.B. Phillips were each offered membership in the League. The Mets declined on account of the fifty-cent tariff, while Reach and Phillips cannot secure sufficient first-class talent to take the risk, although it is rumored that propositions have been made to Ferguson's Troy team, and also to the Providence nine, to locate in Philadelphia as a League club." This author has not found any corroborating evidence to affirm Philadelphia and New York were considered for admittance to the NL at the December meeting; that New York and Philadelphia declined the opportunity; or, that the NL proposed to the Troy and Providence clubs that one of them transfer to Philadelphia. All information this author has examined indicates New York and Philadelphia were offered membership in the League Alliance; both accepted, and no entreaties were made to existing NL teams to have one of them relocate to Philadelphia. "Baseball," *New York Clipper*, December 10, 1881."
37. This condition applied only to Philadelphia because New York was not a member of the American Association or National League in 1882. The city would be represented in both organizations in 1883, just like Philadelphia.
38. "Baseball," *New York Clipper*, December 17, 1881.
39. Rich Westcott, *Philadelphia's Old Ballparks* (Philadelphia: Temple University Press, 1996), 9–10.
40. Robert D. Warrington, "Philadelphia in the 1881 Eastern Championship Association," *Baseball Research Journal*, Vol. 48, No 1 (Spring, 2019), 78–85.
41. Phillips announced in October 1881 that the Philadelphias wanted to lease the grounds for the upcoming season. He stated all existing buildings would be demolished as would the fence surrounding the lot. The baseball diamond also would be reconfigured to increase the distance of center field. He estimated the costs of these changes at "two to three thousand dollars." *New York Clipper*, October 15, 1881.
42. Reach may have been told this initially by the owner of the land to pressure him into offering more money to rent it.
43. That Reach intended to lease Recreation Park for his ball club is recorded in "The Philadelphia Club," *New York Clipper*, December 24, 1881. The initial unavailability of the ballpark and Reach's negotiations to use the circus lot at Broad and Federal Streets are noted in "Baseball," *New York Clipper*, January 7, 1882.
44. Westcott records the dimensions of the playing fields at: 330 feet down the left field line; 369 feet to straightaway center field; 369 feet

to right-center; and, 247 feet down the right field line. Seventy-nine feet separated home plate from the grandstand behind it. The sharply disparate dimensions of the playing field were caused by the contorted shape of the land on which it was located.

45. "The Game in Philadelphia," *New York Clipper*, April 1, 1882. An earlier depiction of the ballpark contained slightly different figures for seating capacities of the grandstand and bleachers, and also furnished additional information about the ballpark's features: "The seating capacity will be about 3,000. Including 1,300 covered seats in a new grandstand which is to be erected. The center portion of the stand, containing 500 seats, will be reserved for subscribers, season ticket holders and ladies. Along the rightfield side open seats—with footrests—for 1,000 persons, and along the leftfield side the same seats for 700 people will be erected. A reporters' stand will be constructed on top of the other stand with accommodations for twenty-five persons (press and visiting club alone)…A clubroom will be under the west end of the stand, and will include dressing room with closets, washbasins and water closets. At centerfield will be erected a large blackboard, on which will be displayed the scores of innings of League and League Alliance games being played on the days the home teams play." *New York Clipper*, December 24, 1881.

46. In preparing Recreation Park to be his team's home, Reach also had the grounds arranged for other sports that could be played on off days of the baseball season. As one newspaper reporter noted, "Tracks for foot racing, bicycling, etc., have been prepared, and the ground is so arranged that almost every known field sport can be indulged in upon it." *New York Clipper*, April 1, 1882.

47. Like Reach's decision to improve Recreation Park before the start of the 1882 season, management of the Athletics also invested significant sums to upgrade Oakdale Park. The grounds were sodded and leveled, and a new border fence and grandstand erected. The grandstand, as described in a contemporary newspaper account, was two hundred feet long and sat 1,500 people. It was divided into three sections, including one for season ticket holders that had cane-seated chairs, and another reserved for ladies and gentlemen accompanying them. The reporters' stand was placed on top of the pavilion and situated to the rear of the catcher's position. It held 20 reporters. "The Athletics Club," *New York Clipper*, February 18, 1882. Oakdale Park was located on a plot of land bordered by Huntingdon Street, 11th Street, Cumberland Street, and 12th Street in Philadelphia. The AA Athletics used it as their home ballpark for only one year. The club moved to the Jefferson Street Grounds for the 1883 season. Oakdale Park was torn down shortly thereafter. https://en.wikipedia.org/wiki/Oakdale_Park.

48. "Baseball," *New York Clipper*, January 14, 1882. As indicated in note 46, when Recreation Park was rehabilitated by Al Reach, the grounds were designed so that sporting events other than baseball could be played at the facility.

49. *New York Clipper*, February 18, 1882.

50. " Opening the Season in Philadelphia," *New York Clipper*, April 15, 1882.

51. Box scores appearing in the *Philadelphia Inquirer*, *New York Clipper* and *The New York Times* between May–October 1882 were examined to assess the Philadelphia club's regular starting lineup during that period.

52. The following sources provided information on the careers of baseball players identified in the Philadelphia club's lineup: Baseball-Reference.com; Baseball-Almanac.com; Nemec, *Great Encyclopedia*.

53. Pop Corkhill was badly injured in a game against Boston on October 7 and was out for the rest of the season. "Field Sports," *Philadelphia Inquirer*, October 9, 1882.

54. Ibid. Tim Manning began the 1882 season with the Providence Grays but was released by that team in June and signed by Philadelphia. "Baseball," *New York Clipper*, June 24, 1882. Corkhill had no big league experience prior to the 1882 season, but would go on to play with teams in the AA and NL into the early 1890s. https://www.baseball-reference.com/players/c/corkhpo01.shtml. John Manning and Tim Manning were not closely related. The former was born in Braintree, Massachusetts in December, 1853, and the latter was also born in

December 1853, but in Henley-on-the-Thames, England. Nemec, *Great Encyclopedia*, 694, 730.

55. Two of the players inserted at catcher early in the season to evaluate their talent were Bill McCloskey and Marshall Quinton. Neither lasted very long. Both men appeared as catcher in the Philadelphia lineup during a game played on April 12, 1882, against the Atlantics of Brooklyn. When Philadelphia switched pitchers in the eighth inning, the catchers were also changed. "Baseball," *New York Clipper*, April 22, 1882. Another player given a tryout as catcher was FNU Morris. One of the reasons he lasted only a short period with the club may have been his demeanor. In a game played on June 14, Morris was ordered off the field by team captain John Manning "for disobeying orders." "An Easy Victory," *Philadelphia Inquirer*, June 15, 1882.

56. "Baseball," *New York Clipper*, September 9, 1882.

57. "Baseball," *New York Clipper*, July 29, 1882. Phillips' plan did not work out. Indianapolis was not a member of the AA in 1883. The city joined the association for the 1884 season, but Phillips was not the manager. Nemec, *Great Encyclopedia*, 205, 231.

58. Nemec.

59. Nemec, 743.

60. The three players were John Corcoran, Al Bushong, and Ed Whiting. Corcoran and Bushong performed most of the catching chores during the last two months of the season, while Whiting appeared in only one game (October 21). Barnie filled in periodically. *New York Clipper*, various dates in September and October 1882.

61. "The Philadelphia Club," *New York Clipper*, January 13, 1883. The players and their game totals were: John Manning (139), William McClellan (132), Fred Lewis (129), Arlie Latham (127), Pop Corkhill (125), Jack Neagle (99), Mike Moynahan (95), and Tim Manning (92).

62. Interestingly, none of the players who were with the ECA's Phillies in 1881 appeared with Philadelphia in 1882; however, there were reports that two of those players, Frank Berkelbach and John Shetzline, had signed with the club. Berkelbach, according to these reports, was engaged by the team to replace Gid Gardner after the latter had been dismissed. At the time, Berkelbach had been playing for the Burlington, NJ, club, one of the teams Philadelphia had played during the season. Berkelbach's signing is reported in "Notes," *Philadelphia Inquirer*, August 12, 1882, and "Baseball" *New York Clipper*, August 12, 1882. Shetzline's signing with Philadelphia is mentioned in, "Baseball," *New York Clipper*, April 29, 1882.

63. This information is derived from examining box scores of games played by Philadelphia during the 1882 season as reported in various dates of the *Philadelphia Inquirer* and *New York Clipper* newspapers.

64. That Battin was released by Philadelphia and signed with Brooklyn, see, "Baseball," *New York Clipper*, June 24, 1882. He umpired a game between the St. Louis Browns and the Athletics on July 21. "Baseball," *New York Clipper*, July 29, 1882. Battin played third base for the Alleghanys in a game against the Baltimores on August 14. "Baseball," *New York Clipper*, August 26, 1882.

65. *Philadelphia Inquirer*, August 2, 1882, and *New York Clipper*, August 12, 1882. The use of "dissipation" was almost certainly a euphemism for alcohol abuse. Despite being suspended by Philadelphia, Gardner continued to play baseball at the professional level for other teams in subsequent years. This included playing one game for Philadelphia in 1888, after the club had joined the National League. Nemec, *Great Encyclopedia*, 353, 724, 778.

66. Neagle's prior experience at the professional level had been pitching in two games for Cincinnati in 1879. Nemec, *Great Encyclopedia*, 131.

67. Neagle's number of games started and percentage of overall games pitched were calculated by totaling all games played by Philadelphia in 1882, and separating out the games in which Neagle was identified as the starting pitcher. The exact number Neagle started could not be determined, however, because in a handful of away games against amateur clubs, only the by-inning and final scores or just the final scores were printed in newspaper reports; lineups and box scores were not. For example, the accounts of two games played in New Haven, Connecticut against Yale College on May 3 and 4 listed only the final

scores. "The Second Victory," *Philadelphia Inquirer*, May 4, 1882, "Deserted by Luck," *Philadelphia Inquirer*, May 5, 1882. It is almost certain Neagle began other games in addition to the 67 in which he is known to have been the starting pitcher.

68. In a game on June 2, Chicago "batted Neagle out of his position," and Philadelphia lost 11–9. "The Champions Win," *Philadelphia Inquirer*, June 3, 1882. Yale College got the best of Neagle on July 3, and he was taken out in the 8th inning after giving up seven runs in the 7th and 8th innings. But he was not sent to the bench. Neagle took over left field, while Gid Gardner—who had been playing that position—pitched the rest of the game. Philadelphia actually won the match 12–9. "College Champions Beaten," *Philadelphia Inquirer*, July 4, 1882.

69. Neagle's won-lost-tied record was calculated using the final scores of all the games in which he was known to have been the starting pitcher. *Philadelphia Inquirer* and *New York Clipper*, various dates. In addition, Neagle was used once as a relief pitcher, replacing Neff in a game on July 12. Philadelphia wound up winning the contest against the Brooklyn Atlantics by scoring seven runs in the bottom of the ninth. Neagle got the win. Neff did not pitch again for Philadelphia, and became one of those players who appeared briefly on the team and then disappeared never to return. "Philadelphia vs. Atlantic," *Philadelphia Inquirer*, July 13, 1882.

70. Neagle's pitching load—incredible by today's standards—was hardly unique in 1882. Jim McCormick, a pitcher for the NL's Cleveland Blues, started 67 games that year, 65 of which he completed. Tony Mullane of the AA's Eclipse was the starting pitcher in 55 games in 1882, 51 of which he completed. Nemec, *Great Encyclopedia*, 181, 187.

71. Neagle's injury and resulting absence from the lineup is noted in "Baseball," *New York Clipper*, May 27, 1882. To cover for the missing Neagle, Philadelphia put Gid Gardner—an outfielder who was also a part-time pitcher—in the box. He started three consecutive games on May 22, 24, and 26. Philadelphia lost the first one but won the other two. Gardner had not pitched earlier in the season and would start only one other game (June 15) thereafter for the club. *Philadelphia Inquirer* and *New York Clipper*, various dates.

72. For example, Neagle played right field in an April 20 game against Troy while Hardie Henderson tended to the pitching duties. "Troy's Second Triumph," *Philadelphia Inquirer*, April 21, 1882. Neagle patrolled left field on May 1 while Henderson pitched in a game against the Merritt amateur club. "The Philadelphia Nine Beat the Merritts Eight to Nothing," *Philadelphia Inquirer*, May 2, 1882.

73. Interest in Neagle by the Eclipse club was first reported in mid-August. *New York Clipper*, August 12, 1882. That the talks had broken down were revealed a week later. "Baseball," *New York Clipper*, August 19, 1882.

74. Neagle went 1–7 for Philadelphia, 1–4 for the Orioles, and 3–12 for the Alleghenys. He went 11–26 with Alleghany the next year, his final one in the big leagues. Perhaps all those pitches he threw in 1882 wore his arm out. https://www.baseball-reference.com/players/n/neaglja01.shtml.

75. Nemec, *Great Encyclopedia*, 781.

76. Henderson's number of games started and percentage of overall games pitched were calculated the same way Neagle's were, as indicated in note 67. *Philadelphia Inquirer* and *New York Clipper*, various dates. As with Neagle, it is almost certain Henderson was the starting pitcher in other games in addition to the 52 he is known to have begun, for the same reason. For example, only final scores were listed for away games Philadelphia played against the Anthracite Club in Pottsville, Pennsylvania, and the Harrisburg Club on September 18 and 19 respectively. Since Neagle started the previous game on September 14, it's highly probable Henderson pitched on the 18 or 19. Henderson's win-loss-tied record was calculated in the same manner as Neagle's as described in note 69. "Baseball," *New York Clipper*, September 23, 1882 and September 30, 1882.

77. The single game Henderson started but did not finish occurred on June 14. He was relieved in the eighth inning by Gid Gardner. The switch

may have been based on Henderson's catcher, Morris, being removed from the game by team captain John Manning for disobeying orders. When Latham replaced Morris, Gardner took Henderson's place as pitcher. Gardner pitched the final two frames in a game Philadelphia won. *Philadelphia Inquirer*, June 15, 1882.

78. For example, Henderson played right field in a game against Atlantic City, NJ, on September 7. "Sall to the Front," *Philadelphia Inquirer*, September 8, 1882.

79. https://www.baseball-reference.com/players/h/hendeha01.shtml.

80. Buffington's identity remains something of a mystery since his first name was not revealed in newspaper reporting, and no pitchers with that last name are listed in compendiums of 19 century baseball players. It is this author's view that the player's last name was misspelled in contemporary accounts, and the individual is actually Charlie Buffinton. According to his career statistics, Buffinton began his professional career with the Boston Red Caps, pitching his first game on May 17, 1882. What probably transpired was that Buffinton pitched for Philadelphia in April and then left the club to play for Boston, a team with whom he would remain through the 1886 season. Buffinton returned to Philadelphia to pitch for Al Reach's team from 1887–89. Nemec, *Great Encyclopedia*, 769. http://www.baseball-almanac.com/players/player.php?p=buffich01.

81. "Baseball," *Philadelphia Inquirer*, April 12, 1882. See note 80 regarding "Buffington."

82. "Baseball," *Philadelphia Inquirer*, April 24, 1882. See note 80 regarding "Buffington."

83. "Two Easy Victories," *Philadelphia Inquirer*, September 7, 1882; *Philadelphia Inquirer*, September 8, 1882.

84. Nemec, *Great Encyclopedia*, 765.

85. According to an article in the *New York Clipper* newspaper summarizing the results of the 1882 campaign, Philadelphia played 144 games in which the club went 72–66–6. *New York Clipper*, January 13, 1883.

86. Helander.

87. "Baseball," *New York Clipper*, August 5, 1882.

88. *Clipper*.

89. "Three More Games," *Philadelphia Inquirer*, May 18, 1882.

90. "Major League Baseballs Have a Short Shelf-life," FOXsports.com, June 30, 2012. http://www.foxsports.com/north/story/major-league-baseballs-have-a-short-shelf-life-062912.

91. After the Metropolitans clinched the League Alliance Championship on July 26, no additional games were scheduled against Philadelphia, and the teams did not play each other for over a month. It was only with the creation of a new 12-game series to vie for the silver trophy that the teams resumed their contests.

92. "Sports of the Field," *Philadelphia Inquirer*, September 4, 1882.

93. The "massive silver punch bowl" was described as follows: "On the top is the figure of a pitcher in the act of delivering a ball. On the sides are handles representing miniature bats. On the back is a representation of an entire ballfield with raised figures representing the nine players in their respective positions. The front side is left unchased for the appropriate inscription when the trophy shall have been won." "Baseball," *New York Clipper*, September 9, 1882.

94. "A Close Game," *Philadelphia Inquirer*, October 25, 1882. "A Victory for the Metropolitans," *The New York Times*, October 26, 1882.

95. "A Tie for the Trophy," *Philadelphia Inquirer*, October 26, 1882.

96. "Baseball," *New York Clipper*, November 4, 1882.

97. "Baseball," *New York Clipper*, March 18, 1882.

98. The first game ever played by the League Alliance Philadelphia team was against the NL's Providence Grays. It took place at Recreation Park on April 8, 1882, with the visitors coming out on top 3–0. The uniform worn by the Philadelphias was described as follows: "On this occasion they entered the field attired in the handsomest uniform ever worn by a Philadelphia team, the dress being similar—except in caps—to that worn by the old Cincinnati and the Boston 'Red Stockings,' the cap being a handsome improvement." *New York Clipper*, April 15, 1882.

99. "Baseball," *New York Clipper*, April 15, 1882. The article lists the opponents and dates for all games that had been scheduled at that point between Philadelphia and NL clubs.

100. The October 10 game against Detroit was held at the Mount Holly, New Jersey fair. A makeshift baseball diamond was created on a racetrack, which, as one newspaper noted, "was not at all adapted to the requirements of the game." Still, the event drew a respectable 3,000 spectators, who saw a slugfest that Detroit won 13–9. Mount Holly is substantially closer to Philadelphia than Detroit, so it is counted as a home game for Philadelphia in Appendix A. "Our National Game," *Philadelphia Inquirer*, October 11, 1882.

101. "At the Recent League Meeting," *New York Clipper*, March 18, 1882.

102. "At the Annual Meeting of the League," *New York Clipper*, March 18, 1882.

103. "Baseball," *New York Clipper*, March 18, 1882.

104. "At the Recent League Meeang," *New York Clipper*, March 18, 1882. Al Reach and John Day were warned that if the financial guarantees NL owners sought were not accepted, then league clubs would be free to play games against other teams in Philadelphia and New York. Recognizing how financially injurious it would be for their clubs if they lost the exclusive right to play NL teams in their cities, Reach and Day reluctantly acquiesced.

105. "At the Annual Meeting," *New York Clipper*, March 18, 1882.

106. "Baseball," *New York Clipper*, April 1, 1882. The Athletics made a similar announcement.

107. "Baseball," *The New York Times*, September 3, 1882.

108. "Baseball," *New York Clipper*, September 9, 1882. Bancroft's figures indicate that Detroit not receive its $100 minimum payment based on the gate receipts for each game. Whether home clubs had to make up the difference out of their own pockets or Detroit had to accept less than the minimum is unclear. Bancroft's numbers, it should be noted, are somewhat misleading. Philadelphia had a much larger population base from which to draw fans compared to the other cities mentioned. Moreover, in addition to being small-market cities, Troy and Worcester were out of the pennant race when these games were played, giving fans less incentive to go to the ballpark to cheer on their hometown crews.

109. Some reporters took a charitable view of Philadelphia's struggles to win games against established professional teams. One opined, for example, "The oft-repeated defects of the Philadelphias have failed to do justice to the team because of newly organized and unpracticed players...The Philadelphia Club have earned a position in the ranks of the strong professional teams of the season, and they should maintain it as credibly as they have won it." "The Philadelphias First League Victory," *New York Clipper*, May 6, 1882. In all fairness to Reach's club, moreover, it should be noted Worcester won only 18 games against League opponents while losing 66. Nemec *Great Encyclopedia*, 176.

110. Fans' willingness to populate the stands at Recreation Park was noted in game reports. One article observed, for example, "In Philadelphia the summer has developed a deeper interest in ball playing than has been the case for some years back." "Is Baseball Waning?," *New York Clipper*, August 5, 1882.

111. "Baseball," *New York Clipper*, May 20, 1882.

112. "Baseball," *New York Clipper*, May 3, 1882. It is not clear how the issue of retaining all admittance fees vice splitting them was resolved.

113. Of the nearly 10,000 people who jammed the stands at Oakdale Park to watch the game, the *New York Clipper*, newspaper provided a remarkably precise figure—8,261—who actually paid admission for entrance. The rest, presumably, were guests of the club or individuals who snuck into the ballpark without paying the fee. "Baseball," *New York Clipper*, May 27, 1882.

114. "On Field and Water," *Philadelphia Inquirer*, May 22, 1882.

115. "Ten Innings," *Philadelphia Inquirer*, May 23, 1882. Reporting in the game summary that "a thousand more witnessed the contest from the windows and roofs of the surrounding houses" is especially noteworthy because it is the first recorded instance—based on this author's research—of spectators watching a baseball game from houses located around the periphery of a ballpark in Philadelphia. Fans were charged ten cents to sit on the roofs vice twenty-five cents to sit in the ballpark. "Baseball," *The New York Times*, September 3, 1882. The practice became much more famous at Shibe Park when homeowners along 20th Street opposite the right field wall built stands on their roofs and removed their second-story windows so fans unable to get into the ballpark or unwilling to pay the admittance fee could watch a game while paying a lesser price to do so. They were called the "rooftop squatters." Lawrence S. Ritter, *Lost Ballparks: A Celebration of Baseball's Legendary Fields* (New York: Penguin Books, 1992), 180–81.

116. *Philadelphia Inquirer*, May 23, 1882.

117. Nemec, *Great Encyclopedia*, 166–67.

118. "Baseball," *New York Clipper*, June 17, 1882.

119. "Upholding a Contract Breaker," *New York Clipper*, December 31, 1881.

120. "Baseball," *New York Clipper*, June 3, 1882.

121. *Clipper*. The prohibition on playing Detroit applied to all AA clubs.

122. *Clipper*.

123. Troy played virtually the entire 1882 campaign with Detroit, but latched on with Providence for four games at the end of the season. In 1883, he was on the roster of the NL's New Yorks, and then finished his major league career playing for the Metropolitans of the American Association in 1884–85. https://www.baseball-reference.com/players/t/troyda01.shtml.

124. "Baseball," *New York Clipper*, June 24, 1882.

125. "Another Victory for Troy," *Philadelphia Inquirer*, October 3, 1882.

126. *Inquirer*.

127. *Inquirer*.

128. *New York Clipper*, June 24, 1882.

129. Helander.

130. Unfortunately, newspaper accounts of the Philadelphias' games against amateur teams rarely contain attendance figures. One exception is the contest against the Actives that occurred in Reading, Pennsylvania on September 16. Approximately 1,000 people watched the visiting team bash the hometown crew 10–1. "Baseball on Saturday," *Philadelphia Inquirer*, September 18, 1882.

131. How often, if at all, the Philadelphias would travel to play an away game against an amateur team almost certainly depended in part on the seating capacity of the latter's ballpark. It had to have enough seats to make the game potentially profitable through admission fees.

132. "Baseball," *New York Clipper*, May 13, 1882.

133. "Baseball," *New York Clipper*, September 23, 1882.

134. "Easy Victory," *Philadelphia Inquirer*, April 13, 1882; "Baseball," *Philadelphia Inquirer*, April 17, 1882.

135. "Baseball," *Philadelphia Inquirer*, May 2, 1882.

136. "A Disappointed Crowd," *Philadelphia Inquirer*, June 14, 1882.

137. *New York Clipper*, June 24, 1882.

138. "A Novel Match," *Philadelphia Inquirer*, July 20, 1882; "Baseball," *New York Clipper*, July 29, 1882.

139. "Champions Beaten," *Philadelphia Inquirer*, August 17, 1882.

140. "Champions 'Chicagoed,'" *Philadelphia Inquirer*, August 18, 1882. "Chicagoed" was a term used during the period to indicate a team had been shut out in a baseball game.

141. Nemec, *Beer and Whiskey*, 44.

142. "Baseball," *New York Clipper*, July 15, 1882.

143. "Baseball Matters," *The New York Times*, September 25, 1882.

144. *The New York Times*.

145. "The Late League Meeting," *New York Clipper*, September 30, 1882. A more complete accounting of what happened at the September 22 meeting with a focus on Troy's and Worcester's denials of their willingness to leave the League can be found in "Baseball," *The New York Times*, September 26, 1882.

146. "Two Good Games," *Philadelphia Inquirer*, October 5, 1882.

147. "Beaten by Boston," *Philadelphia Inquirer*, October 7, 1882. Hayes jumped after the season to the American Association, playing for the Alleghenys in 1883–84. Nemec, *Great Encyclopedia*, 749.

148. Nemec, *Beer and Whiskey*, 44.

149. John Day and James Mutrie formed a second club called the New Yorks—also referred to as Gothams—that joined the NL in 1883. John Clapp was appointed team manager. The franchise's nickname evolved into Giants by 1888, and the club stayed in New York until relocating to San Francisco after the 1957 season. https://en.wikipedia.org/wiki/History_of_the_New_York_Giants_(baseball). The Metropolitans folded after the 1887 season. Nemec, *Beer and Whiskey*, 147.

150. "Baseball," *Philadelphia Inquirer*, December 8, 1882.

151. Lieb and Baumgartner, 12–13. The authors state, "It didn't take much of a sales talk to sell Reach on the idea of a Philadelphia National League Club."

152. "Baseball," *New York Clipper*, October 7, 1882.

153. 1883 Philadelphia Phillies Schedule, Baseball Almanac. http://www.baseball-almanac.com/teamstats/schedule.php?y=1883&t=PHI.

154. This loss may have been offset somewhat by the fact that games against NL clubs attracted a greater number of spectators to the ballpark than matches against amateur teams.

155. Nemec, *Great Encyclopedia*, 197. Reach's campaign to attract fans to Recreation Park in 1883 was not made easier by the fact the Athletics won the AA championship that year.

156. Lieb and Baumgartner, 16–17.

157. Lieb and Baumgartner, 15–16.

158. To alleviate the financial, legal and administrative responsibilities of owning the club once it gained membership in the National League, Reach took on a co-owner. His name was John I. Rogers, a well-connected lawyer with deep political connections. Reach became president of the franchise, and Rogers took on the positions of treasurer and secretary. Jordan, 6.

159 *New York Clipper*, April 15, 1882. Adding "Sporting Association" and "Exhibition Company" to the franchise's title reflected Reach's determination to organize profitable sporting events at Recreation Park beyond baseball.

160. For a major league baseball clubs not to have an "official" nickname was characteristic of the era. Unless the moniker was derived from a franchise's corporate name, like the Metropolitan of New York, sobriquets were conferred upon teams by sportswriters who covered them, and the names emerged—and sometimes changed—over time.

161. Donald Honig, *The Philadelphia Phillies: An Illustrated History* (New York: Simon & Schuster, 1992), 15.

162. "Baseball," *Philadelphia Inquirer*, June 25, 1881.

163. Interestingly, the nickname "Phils" is never linked to Reach's team during the period in newspaper reporting. Yet, the commonly used moniker of the Metropolitans was "Mets." See, for example, "The Metropolitans Win," *The New York Times*, September 9, 1882. The shorthand Phils has long been the secondary sobriquet of the franchise and was even adopted officially in 1942; however, it was dropped after that year and resumed its unofficial status. Jordan, 87.

164. Lieb and Baumgartner are among the authors who misdate the creation of the Phillies' nickname and its association with the Philadelphia NL franchise. Unfortunately, their history of the Phillies is riddled with errors, especially in describing the formation of the ballclub. They never mention the team's participation in the League Alliance in 1882, and state the first time NL officials approached Reach about owning a franchise was in early 1883. The authors also write that work on repairing Recreation Park as the new home of the Phillies didn't begin until 1883. As this article has sought to demonstrate, all of this information is inaccurate. Lieb and Baumgartner, 12–13.

165. "Beaten by One Run," *Philadelphia Inquirer*, April 14, 1882.

166. "The 'Phillies' Beaten," *Philadelphia Inquirer*, July 15, 1882.

167. "Baseball," *New York Clipper*, September 23, 1882.

168. "Philadelphias" appears in "Baseball," *The New York Times*, May 9, 1882. "Philadelphia Club" is contained in the following newspaper game account, "The Philadelphia Club Beaten," *The New York Times*, July 30, 1882. "Philadelphia nine" was used in the following article, "Baseball," *The New York Times*, September 13, 1882.

169. Nemec, *Great Encyclopedia*, 197, 221, 266.

170. Donald Dewey and Nicholas Acocella, *Total Ballclubs: The Ultimate Book of Baseball Teams* (Toronto: Sport Media Publishing, 2005), 455.

171. Lieb and Baumgartner, 13.

172. Nemec, *Great Encyclopedia*, 7–81. According to Nemec, the following Philadelphia clubs identified by their names were members of the National Association during its five-year existence: Athletics (1871–74), White Stockings (1873), Pearls (1874–75), and Centennials (1875).

173. Philadelphia's entry in the Players' League was called the Philadelphia Players League team or the Philadelphias, but that didn't happen until 1890, and the league lasted only one year. Nemec, *Great Encyclopedia*, 429.

174. Warrington, 78–85.

APPENDIX A. 1882 Phillies League Alliance Schedule

Date	Opponent	Score	Decision	Attendance	H/A	Date	Opponent	Score	Decision	Attendance	H/A
4/8	Providence	0–3	L	3,000	H	5/4	Yale College (CT)	0–12	L	N/A	A
4/11	Providence	6–19	L	N/A	H	5/8	Metropolitans	8–6	W	N/A	A
4/12	Atlantics (Brooklyn)	15–1	W	"Very slim attendance"	H	5/9	Worcester	0–2	L	1,500	H
4/13	Princeton College (NJ)	7–8	L	N/A	H	5/16	Metropolitans	4–5	L	1,200	H
4/14	Worcester	3–5	L	800	H	5/17	Metropolitans	6–12	L	1,300	H
4/15	Worcester	3–6	L	1,000	H	5/18	Merritt (Camden, NJ)	8–1	W	N/A	A
4/17	Worcester	2–3	L	1,000	H	5/19	Providence	1–9	L	1,200	H
4/18	Troy	5–11	L	"Small audience"	H	5/20	Athletics	7–6	W	10,000	A
4/20	Troy	5–8	L	400	H	5/22	Athletics	6–5	W	7,000–8,000	H
4/21	Quaker City (Philadelphia)	7–1	W	N/A	A	5/24	Boston	10–9	W	1,000	H
4/22	Young America (Philadelphia)	11–0	W	"Not Large"	H	5/26	Merritt (Camden, NJ)	4–0	W	500	H
4/24	Chicago	1–4	L	2,000	H	5/27	Metropolitans	2–0	W	1,200	H
4/25	Chicago	1–8	L	1,500	H	5/29	Detroit	2–6	L	3,000	H
4/26	Chicago	2–11	L	200	H	5/30	Metropolitans	5–6	L	4,000	H
4/27	Boston	12–12	T	"Very slim crowd"	H	5/31	Dartmouth College (NH)	30–1	W	N/A	H
4/28	Boston	2–3	L	1,500	H	6/2	Chicago	9–11	L	2,000	H
4/29	Boston	4–5	L	2,500	H	6/3	Cleveland	3–5	L	2,000	H
5/1	Merritt (Camden, NJ)	8–0	W	1,500	H	6/5	Worcester	4–3	W	1,500	H
5/2	Princeton College (NJ)	9–5	W	N/A	A	6/6	Clipper (Philadelphia)	8–0	W	500	H
5/3	Yale College (CT)	6–2	W	N/A	A	6/7	Metropolitans	0–13	L	1,000	A

(Continued on following page)

APPENDIX A. 1882 Phillies League Alliance Schedule (*continued*)

Date	Opponent	Score	Decision	Attendance	H/A	Date	Opponent	Score	Decision	Attendance	H/A
6/8	Boston	3–7	L	N/A	H	8/18	Troy	6–1	W	2,000	H
6/9	Metropolitans	1–7	L	500	A	8/19	Troy	2–0	W	4,000	H
6/10	Metropolitans	5–0	W	1,500	H	8/21	Cleveland	0–6	L	3,000	H
6/12	Metropolitans	12–5	W	2,500	H	8/22	Cleveland	5–0	W	1,000	H
6/13	Picked Nine	12–5	W	1,000	H	8/23	Buffalo	5–3	W	4,000	H
6/14	Alaskas (New York City)	16–8	W	500	H	8/24	Atlantic City (NJ)	7–6	W	1,000	H
6/15	Alaskas (New York City)	5–2	W	"Small crowd"	H	8/25	Detroit	0–5	L	2,500	H
6/17	Buffalo	5–9	L	3,000	H	8/26	Detroit	7–6	W	3,000–4,000	H
6/19	Buffalo	1–4	L	2,000	H	8/28	Buffalo	0–6	L	2,500	H
6/20	Trenton (NJ)	8–1	W	N/A	A	8/29	Buffalo	8–7	W	2,000	H
6/21	Burlington (NJ)	9–3	W	500	H	8/30	Providence	10–8	W	2,000+	H
6/22	Metropolitans	13–6	W	1,200	A	8/31	Metropolitans	15–8	W	"Fair sized"	A
6/23	Metropolitans	2–7	L	N/A	A	9/1	Metropolitans	6–5	W	N/A	A
6/24	Metropolitans	2–2	T	2,500	H	9/2	Metropolitans	4–1	W	4,000	H
6/26	Metropolitans	2–3	L	4,000	H	9/4	Metropolitans	8–6	W	2,500	H
7/1	Metropolitans	1–5	L	2,500	H	9/5	Atlantic City (NJ)	13–2	W	N/A	H
7/3	Yale College (CT)	12–9	W	1,500	H	9/6	Houston (Thurlow, PA)	13–3	W	"Very small"	H
7/4	Trenton	22–3	W	700	H	9/7	Atlantic City (NJ)	5–2	W	N/A	H
7/7	Trenton	8–3	W	N/A	A	9/8	Metropolitans	1–3	L	N/A	A
7/8	Boston	7–9	L	"Large number"	H	9/9	Metropolitans	4–8	L	1,200	A
7/10	Providence	0–5	L	2,000	H	9/12	Metropolitans	3–4	L	1,500	H
7/11	Burlington (NJ)	8–2	W	N/A	A	9/13	Metropolitans	3–4	L	500	A
7/12	Atlantics (Brooklyn)	8–3	W	N/A	H	9/14	Metropolitans	6–8	L	N/A	A
7/13	Atlantics (Brooklyn)	4–3	W	N/A	H	9/15	Trenton (NJ)	9–0	W	N/A	A
7/14	Troy	3–5	L	1,000	H	9/16	Actives (Reading, PA)	10–1	W	1,000	A
7/15	Troy	5–6	L	2,000	H	9/18	Anthracite Club (Pottsville, PA)	10–2	W	N/A	A
7/17	Metropolitans	1–11	L	N/A	A	9/19	Harrisburg (PA)	19–10	W	N/A	A
7/18	Metropolitans	8–11	L	700	A	9/21	Troy	3–3	T	N/A	H
7/19	Orion (Philadelphia—"Colored")	17–1	W	2,000	H	9/27	Boston	1–4	L	1,000	H
7/20	Actives (Reading, PA)	9–3	W	300	H	9/28	Providence	3–6	L	800	H
7/21	Boston	1–4	L	1,000	H	9/29	Old Athletic (Philadelphia)	12–6	W	4,300	H
7/22	Boston	3–6	L	N/A	H	9/30	Troy	2–4	L	N/A	H
7/24	Metropolitans	1–2	L	1,000	H	10/2	Troy	2–8	L	1,000	H
7/25	Burlington (NJ)	5–0	W	500	H	10/3	Troy	2–3	L	800	H
7/26	Metropolitans	6–8	L	1,000	H	10/4	Buffalo	6–10	L	1,200	H
7/27	Atlantic (Brooklyn)	9–6	W	500	H	10/5	Buffalo	4–6	L	1,500	H
7/28	Metropolitans	5–0	W	N/A	A	10/6	Boston	1–7	L	N/A	H
7/29	Metropolitans	2–7	L	N/A	A	10/7	Boston	4–7	L	1,500	H
8/1	Cleveland	9–16	L	N/A	H	10/9	Detroit	3–3	T	1,500	H
8/2	Chicago	13–0	W	300	H	10/10	Detroit	9–13	L	3,000	H
8/3	Detroit	4–3	W	1,500	H	10/13	Cleveland	1–2	L	N/A	H
8/5	Buffalo	3–13	L	3,000	H	10/14	Buffalo	5–4	W	N/A	H
8/7	Providence	3–2	W	2,000	H	10/16	Buffalo	4–4	T	800	H
8/8	Cleveland	7–3	W	1,500	H	10/18	Merritt (Camden, NJ)	5–1	W	800	H
8/9	Atlantic City (NJ)	17–3	W	800	H	10/20	Cleveland	1–1	T	1,000	H
8/11	Detroit	9–10	L	N/A	H	10/21	Cleveland	2–6	L	1,000	H
8/12	Detroit	5–4	W	4,000	H	10/23	Metropolitans	4–2	W	300	H
8/14	Chicago	1–10	L	3,000	H	10/24	Metropolitans	1–0	W	800	H
8/16	Atlantics (Canada)	7–4	W	800	H	10/25	Metropolitans	4–9	L	1,000	H
8/17	Atlantics (Canada)	2–0	W	800	H						

Contributors

ART AHRENS is a longtime contributor to SABR's publications, spanning 1973 to present. He lives in Chicago.

RON BACKER is an attorney who is an avid fan of both movies and baseball. He has written five books on film, the most recent being *Baseball Goes to the Movies*, published in 2017 by Applause Theatre and Cinema Books. A long-suffering Pirates fan, Ron lives in Pittsburgh, Pennsylvania.

JOHN C. BARNES, PhD, is an associate professor in the sports administration program at the University of New Mexico. His book, *Same Players, Different Game: An Examination of the Commercial College Athletics Industry*, will be available in 2020. He holds a Bachelor of Science degree in physical education from California State Polytechnic University, Pomona; a Master of Science degree in kinesiology from University of Nevada, Las Vegas; and a PhD in sports administration from the University of New Mexico.

ED COEN is a Senior Nuclear Engineer with Enercon Services Inc. who, in his spare time, follows the Milwaukee Brewers, reads SABR publications, and occasionally contributes to them. He has been a SABR member since 1984. His email address is edcoen82@gmail.com. His research interests include Milwaukee baseball, nineteenth century baseball, and team nicknames.

CONNELLY DOAN, MA, is a Data Analyst in the San Francisco Bay Area who has applied his professional skills to the game of baseball, both personally and for RotoBaller.com. He has been a SABR member since 2018. He can be reached on Twitter (@ConnellyDoan) and through email (doanco01@gmail.com).

CAMPBELL GIBSON, PhD, is a retired Census Bureau demographer. His first article in the *BRJ* was "Simon Nicholls: Gentleman, Farmer, Ballplayer" published in Vol. 18 (1989).

DONNA L. HALPER, PhD is a media historian, author of six books and many articles (including chapters in a number of SABR books). A former broadcaster and journalist, she is an Associate Professor of Communication and Media Studies at Lesley University in Cambridge, Massachusetts.

DOUGLAS JORDAN is a professor at Sonoma State University in Northern California where he teaches corporate finance and investments. He has been a SABR member since 2014 and has been contributing articles to BRJ since 2014. He runs marathons when he's not watching or writing about baseball. You can contact him at jordand@sonoma.edu.

After planning the World Series Trophy Tour for the Chicago Cubs in 2016, **KATIE KRALL** received a SABR membership from her twin sister as a present for her work with the team. In February 2018, she was selected as part of the inaugural class of the Major League Baseball (MLB) Diversity Fellowship. The program is designed to promote women and people of color into front office executive roles. Krall works in the League Economics & Operations department at the Commissioner's Office in New York City and assists with player transactions, contracts, on-field discipline, and salary arbitration.

BARRY KRISSOFF is an Adjunct Associate Professor of Economics at the University of Maryland Global Campus. His first article in the *BRJ*, "Society and Baseball Face Rising Income Inequality," was a finalist for the 2014 SABR Analytics Conference Research Awards in the category of Historical Analysis/Commentary. He continues to look forward to a World Series victory in Washington, DC—maybe this is the year! Contact information: bcybermetric@hotmail.com.

JON C. NACHTIGAL, PhD, is an assistant softball coach at Purdue University Fort Wayne. He received a doctorate in sport administration from the University of New Mexico and has taught sport management at Simpson College and New Mexico. He publishes softball research at FastpitchAnalytics.com.

BILL NOWLIN has served on SABR's Board of Directors since 2004. He has kept busy writing and helping edit biographies for BioProject, and is particularly active helping edit books for SABR's publications program. He lives in Cambridge, Massachusetts, and spends a great deal of time at Fenway Park.

PETE PALMER is the co-author with John Thorn of *The Hidden Game of Baseball* and co-editor with Gary Gillette of *The Barnes and Noble ESPN Baseball Encyclopedia* (five editions). Pete worked as a consultant to Sports Information Center, the official statisticians for the American League 1976–87. Pete introduced on-base average as an official statistic for the American League in 1979 and invented on-base plus slugging (OPS), now universally used as a good measure of batting strength. Among his many accolades, he won the SABR Bob Davids award in 1989 and was selected as a charter member of the Henry Chadwick Award.

DAVID W. SMITH joined SABR in 1977 and has made research presentations at over 20 national SABR conventions. In 2001 at SABR31, he won the *USA Today Sports Weekly* Award for his presentation on the 1951 NL pennant race. In 2016 he won the Doug Pappas Award for his presentation on closers. In 2005 he received SABR's highest honor, the Bob Davids Award, and in 2012 he was honored with the Henry Chadwick award. He is founder and president of Retrosheet and an Emeritus Professor of Biology at the University of Delaware.

GEORGE S. RIGAKOS is Professor of the Political Economy of Policing at Carleton University, where he also manages the university's baseball program.

DANIEL ROUSSEAU is a Philadelphia-based writer. His work has appeared in *Cimarron Review*, *The Briar Cliff Review*, and *Salon*, among others. He has been a finalist for the Frank McCourt Memoir Prize, and his essay "Retrieving Charlie Gehringer" received a notable citation in *Best American Essays 2018*.

MARK RUCKER is a photographic historian and a long time SABR member. He was co-founder of SABR's 19th Century Research Committee with John Thorn, and has been involved in publishing since the mid-1970s. His companies Transcendental Graphics and The Rucker Archive provide access to rare and surprising images from long ago.

MITCHELL THOMPSON is a second year statistics student majoring in mathematics at Carleton University.

ROBERT D. WARRINGTON is a native Philadelphian who writes about the city's baseball past.

  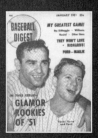 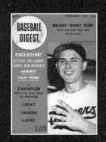 

Friends of SABR

You can become a Friend of SABR by giving as little as $10 per month or by making a one-time gift of $1,000 or more. When you do so, you will be inducted into a community of passionate baseball fans dedicated to supporting SABR's work.

Friends of SABR receive the following benefits:
- ✓ Annual Friends of SABR Commemorative Lapel Pin
- ✓ Recognition in This Week in SABR, SABR.org, and the SABR Annual Report
- ✓ Access to the SABR Annual Convention VIP donor event
- ✓ Invitations to exclusive Friends of SABR events

SABR On-Deck Circle - $10/month, $30/month, $50/month

Get in the SABR On-Deck Circle, and help SABR become the essential community for the world of baseball. Your support will build capacity around all things SABR, including publications, website content, podcast development, and community growth.

A monthly gift is deducted from your bank account or charged to a credit card until you tell us to stop. No more email, mail, or phone reminders.

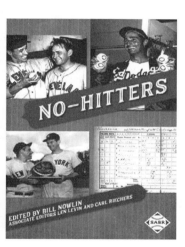

Join the SABR On-Deck Circle

Payment Info: _____Visa _____Mastercard

Name on Card: _____

Card #: _____

Exp. Date: _____ Security Code: _____

Signature: _____

○ $10/month

○ $30/month

○ $50/month

○ Other amount _____

Go to sabr.org/donate to make your gift online

New Books from SABR

Part of the mission of the Society for American Baseball Research has always been to disseminate member research. In addition to the *Baseball Research Journal*, SABR publishes books that include player biographies, historical game recaps, and statistical analysis. All SABR books are available in print and ebook formats. SABR members can access the entire SABR Digital Library for free and purchase print copies at significant member discounts of 40 to 50% off cover price.

JEFF BAGWELL IN CONNECTICUT:
A Consistent Lad in the Land of Steady Habits
This volume of articles, interviews, and essays by members of the Connecticut chapter of SABR chronicles the life and career of Connecticut's favorite baseball son, Hall-of-Famer Jeff Bagwell, with special attention on his high school and college years.
Edited by Karl Cicitto, Bill Nowlin, & Len Levin
$19.95 paperback (ISBN 978-1-943816-97-2)
$9.99 ebook (ISBN 978-1-943816-96-5)
7"x10", 246 pages, 45 photos

1995 CLEVELAND INDIANS:
The Sleeping Giant Awakens
After almost 40 years of sub-.500 baseball, the Sleeping Giant woke in 1995, the first season the Indians spent in their new home of Jacob's Field. The biographies of all the players, coaches, and broadcasters from that year are here, sprinkled with personal perspectives, as well as game stories from key matchups during the 1995 season, information about Jacob's Field, and other essays.
Edited by Joseph Wancho
$19.95 paperback (ISBN 978-1-943816-95-8)
$9.99 ebook (ISBN 978-1-943816-94-1)
8.5"X11", 410 pages, 76 photos

TIME FOR EXPANSION BASEBALL
The LA Angels and "new" Washington Senators ushered in MLB's 1960 expansion, followed in 1961 by the Houston Colt .45s and New York Mets. By 1998, 10 additional teams had launched: the Kansas City Royals, Seattle Pilots, Toronto Blue Jays, and Tampa Bay Devil Rays in the AL, and the Montreal Expos, San Diego Padres, Colorado Rockies, Florida Marlins, and Arizona Diamondbacks in the NL. *Time for Expansion Baseball* tells each team's origin and includes biographies of key players.
Edited by Maxwell Kates and Bill Nowlin
$24.95 paperback (ISBN 978-1-933599-89-7)
$9.99 ebook (ISBN 978-1-933599-88-0)
8.5"X11", 430 pages, 150 photos

BASE BALL'S 19TH CENTURY "WINTER" MEETINGS 1857-1900
A look at the business meetings of base ball's earliest days (not all of which were in the winter). As John Thorn writes in his Foreword, "This monumental volume traces the development of the game from its birth as an organized institution to its very near suicide at the dawn of the next century."
Edited by Jeremy K. Hodges and Bill Nowlin
$29.95 paperback (ISBN 978-1-943816-91-0)
$9.99 ebook (ISBN978-1-943816-90-3)
8.5"x11", 390 pages, 50 photos

MET-ROSPECTIVES:
A Collection of the Greatest Games in New York Mets History
This book's 57 game stories—coinciding with the number of Mets years through 2018—are strictly for the eternal optimist. They include the team's very first victory in April 1962 at Forbes Field, Tom Seaver's "Imperfect Game" in July '69, the unforgettable Game Sixes in October '86, the "Grand Slam Single" in the 1999 NLCS, and concludes with the extra-innings heroics in September 2016 at Citi Field that helped ensure a wild-card berth.
edited by Brian Wright and Bill Nowlin
$14.95 paperback (ISBN 978-1-943816-87-3)
$9.99 ebook (ISBN 978-1-943816-86-6)
8.5"X11", 148 pages, 44 photos

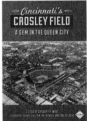

CINCINNATI'S CROSLEY FIELD:
A Gem in the Queen City
This book evokes memories of Crosley Field through detailed summaries of more than 85 historic and monumental games played there, and 10 insightful feature essays about the history of the ballpark. Former Reds players Johnny Edwards and Art Shamsky share their memories of the park in introductions.
Edited by Gregory H. Wolf
$19.95 paperback (ISBN 978-1-943816-75-0)
$9.99 ebook (ISBN 978-1-943816-74-3)
8.5"X11", 320 pages, 43 photos

MOMENTS OF JOY AND HEARTBREAK:
66 Significant Episodes in the History of the Pittsburgh Pirates
In this book we relive no-hitters, World Series-winning homers, and the last tripleheader ever played in major-league baseball. Famous Pirates like Honus Wagner and Roberto Clemente—and infamous ones like Dock Ellis—make their appearances, as well as recent stars like Andrew McCutchen.
Edited by Jorge Iber and Bill Nowlin
$19.95 paperback (ISBN 978-1-943816-73-6)
$9.99 ebook (ISBN 978-1-943816-72-9)
8.5"X11", 208 pages, 36 photos

FROM SPRING TRAINING TO SCREEN TEST:
Baseball Players Turned Actors
SABR's book of baseball's "matinee stars," a selection of those who crossed the lines between professional sports and popular entertainment. Included are the famous (Gene Autry, Joe DiMaggio, Jim Thorpe, Bernie Williams) and the forgotten (Al Gettel, Lou Stringer, Wally Hebert, Wally Hood), essays on baseball in TV shows and Coca-Cola commercials, and Jim Bouton's casting as "Jim Barton" in the *Ball Four* TV series.
Edited by Rob Edelman and Bill Nowlin
$19.95 paperback (ISBN 978-1-943816-71-2)
$9.99 ebook (ISBN 978-1-943816-70-5)
8.5"X11", 410 pages, 89 photos

To learn more about how to receive these publications for free or at member discount as a member of SABR, visit the website: sabr.org/join